IMAGES
of America

PLYMOUTH STATE COLLEGE

IMAGES
of America

PLYMOUTH STATE COLLEGE

Bruce D. Heald, Ph.D.

ARCADIA
PUBLISHING

ISBN 0-7385-0184-0

Published by Arcadia Publishing
Charleston, South Carolina

Printed in the United States of America

Library of Congress Catalog Card Number: 99-63937

For all general information, please contact Arcadia Publishing:
Telephone 843-853-2070
Fax 843-853-0044
E-mail sales@arcadiapublishing.com
For customer service and orders:
Toll-Free 1-888-313-2665

Visit us on the internet at www.arcadiapublishing.com

Presidents of Plymouth State College

Silas H. Pearl (1871–1873)
Horatio O. Ladd (1873–1876)
Ambrose P. Kelsey (1876–1879)
Henry Pitt Warren (1879–1883)
Charles Collins Rounds (1883–1896)
Alfred Hills Campbell (1896–1900)
James E. Klock (1900–1911)
Ernest Leroy Silver (1911–1946)
Howard R. Jones (1946–1951)
Harold Eldred Hyde (1951–1977)
Kasper C. Marking (1977–1983)
Madie Barrett, Interim (1983–1984)
William J. Farrell (1984–1992)
Theodora J. Kalikow, Interim (1992–1993)
Donald P. Wharton (1993–)

CONTENTS

SPECIAL THANKS IS EXTENDED TO THE FOLLOWING
FOR THEIR ASSISTANCE IN MAKING THIS HISTORIC DOCUMENT POSSIBLE:

David Switzer, Ph.D., Chair, Social Science
Donald P. Wharton, Ph.D., President
A. Robin Bowers, Ph.D., Dean of the College
Elizabeth W. Cheney, M.B.A., Public Relations Program Coordinator
Todd S. Trevorrow, Director of Library Services
Bonnie W. Epstein, Ph.D., English
Thomas Emanuel
Norton R. Bagley, Ph.D.
Plymouth Historical Society
James Hogan
Sandra Ramsey

INTRODUCTION

For more than a century, this educational institution has been a magnet for guiding, inspiring, and motivating its young men and women to academic excellence. Located in central New Hampshire, at the foothills of the White Mountains, this school experienced its beginning when the town of Plymouth, New Hampshire, became a center for a teacher training school under the name "New Hampshire Normal School." The history of Plymouth State College is the story of the labors of earnest, inspired people, striving to raise the standards of education in order that our students might better fulfill their destinies in a progressive America.

The history of the school originally stemmed from the Holmes Plymouth Academy, which dates back to 1808 as a pioneer institution for teacher training. For several years, Samuel Read Hall had labored before the failure of an expected endowment had put an end to his hope of creating an institution solely for the training of teachers. Farsighted men saw that only in separate institutions could high standards of teacher training be maintained. As early as 1836, Rev. Charles Brooks had lectured before the legislature of New Hampshire and throughout the state on the subject of normal schools. An "Act for the establishment and management of a state normal school for the better training of teachers for the common schools of the state," was passed in 1870.

The board of trustees located the school at Plymouth, which had offered the Holmes Plymouth Academy building and other support to the new school. The school was besieged on all sides by enemies—the jealousy of the academies, the usual parsimonious individuals, and those people who always believe that what was good enough for their grandfathers was good enough for their grandchildren.

As early as 1874, at least 20 years before the system was attempted in any other normal school in the country, the grade and high schools of Plymouth had been organized as training schools under the direct supervision of the normal school. The curriculum of the normal school was so arranged as to give continuous, integrated study, not only in the subjects taught, but also in their practical application to the mechanics of the classroom and the needs of the schoolchildren.

The advent of Henry P. Warren in 1879 marked the opening of a new era for the school. He introduced higher standards of admission. The subject-matter content of the normal school courses was broadened. Professional training was extended throughout the curriculum. Charles C. Rounds, who succeeded Mr. Warren, extended the ideas that the latter had introduced. The state began to give more support. A new school building (Rounds Hall) and a new dormitory were erected in 1890.

Shortly after the turn of the century, Henry C. Morrison became the superintendent of Public Instruction in New Hampshire. His keen appreciation of the values and services of the normal school and his understanding of state needs aided the development of the school. In 1911, Ernest L. Silver, with experience as superintendent of schools and as principal of Pinkerton Academy, established a 35-year administration of the school, which saw the school grow to maturity spiritually, professionally, and physically.

As the general level of education throughout the state became higher, entrance requirements were raised. In 1915, high school graduation was made a requirement for entrance. During Dr. Silver's administration, a new emphasis was placed upon practice teaching for elementary students. A training school was opened in 1914 in which the new program, one of carefully correlated learning and teaching, was carried out.

As early as 1905, the normal school had offered a one-year program for college graduates. In 1910, a three-year curriculum for supervisors of music, art, and home economics in elementary and secondary schools were introduced. In 1916, a three-year curriculum for junior high school teachers was begun, and, in 1921, these were followed by a three-year curriculum preparing secondary teachers in history and other social sciences. By 1933 all secondary curricula had been lengthened to four years. Plymouth Normal School had become a teachers college in fact, if not in name. Degrees were first granted to elementary graduates in 1940.

In 1919, the creation of the New Hampshire Board of Education, which centralized all educational activities of the state, added to the prosperity of the normal school. The normal school entered more aggressively than ever into the task of bringing extended training to experienced teachers through summer schools, institutes, and extension courses. In 1927, the American Council of Teachers Colleges made a survey of Plymouth Normal School and rated it a Grade A teachers college; a rating it has since held. In 1937, the state legislature officially recognized the increased stature of the college by changing its designation to Plymouth Teachers College and later, in 1963, to Plymouth State College of the University System of New Hampshire.

Having been a school first housed in an ancient academy building, Plymouth State College is proud of its historic commitment to educating teachers, of its many excellent majors, offering specialization in the liberal arts, and preparing both graduates and undergraduates for the business profession. Plymouth State College demands the very best in its professional programs and its liberal arts majors, but its primary concern is the development of the individual, including the student's moral, social, and intellectual growth. The college measures its excellence, not by the quality of students who enter its doors, but by the quality it adds to those who graduate.

Today, under the leadership of President Donald P. Wharton and the board of trustees, the college believes that every student must receive a well-rounded education as well as specialized instruction in a field. Those who truly have a general education should possess the ability to communicate well, but more important they should know how to integrate their skills and areas of knowledge in encountering specific problems, whether of special topics, or simply in appreciating the beauty of life. As a community, the college has always valued courage, wisdom, kindness, and humor.

Through this rare photographic journey, I have attempted to capture brief moments that encompass some of the physical and academic aspects of student life at the school, i.e. the extra-curricular activities, which have enriched the students' lives, and a few reminiscent moments that reflect the nostalgia and charm so characteristic of the college's extensive history.

—Bruce D. Heald, Ph.D.

One

New Hampshire State Normal School: 1871–1939

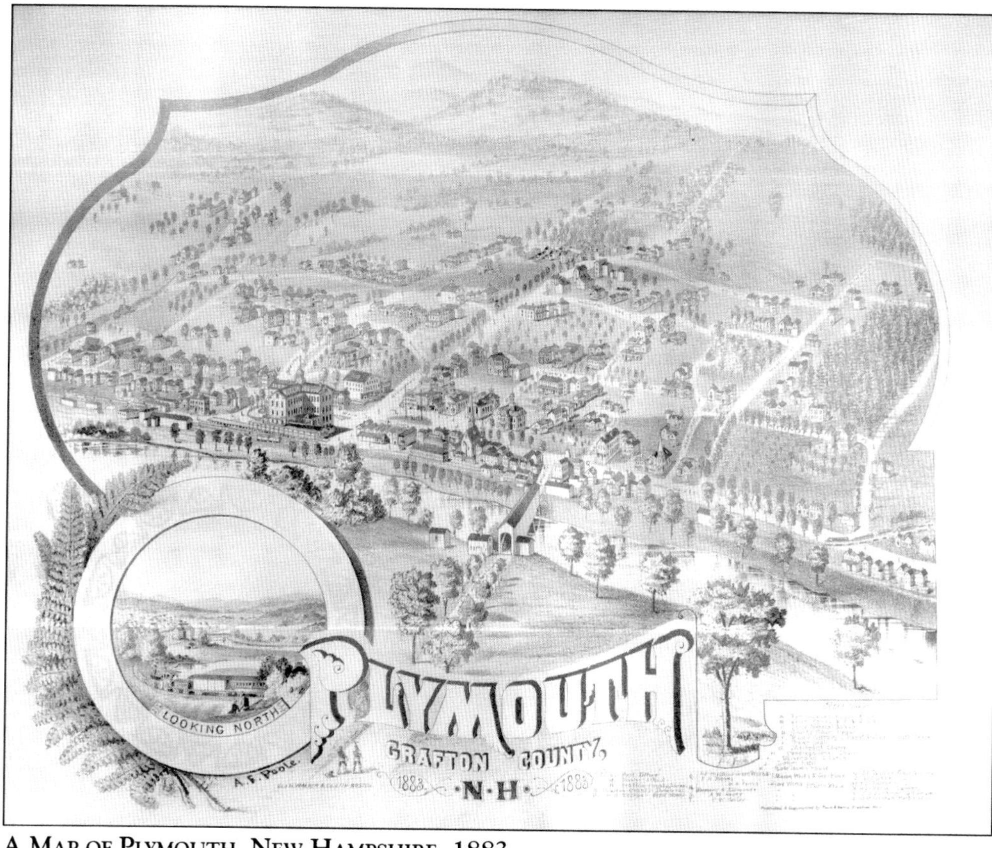

A MAP OF PLYMOUTH, NEW HAMPSHIRE, 1883.

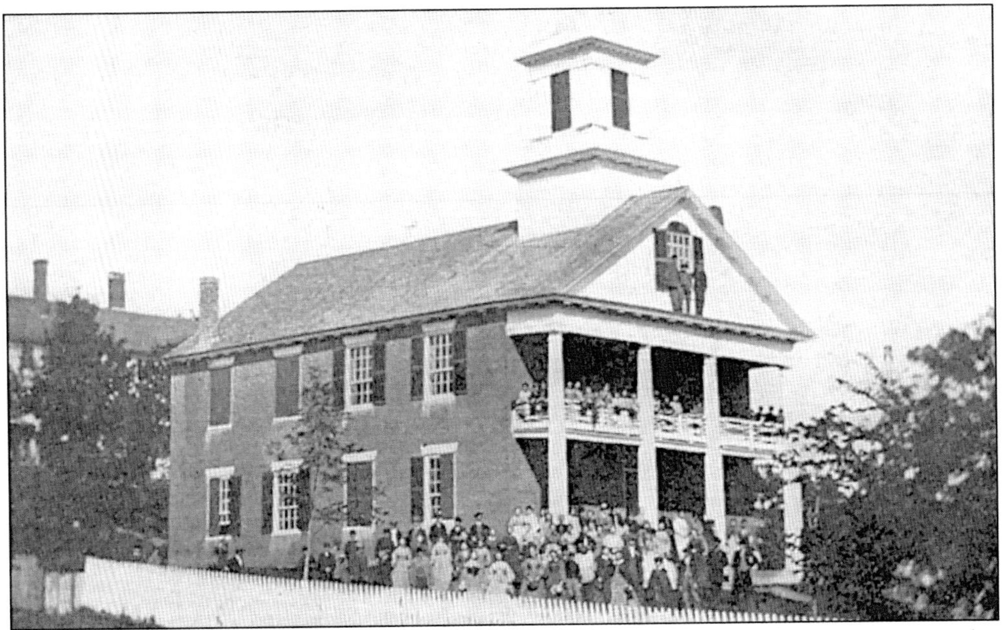

HOLMES PLYMOUTH ACADEMY. The history of Plymouth State College (PSC) stems from this academy that dates from 1808 as a pioneer institution. Revolutionary War soldier Col. Samuel Holmes dedicated himself to the task of raising funds to establish and promote an educational institution. His gifts were appreciated; an Act of Incorporation was granted in 1808 to establish an academy in Plymouth to be named "Holmes Plymouth Academy." Colonel Holmes was president and treasurer of the board of trustees until his death in 1823. Rev. Dr. Samuel Read Hall became the principal of Holmes Plymouth Academy in 1837; he gave the first training for teachers in New Hampshire that year. To Dr. Hall belongs the distinction and honor of being the first person in America to give normal training in the art of teaching.

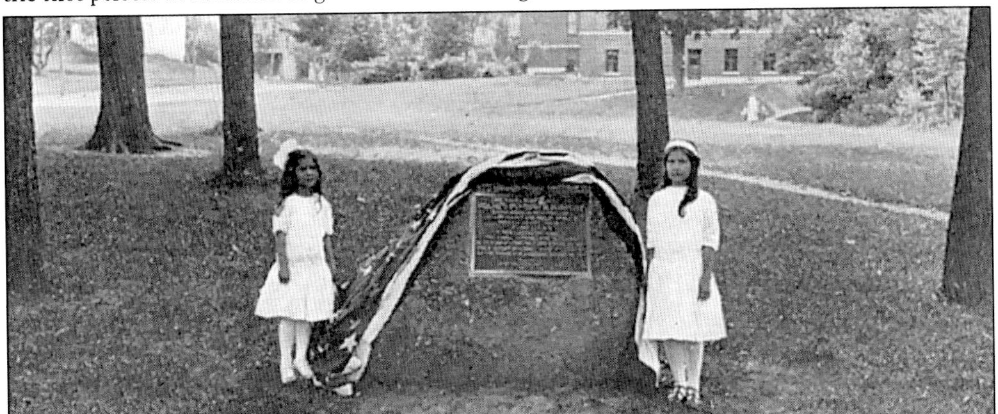

MEMORIAL TABLET AND BOULDER. This tablet marks the site of Holmes Plymouth Academy and New Hampshire's first normal school. This plaque and boulder was presented by the Asquamchumauke Chapter of Daughters of the American Revolution on June 15, 1913. Elizabeth Denman and Thorndike Rubert frame the plaque. This academy had its halcyon days and its period of depression. After years of struggle, the corporation was discontinued and a private school took its place. In 1871, the academy buildings were presented to the state for a normal school, which, after much deliberation by state officials, was opened in Plymouth on March 15, 1871.

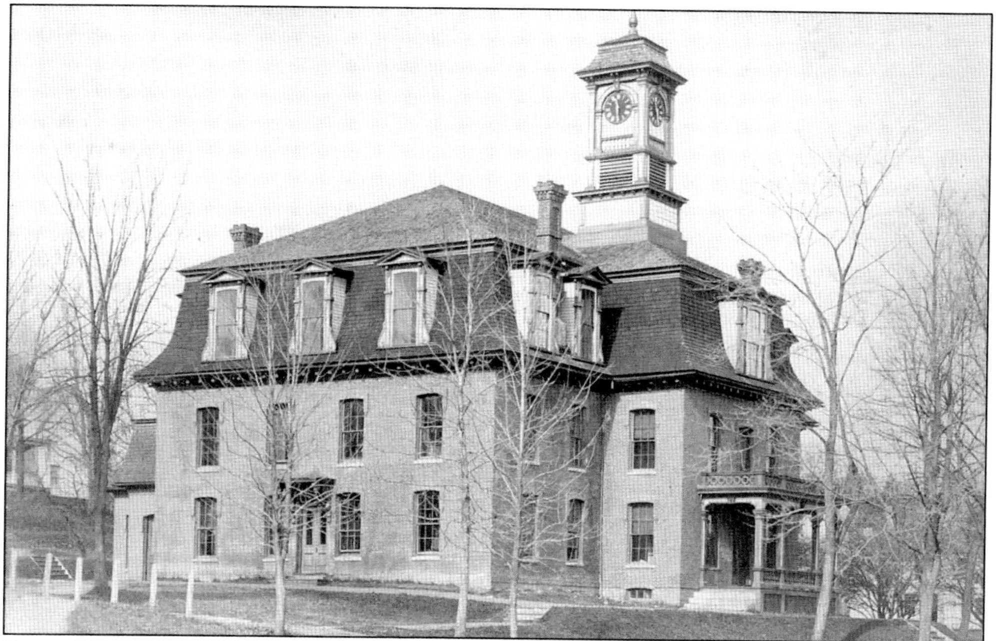

STATE NORMAL SCHOOL AT PLYMOUTH, NEW HAMPSHIRE, C. 1875. A boardinghouse can be seen in the background. In 1870, an act of incorporation for a normal school was granted and a school was born; a commitment for intellectual growth was already well established. This community was on its way to becoming one of the finest educational institutions in New England. The edifice of classical design stood about 70 yards east of the present Rounds Hall, on the line with the old courthouse and the Congregational Church.

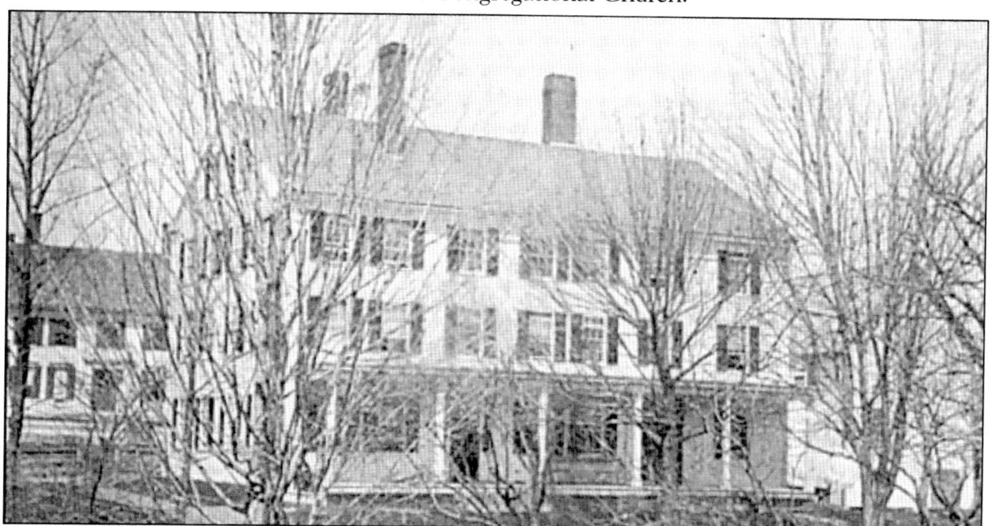

BOARDINGHOUSE FOR SCHOOL IN BACK OF NORMAL SCHOOL BUILDING. This two-story house stood on the site of Rounds Hall that housed approximately 60 occupants; a barn also connected with the boardinghouse. When the school opened, Mr. Denison Burnham conveyed the school building to the state and Mr. John Cutler, the boardinghouse; both buildings were paid for by the town. In June 1871, the legislature appropriated $5,000 for necessary repairs and equipment. Since the sum was insufficient, $8,000 more was granted in 1872; thus the first addition to the old building began in 1871 on the northern site.

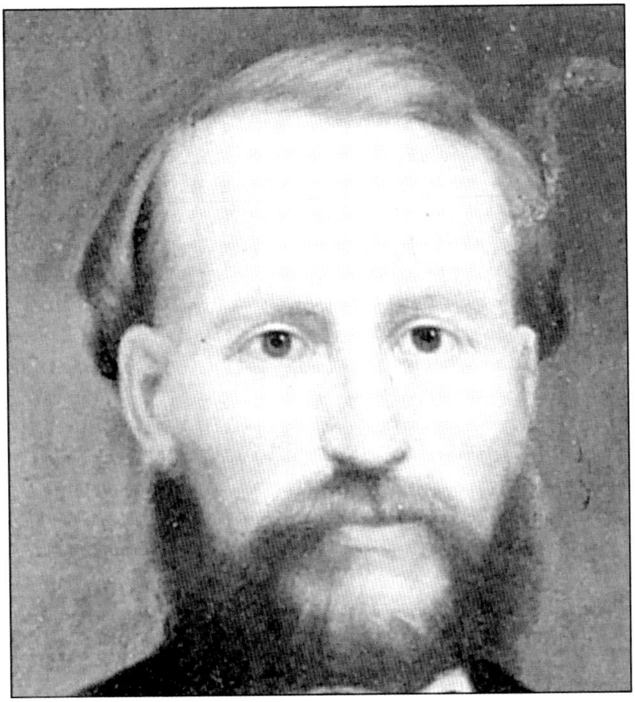

SILAS H. PEARL, 1871–1873. Having located the normal school in Plymouth, the trustees selected Silas Pearl, M.A., as principal and Amos Hadley, M.A., as his assistant. Since Mr. Pearl could not leave his duties at the Normal School at Johnson, Vermont, until later that term, Mr. Hadley opened the first term of the Plymouth Normal School on March 15, 1871 with 80 students. Here, Mr. Pearl laid the foundations for a teacher-training program; he died as the result of overwork, which exemplified his motto, "Better to wear out than to rust out."

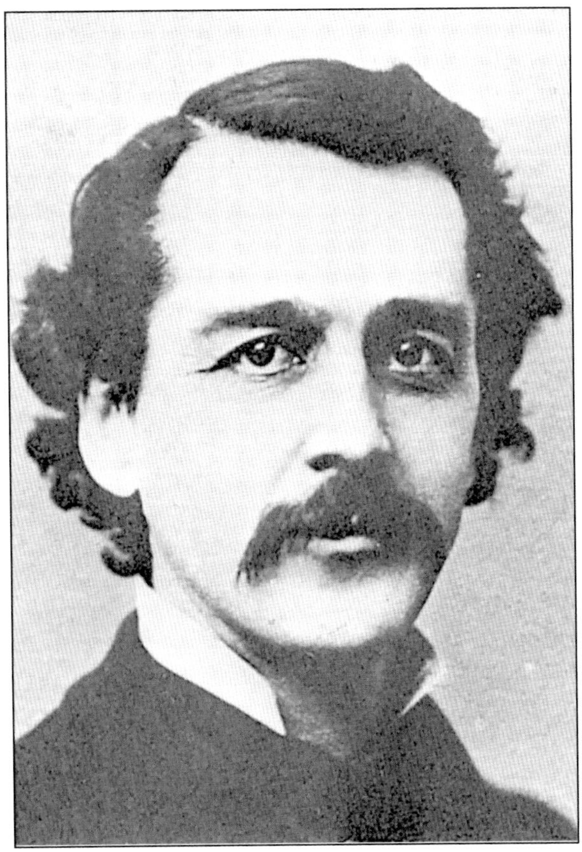

HORATIO O. LADD, 1873–1876. During Reverend Ladd's administration, he emphasized the classical subjects and normal training; he also added four assistants and special instruction in gymnastics, drawing, and instrumental and vocal music. The trustees could boast, "Our normal school is no longer an experiment but a 'fixed fact.' Its objects and importance are now much better understood and appreciated; its active enemies have either surrendered or taken the open field; and the school is fully recognized as a state institution, rightfully claiming public patronage and support." However, the forces of opposition united to almost close the school. From 1876 to 1883, two presidents, namely Ambrose P. Kelsey (1876–1879) and Henry Pitt Warren (1879–1883), led the school through these difficult times.

CHARLES COLLINS ROUNDS, 1883–1896. With the resignation of Mr. Warren in 1883, Dr. Rounds, who had previously been at the normal school in Farmington, Maine, continued the operation of the school. He was assisted by two teachers in the normal department and three teachers in the model schools. He told the legislature that enrollments at the normal school (31 in 1884) would not increase until the school districts of the state had sense enough to employ trained teachers. Since a law of 1883 required teachers at the normal school to take part in teacher institutes throughout the state, his philosophy began to have considerable influence. His tenure of 13 years as principal marks the first of the long-tenured administrations at Plymouth that have had great influence on the education of the state.

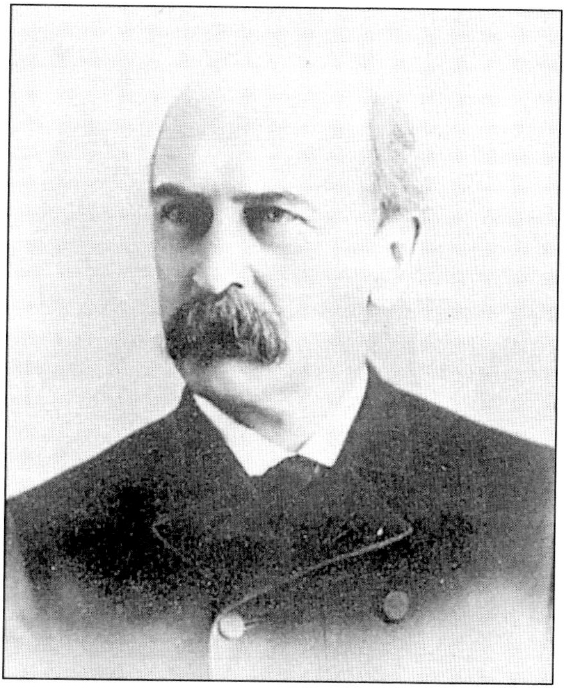

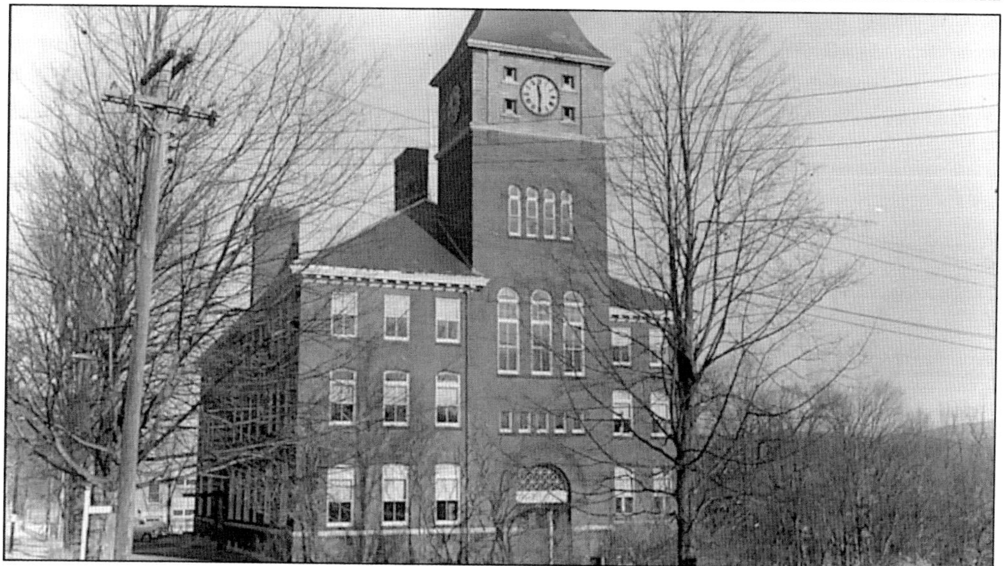

ROUNDS HALL. In 1877, a building committee was appointed by legislative act, which used appropriation from the state, to construct a new addition to the rear of the old school building; however, after study, a select committee decided that a new building was needed. The result was the present Rounds Hall, dedicated August 28, 1892 at 2 p.m. The classrooms were on the top two floors; the library was housed partly in Livermore Hall (which served as assembly hall, study hall, and classroom) and partly in the adjoining classroom. The Plymouth Grade School and High School were housed on the first floor. The school was well equipped with apparatus for teaching the sciences and was furnished with an excellent library of reference books. For the convenience of the students, the public library was easily accessible and well supplied with general literature.

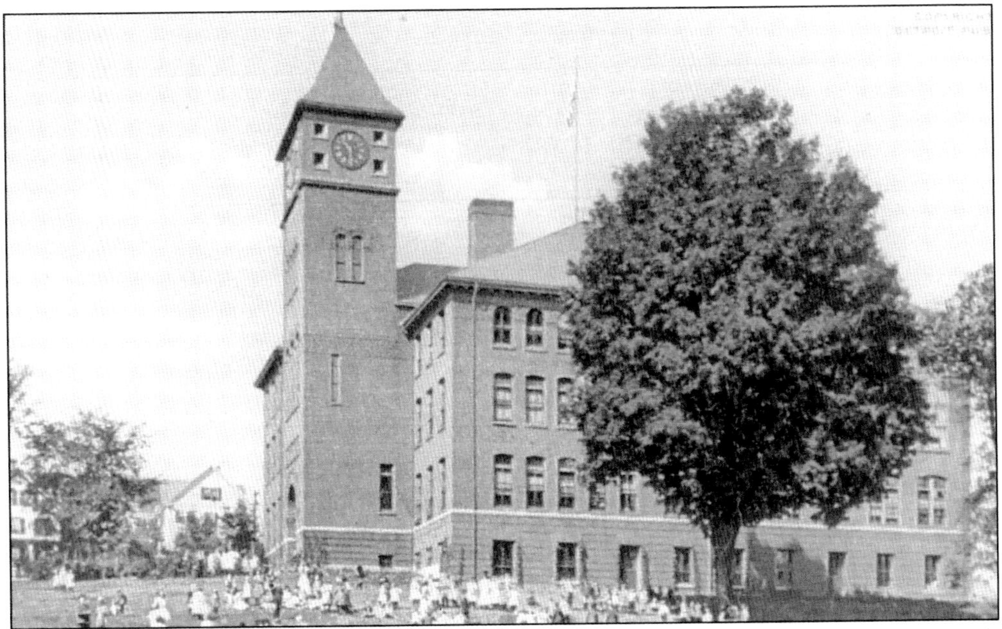

ROUNDS HALL. This edifice is constructed of brick, 112 feet by 80 feet, and three stories high above the basement. It contained recitation rooms, laboratories for nature study, drawing, domestic arts, and music, all constructed and furnished for their special uses, and supplied with practical apparatus and models. In 1887 and 1889, the legislature made "liberal appropriations for new buildings and in the year 1890–91, a schoolhouse and a boarding hall were erected." In 1894, the annual session of the New Hampshire Summer Institute was held in Plymouth under the auspices of the State Department of Public Institution. Courses including Nature Study, Advanced Arithmetic, Penmanship, and Swedish Gymnastics were offered by Dr. Charles C. Rounds and others.

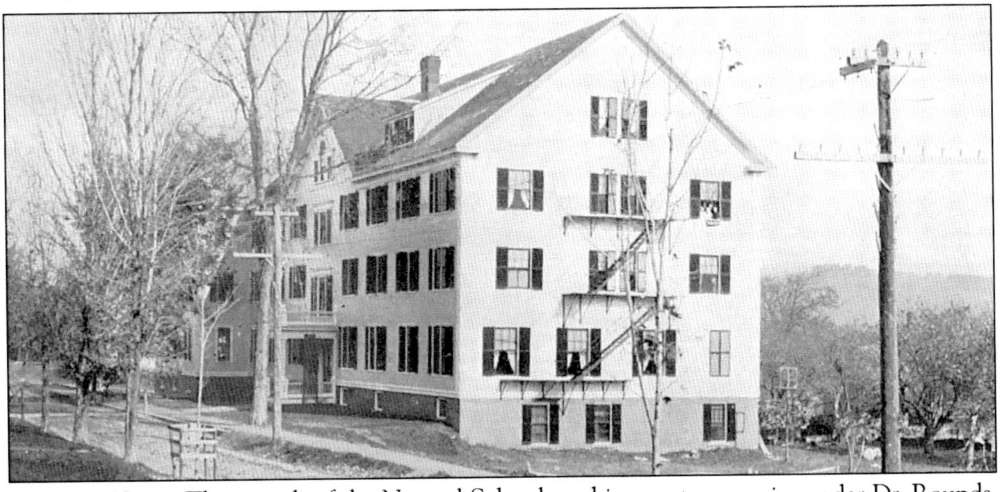

NORMAL HALL. The growth of the Normal School, and its greater promise under Dr. Rounds, caused the legislature to appropriate funds for a new dormitory called Normal Hall. It was situated on the present lawn of Mary Lyon Hall. It was "newly furnished in the best style, warmed by steam, supplied by bath rooms, with hot and cold water on every floor and is in every way healthful and commodious. It is designed to afford the pupils the privileges and advantages of the best social life. It is the home of the principal…" —*PNS Catalogue*, 1892.

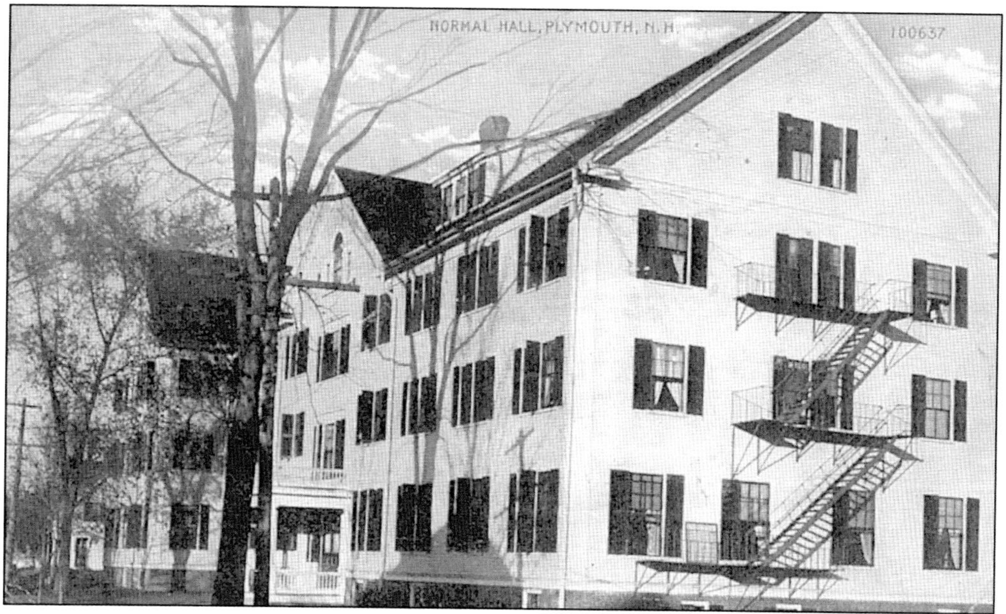

NORMAL HALL. During the turn of the century, the enrollment of the State Normal School increased, approaching 150 students. The town pupils and the normal pupils overcrowded the Normal School; two rooms of the Kidder Block on Main Street were hired to house parts of the local high school. Dormitory accommodations were added in 1913, 1916, 1922, 1925, 1926, 1929, and 1931. It was the policy of the state to provide dormitories since few students commuted. When the Normal Hall was built in the '90s, a gymnasium was included. The catalog for 1908–1909 mentions teams organized in golf, basketball, and tennis.

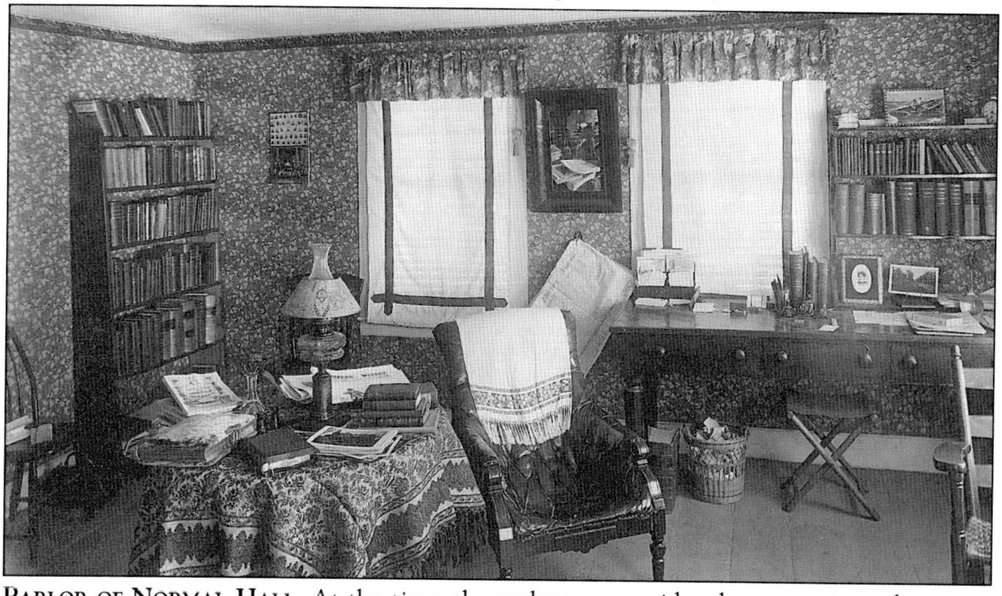

PARLOR OF NORMAL HALL. At the time, the parlor was considered very spacious; the up-to-date facilities and comfort must have added considerably to the student life. It was heated by furnaces and had bathrooms supplied with hot and cold water on every floor. Notice that all the furniture is of the Victorian period. The parlor and other rooms were designed to afford the pupils the privileges and advantages of the best social life.

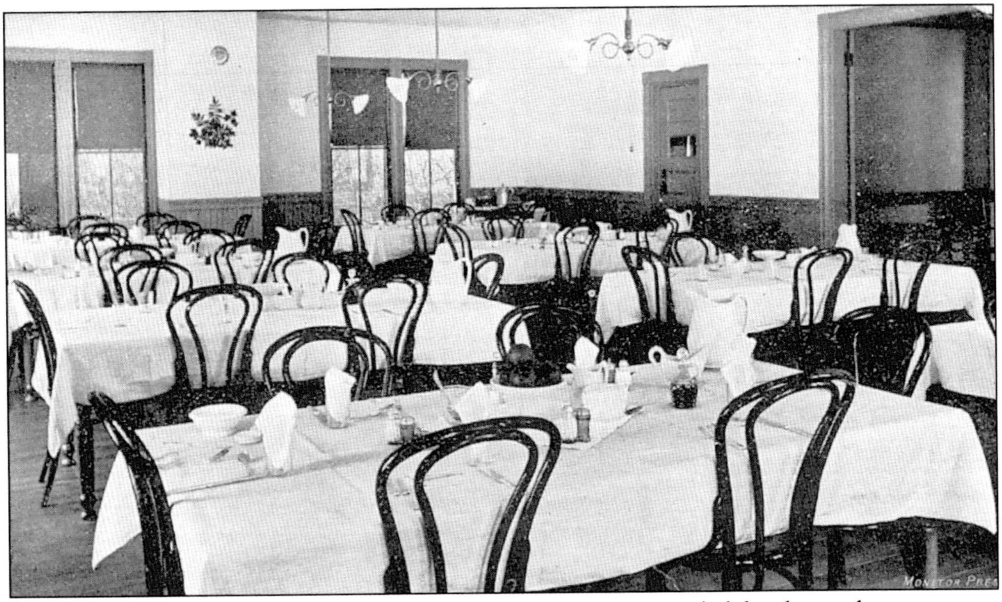

DINING ROOM, 1899. A formal Victorian atmosphere was provided for the students in every respect. Comfort and cleanliness was considered a proper atmosphere for all residents.

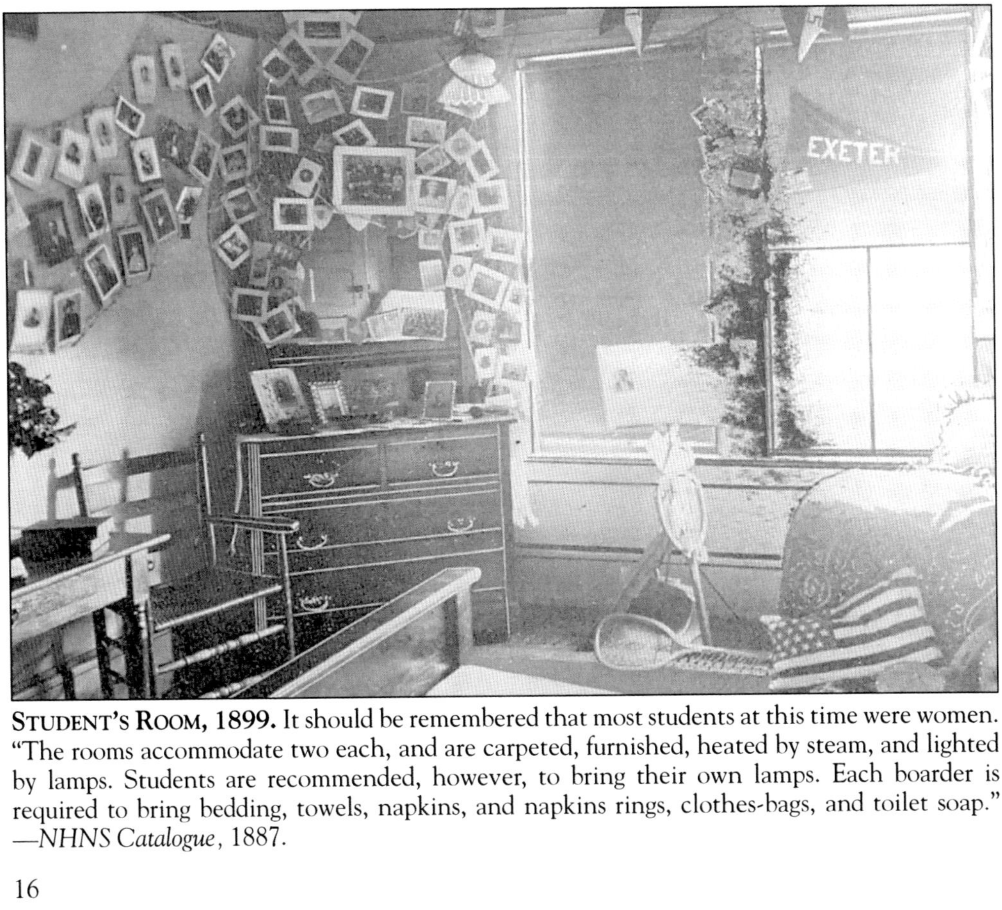

STUDENT'S ROOM, 1899. It should be remembered that most students at this time were women. "The rooms accommodate two each, and are carpeted, furnished, heated by steam, and lighted by lamps. Students are recommended, however, to bring their own lamps. Each boarder is required to bring bedding, towels, napkins, and napkins rings, clothes-bags, and toilet soap." —*NHNS Catalogue*, 1887.

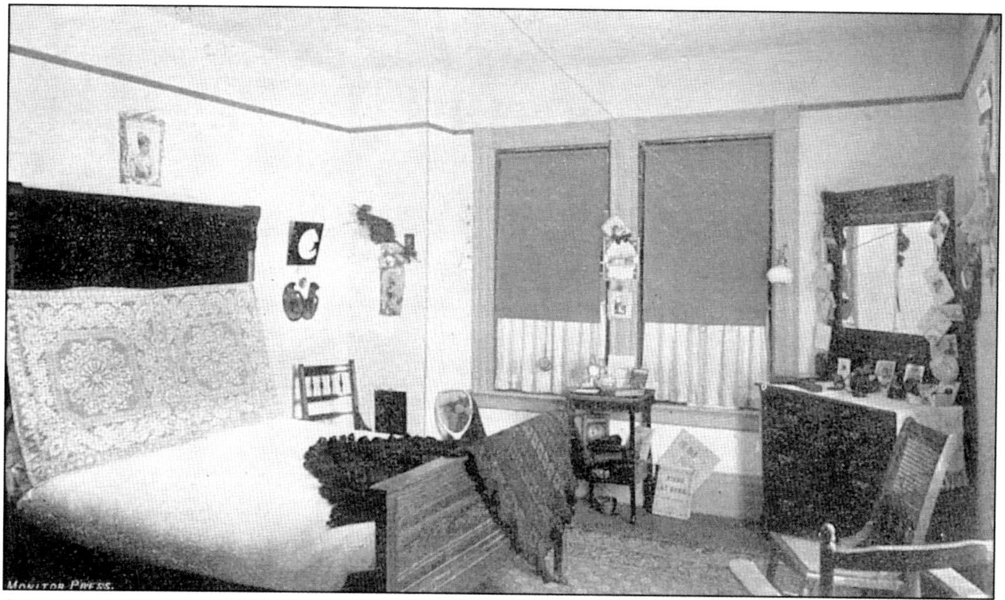

STUDENT'S ROOM, 1892. "Great care has been taken to secure the best sanitary conditions in schoolhouse and boarding-house; the general good health of the school, and the remarkable improvement in the health and strength of some, attest the success of the attempt." —*NHNS Catalogue*, 1887. During the mid-1930s, few male students appeared on campus; thus, many of the dormitory rooms were quite feminine in decoration.

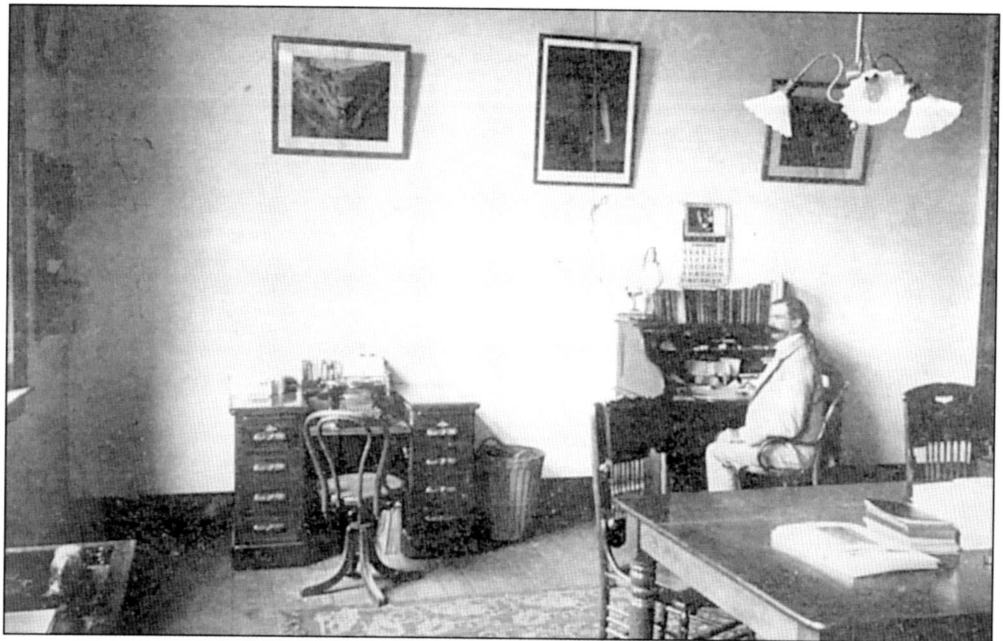

DR. CAMPBELL SITTING IN HIS OFFICE, 1896–1900. During Dr. Campbell's tenure, he added a reading room to the library and greatly increased the library holdings. He continued the work of Dr. Rounds by building up the faculty and by increasingly stressing the importance of degree-holding people. Dr. Campbell departmentalized the faculty and added one person. It was during his term that Normal Hall was finally completely furnished.

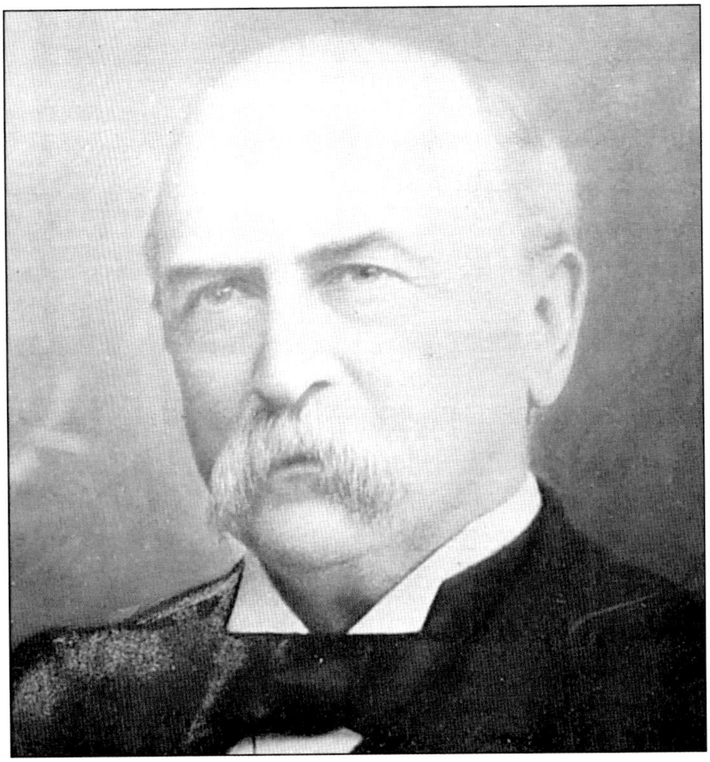

DR. JAMES E. KLOCK, 1900–1911. During the next decade, Dr. Klock served as principal. The trustees said of him that "Mr. Klock's native gifts, a kindliness of heart, a graciousness of speech and manner, an ability to read human nature and to rightly interpret human motives, combined with the power of a cultured mind and long experience as an instructor and superintendent..." fitted him for the post.

DR. ERNEST LEROY SILVER, 1911. During the next 35 years, Dr. Silver served as principal, director, and president. With the advent of this new administration, the trustees completely recognized the educational, administrative, and accounting programs of the school. Dr. Silver was firm but compassionate and his words of advice, admonition, and philosophy through the long period covering two World Wars and the Great Depression point out the role of a teacher. His thoughts turned to "political, economic and social stress." He felt that the "American way of bringing mighty changes should be an orderly one," though he knew revolutionary changes were necessarily afoot. His favorite quotation could have been, "With all thy wisdom get understanding." He told his graduates that they must help on these changes by "beating new paths, finding new truths, and achieving greater deeds of service."

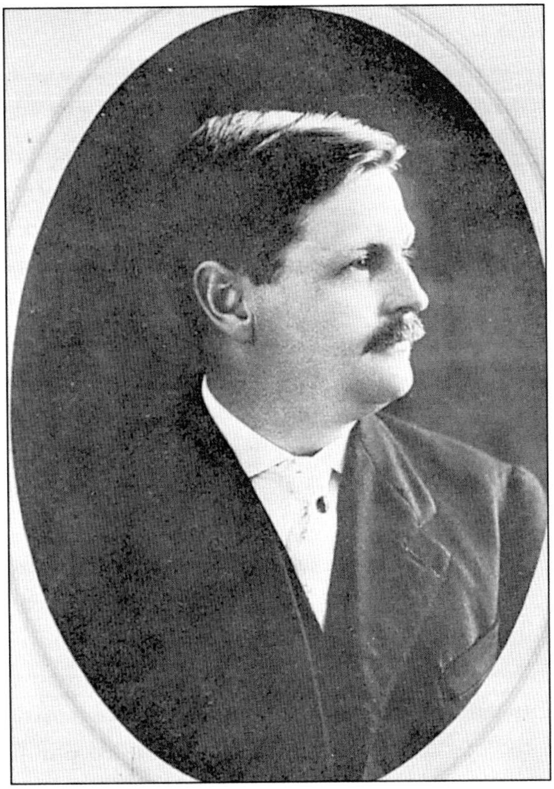

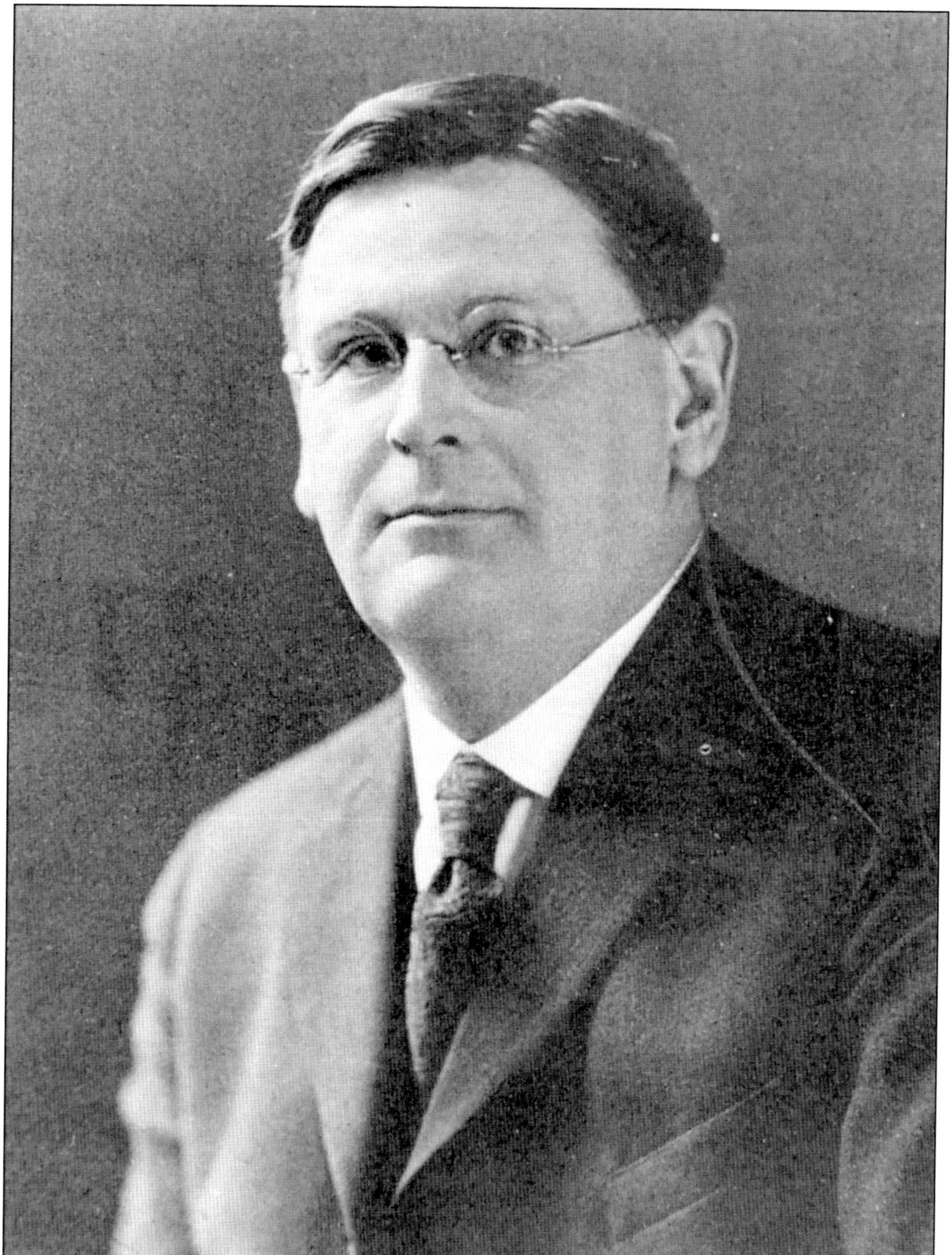

Dr. Ernest L. Silver as Principal, 1911–1946. Robert Frost wrote of Dr. Silver on the occasion of the 75th anniversary of the college and the 35th year of Dr. Silver's presidency: "We all owe Mr. Silver a debt of gratitude for the large and liberal way he encouraged our individualities both as teachers and students under him. I went to Plymouth with him when he began his presidency and I have kept up my friendly interest in the whole 35 years of his unusually long administration. It warms the heart with reassurance to look on at anything that persists so successfully in this world of broken pieces."

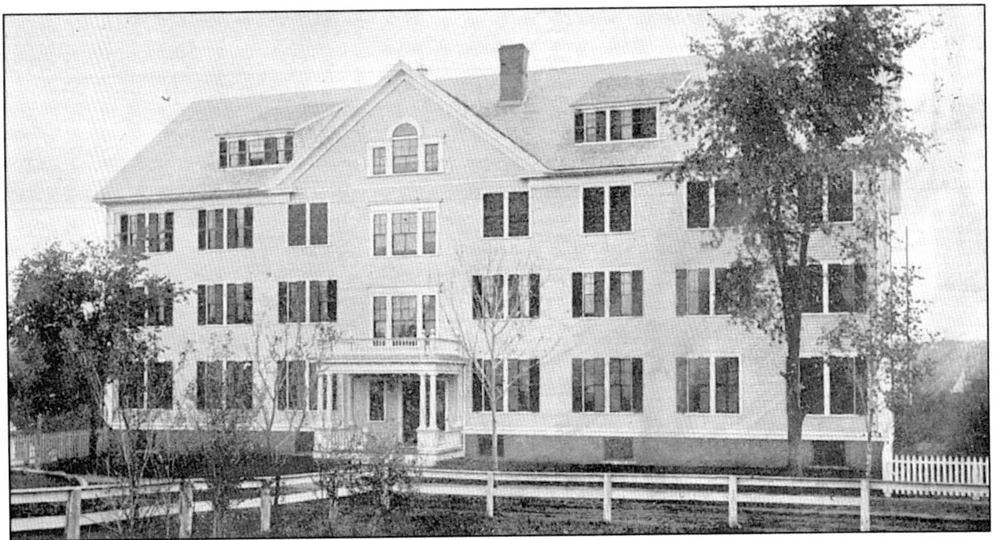

NORMAL HALL. Later, upon the investigation by a building committee, it was found that Normal Hall was in such a condition that it would be cheaper to build a new dormitory rather than repair the old. The legislature of 1913 therefore began appropriation to build a new dormitory immediately behind Normal Hall on land given for that purpose by Amos Kidder, a prominent citizen of Plymouth.

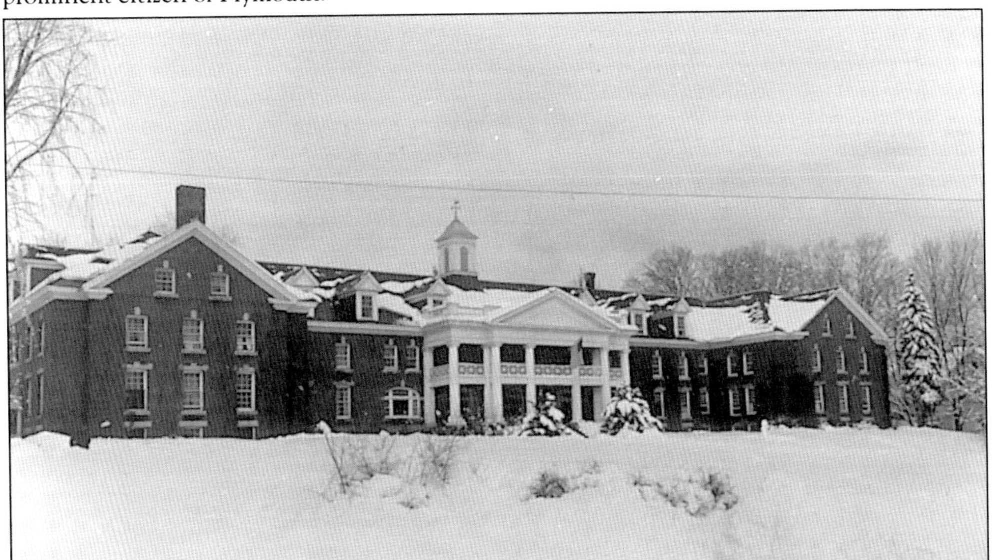

MARY LYON HALL. Appropriations were slow and sometimes insufficient; however, by 1916, this new building was completed. The original building was 100 feet by 45 feet and was three stories high above the basement. It was "newly furnished in the best style, warmed by steam, supplied by bath rooms with hot and cold water on every floor and is in every way healthful and commodious; and in the planning of its parlors and other rooms, as in its arrangements, it is designed to afford the pupils the privileges and advantages of the best social life. It was the home of the principal..." Despite the boasting of the catalog, funds were lacking for some years to completely furnish the building as planned. On the lawn in front of Mary Lyon Hall stood the parsonage of the Congregational Society. Bought in 1924, it served as a dormitory named Carroll Cottage in 1931.

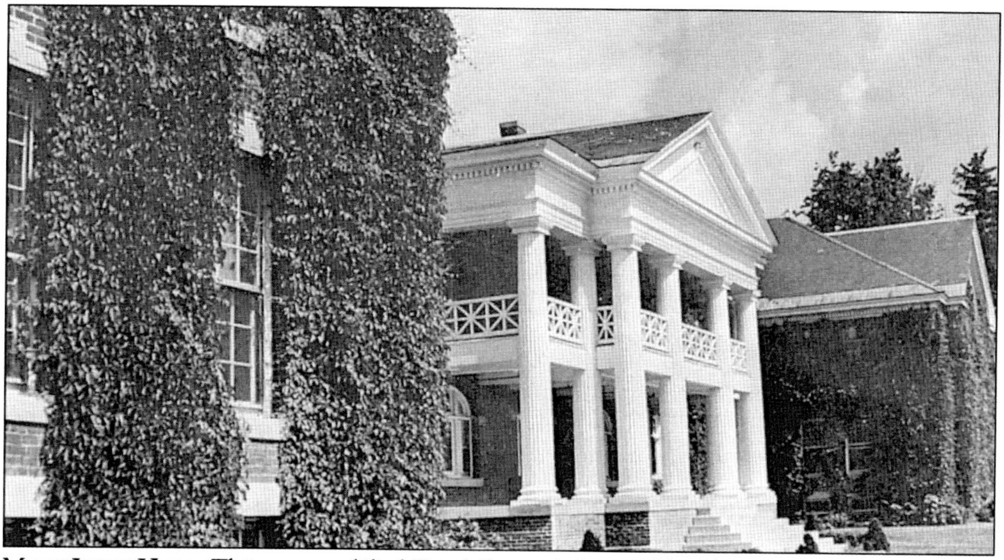

MARY LYON HALL. This new modified Greek Revival-designed building was respectfully named after the female educator who had founded Mount Holyoke College and who had taught in Adam's Female Academy in East Derry, New Hampshire. In the basement, it had a kitchen, rooms for storage and refrigeration, chambers, and two laundries. A "spacious" gymnasium, as well as space for maintenance, were included in the basement. By 1929, this area included two bowling lanes given to Mr. Orton Brown, the president of the State Board of Education. On the first floor, a music room, library, dining room, and serving rooms connected with the kitchen. The second floor contained single and double rooms and bath facilities for students. For many years, the third floor was used as an attic for storage.

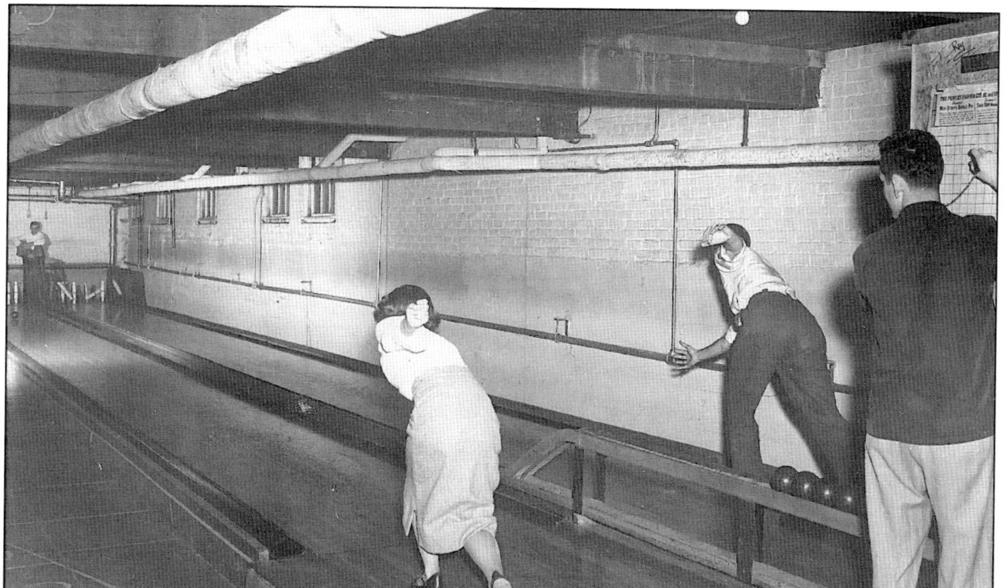

BOWLING ALLEY IN THE BASEMENT OF THE MARY HYON HALL, 1929. "Our gymnasium offers opportunity for exercise and recreation as well as instruction in play, games and folk dancing. Numerous showers and lockers are provided. Two bowling alleys of the finest sort, a gift to the school, are most popular." —*PNS Catalogue*, 1939.

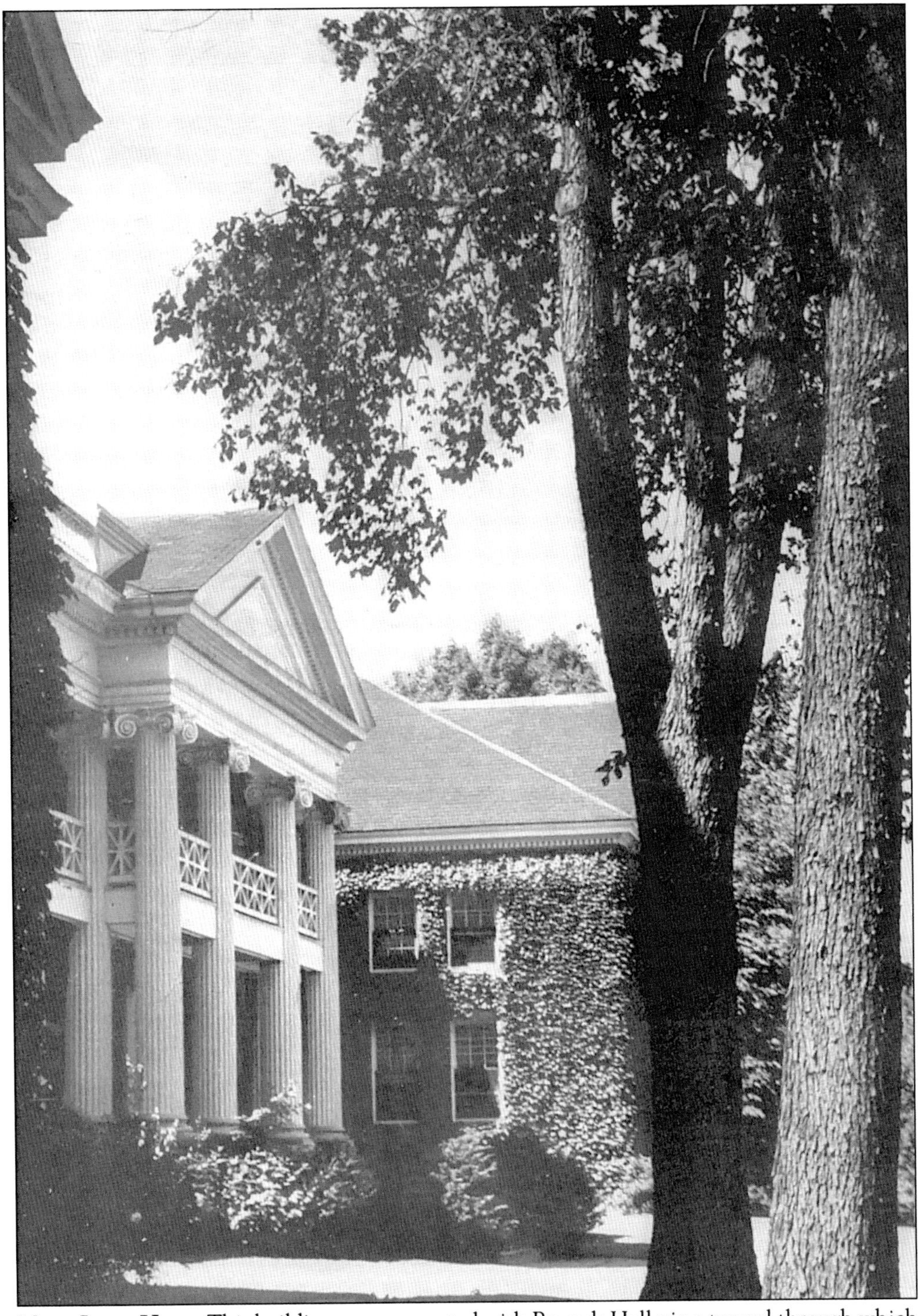

MARY LYON HALL. This building was connected with Rounds Hall via a tunnel through which the steam pipes passed; for many years, students used the passageway to get from the dormitory to classes without having to go outside during inclement weather. The subway was later extended to the Read Hall Dormitory.

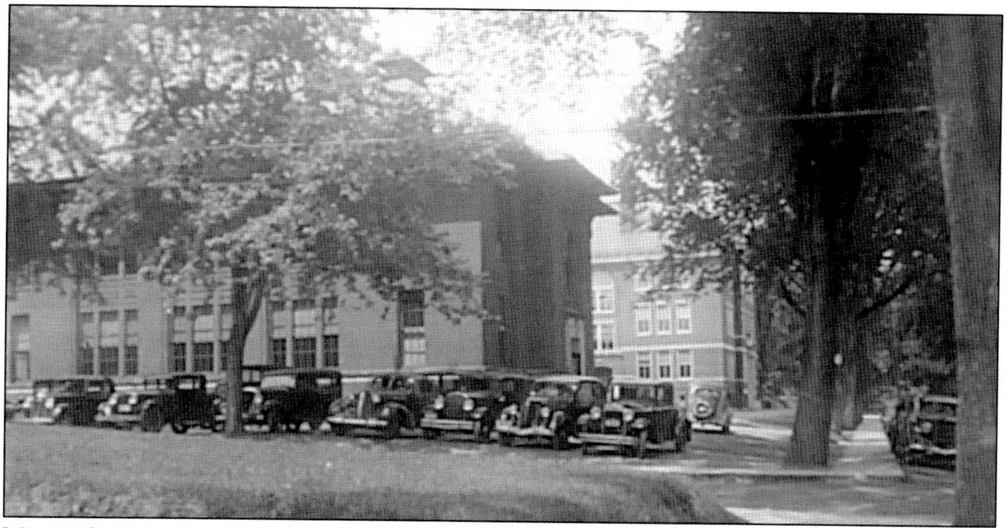

MODEL SCHOOL (NOW MEMORIAL HALL) AND THE OLD HIGH SCHOOL IN THE BACKGROUND. This photograph was probably taken by Dr. Lamson during the early 1930s. Trees lining Summer Street were mostly destroyed by Dutch elm disease and the hurricane of '38. This school was constructed in 1910 at a cost of $40,556.25 as a training elementary school (grades 1 through 8) for the Town of Plymouth. The faculty came from the Normal School and some senior students who practiced teaching in the classroom. When the new grade school was built in 1939 on the corner of High Street, opposite the high school, the seventh and eighth grade attended the Model School until 1963. In 1970, this building was purchased from the Town of Plymouth, and later, in 1974, it was renovated to house the college computer center. Today, it houses the Computer Science and Geography Departments.

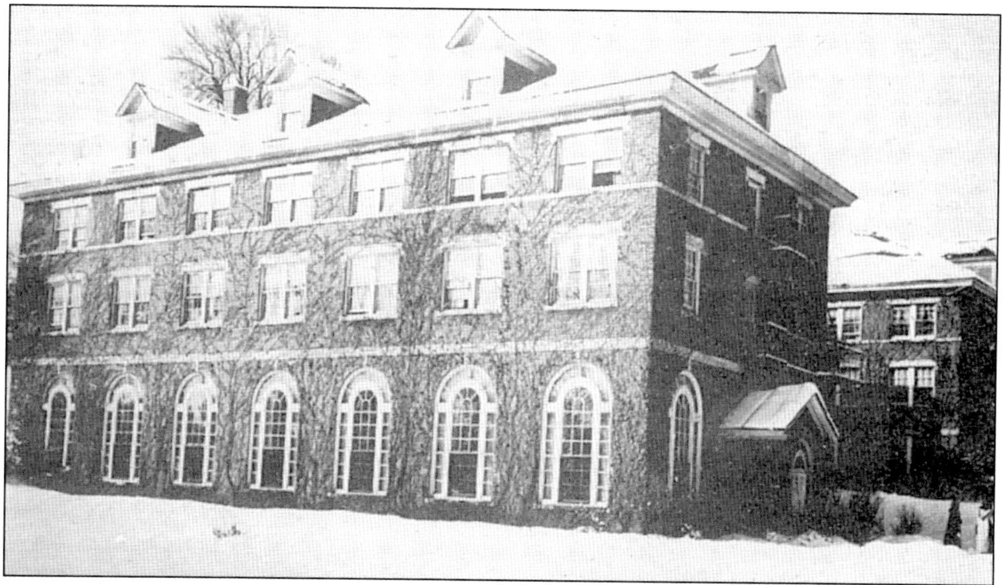

SAMUEL REED HALL DORMITORY AND ENTRANCE TO LAMSON LIBRARY. In 1923, the Peppard House on the corner of Highland Avenue and Highland Street was acquired. The barn was torn down and the first wing of Samuel Read Hall dormitory was constructed on the site. For some years, until further appropriations were forthcoming, students lived in the Peppard House while others lived in the completed wing of Hall Dormitory; the two were connected.

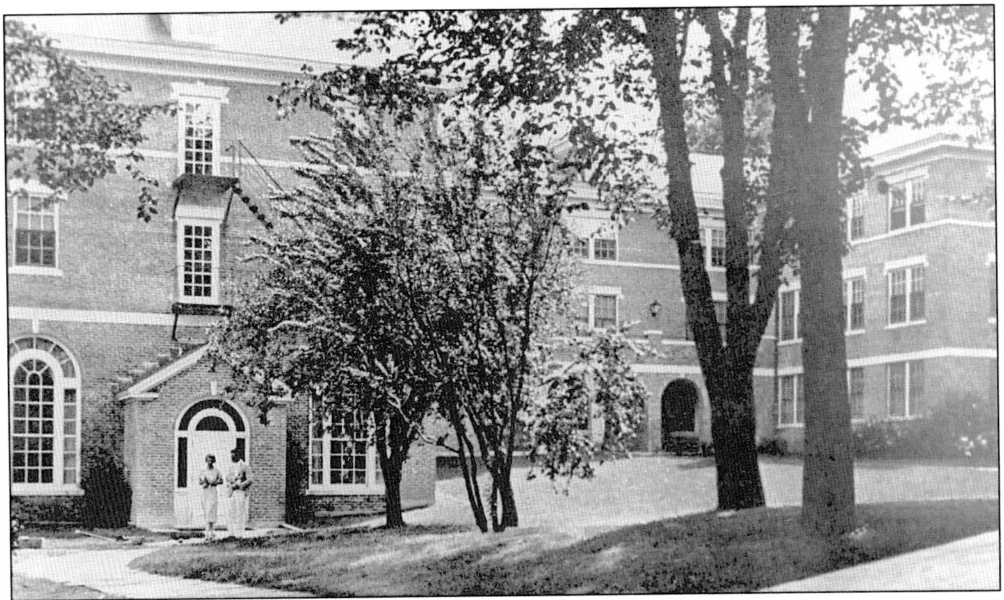

SAMUEL READ HALL DORMITORY AND LAMSON LIBRARY, 1923. The dormitory was completed in 1929 and honored the name of Samuel Read Hall who, in 1837, began the first seminary for training teachers. There were over 40 attractive double rooms as well as a few single rooms in this dormitory. It also contains a large and pleasant student lounge and adjoining sun porch. It later became a lecture hall and then the academic commons.

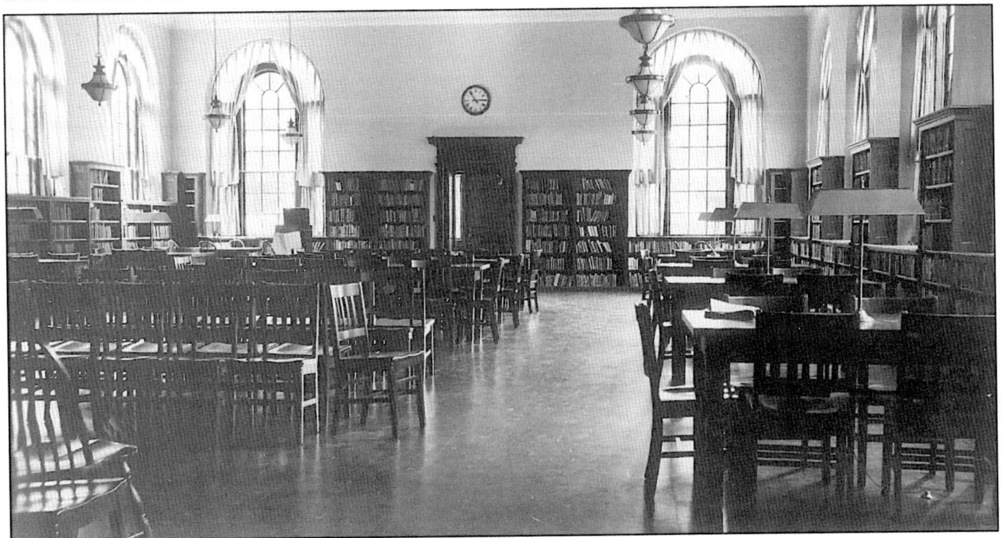

THE INTERIOR OF THE NEW LAMSON LIBRARY. This library was located on the lower floor of a new wing of Samuel Read Hall Dormitory and was opened in March of 1932. When the new wing to Hall Dormitory was added, it included the first planned library facility in the school's history. It was an extraordinary honor to name this library for Dr. Lamson since he was still an active faculty member. When Dr. Lamson spoke at the dedication of this new library on December 8, 1932, the text for his remarks was as follows: "*Thirty Years of Hoping or a Dream Come True.*" For many years the library was located in Hall Dormitory. It contained students' rooms, a matron's office, a little theater, a library, and some classrooms. As a result of building this new library, space in Rounds Hall was freed for other purposes.

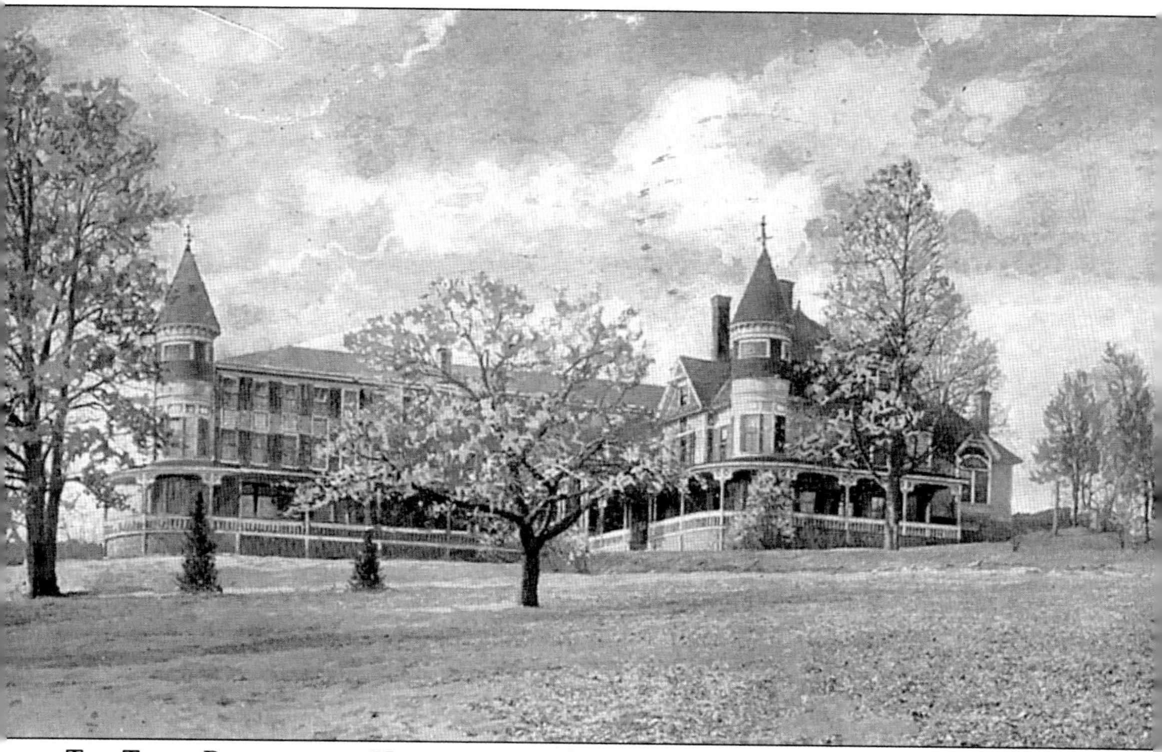

THE THIRD PEMIGEWASSET HOTEL, 1913. When the Mary Lyon Hall was constructed, the Normal Hall was moved from its original location on Highland Avenue to the east wing of the Pemigewasset Hotel. The feat of moving such a large structure was considered a large undertaking, especially when you consider that part of the journey was uphill. The capacity of the hotel was greatly increased after the addition. In 1965, a dormitory named Pemigewasset Hall was to occupy this site.

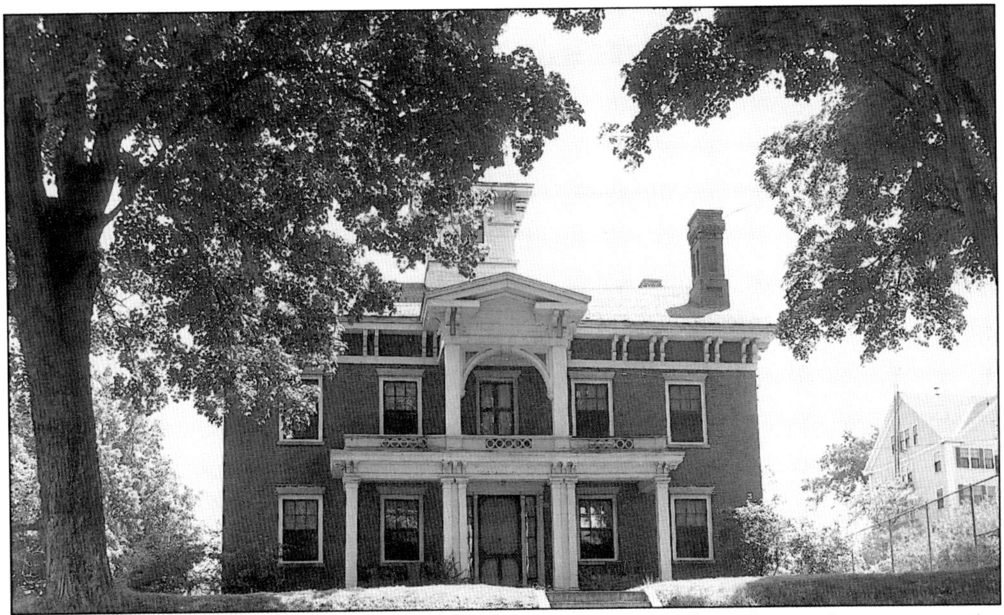

RUSSELL HOUSE, 1925. Due to the increasing enrollment of students for teacher training, the home of the Russell family was purchased for a dormitory. This red brick colonial mansion on Highland Street, with its kitchen erected in 1797 and the entire structure completed in 1825, is now a landmark that crowns the slope of the campus. Dr. Silver, president of the Normal School, preserved every architectural feature, including the unsupported staircase with its newel post that contained a small disk of ivory to prove that the house was free from debt. In 1967–68, this building was remodeled to accommodate Alumni, Admissions Offices, Public Relations, Social Science Department, and Director of Student Teaching.

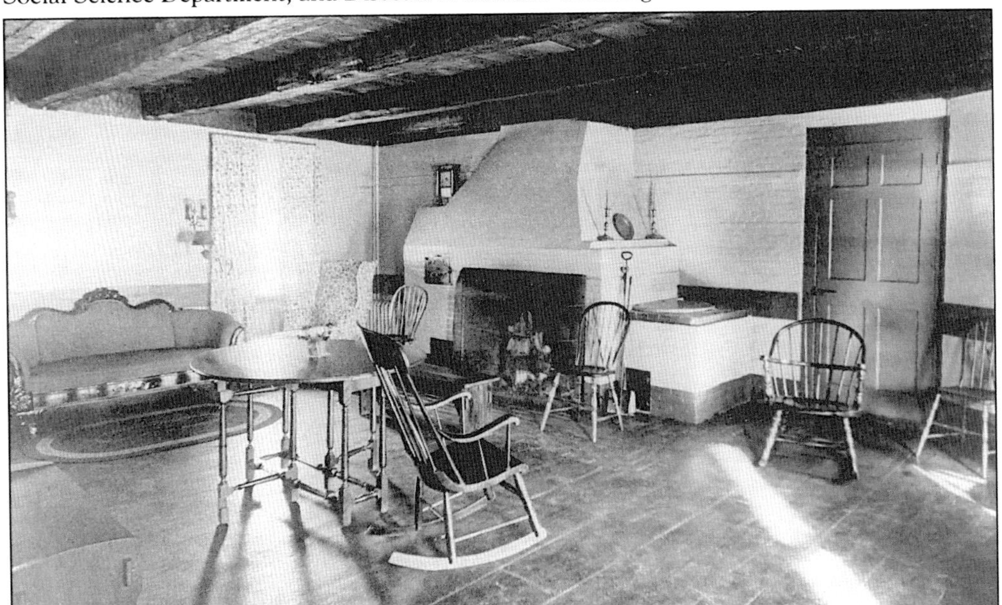

INTERIOR OF RUSSELL HOUSE. The kitchen, with its fireplace and hewn timbers, was converted into a living room for the students. The folding inside shutters at the front windows and the marble mantel for the fireplace remain intact today.

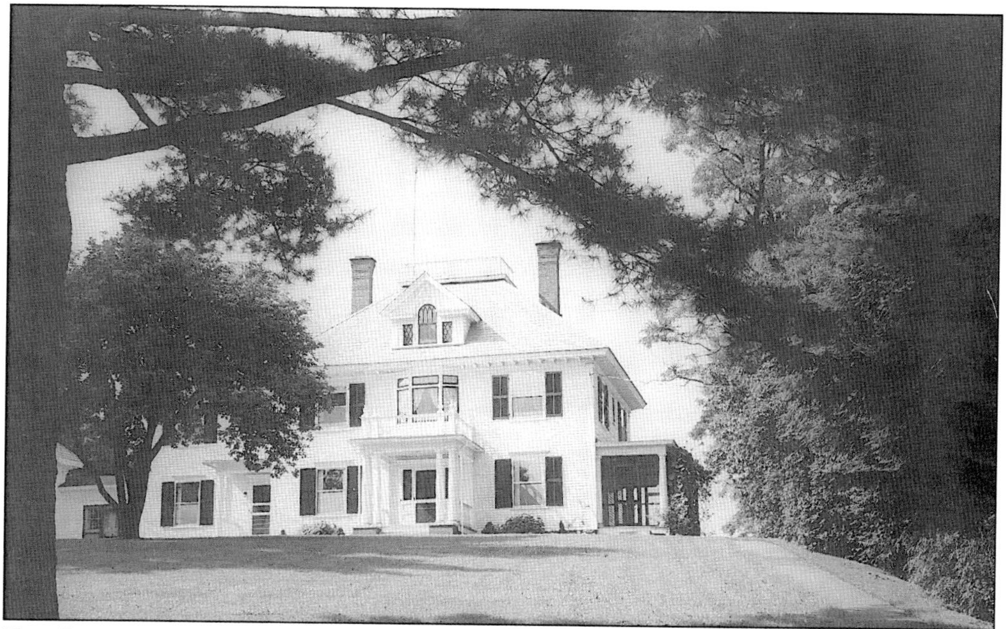

The President's House. The new president's house was acquired from the Shephard family in 1928. The interior was changed considerably during the Hyde administration to provide for greater office space, occasioned by the growth of the college administrative personnel. This house was originally built in 1904.

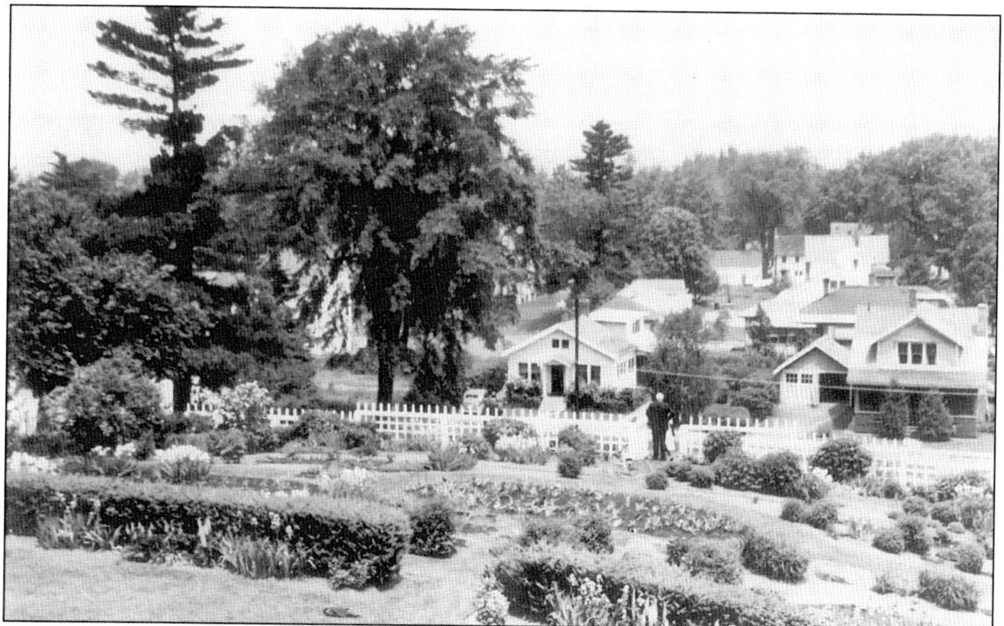

Garden at the President's House, 1929. At the north side of the president's home, a large vegetable garden had flourished. With the assistance of Prof. Robert Boyd, the landscape was changed into a beautiful garden with rose buds and borders of flowering shrubs that displayed the innate love for beauty held by Dr. Silver for many years. Frequently, afternoon teas for students and friends were enjoyed in this garden. One to be especially remembered occurred when Mr. and Mrs. Robert Frost were special guests.

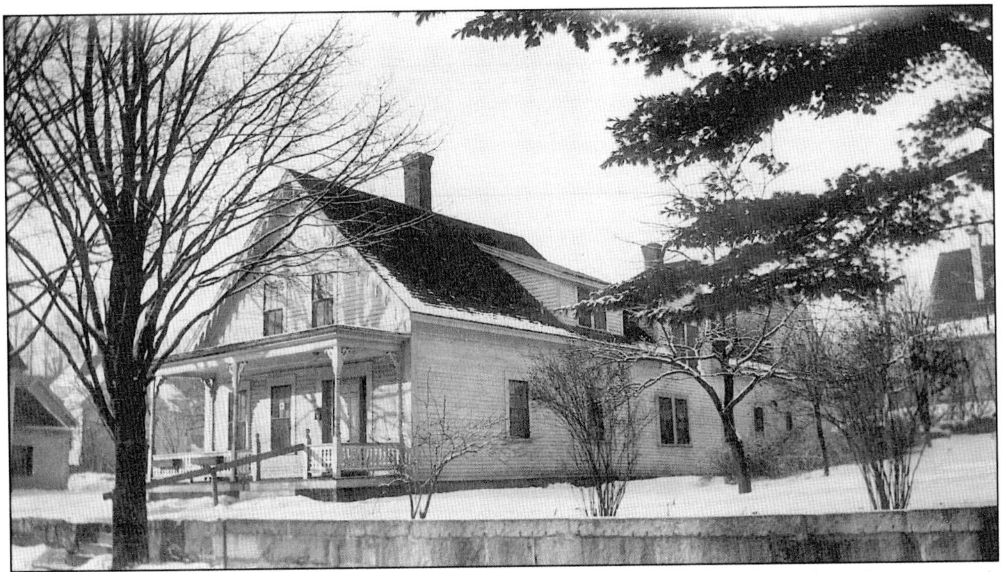

PERKINS HOUSE, 1925. This house, located on College Row, was purchased as a men's dormitory in 1925; remodeled in 1926, it accommodated 19 students. In 1931, it was renamed Grafton Hall after the county of Grafton, New Hampshire. This structure was later torn down to make way for Blair Hall.

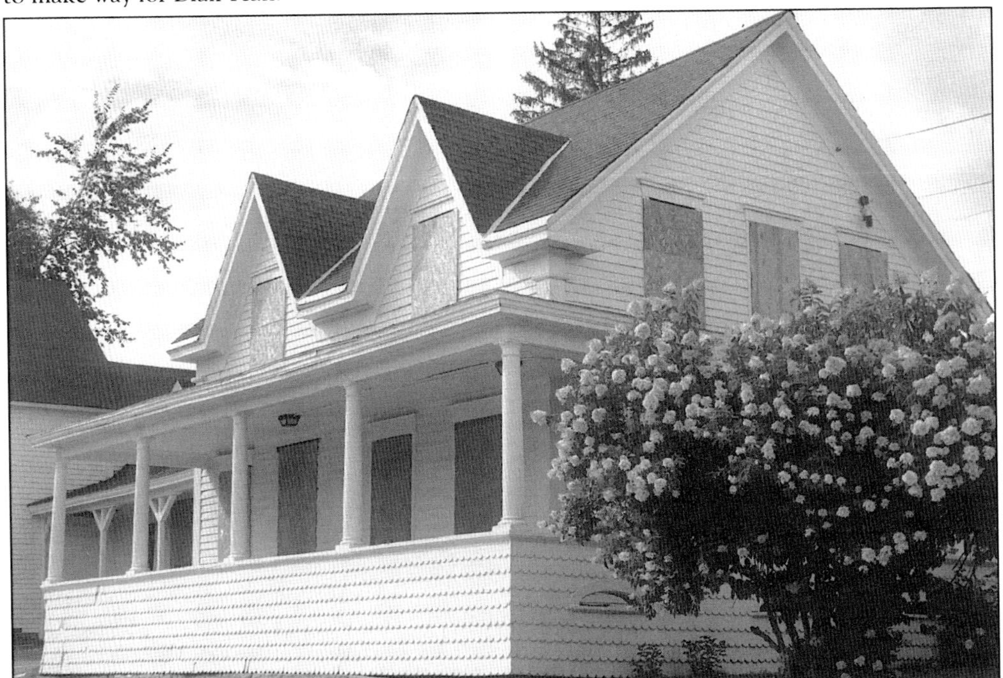

KLOCK HOUSE In 1904, the state purchased a house opposite Normal Hall as a home for the principal. This house became the home of the Klock family; later, Dr. Silver lived there. Since Dr. Silver's wife was ill during the early years of his administration and could not come to Plymouth, he asked the Robert Frost family to share their home with him while he taught at the school. A suitable plaque has been placed on the wall marking the residence of America's poet laureate in this house.

DR. SILVER STANDING BESIDE THE ROBERT FROST COTTAGE, 1926. In 1924, this house became part infirmary and part dormitory, until 1973 when the infirmary took the building over completely.

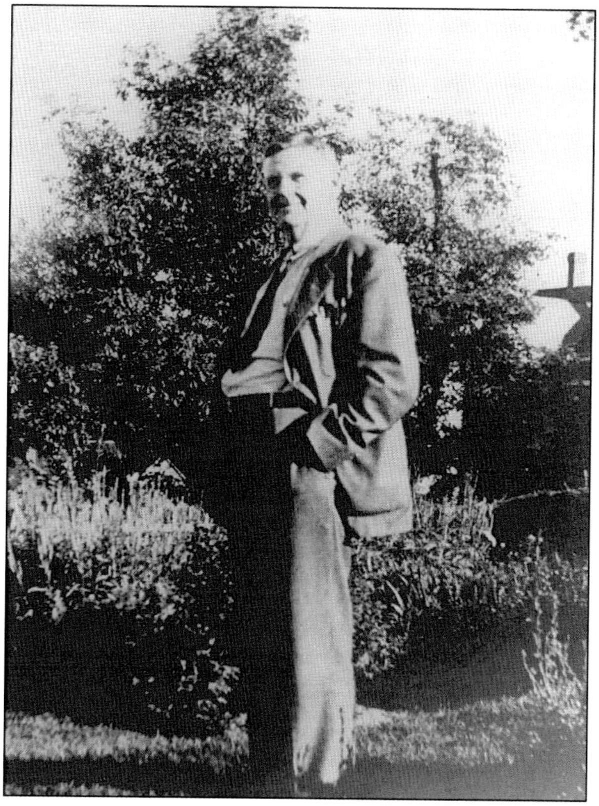

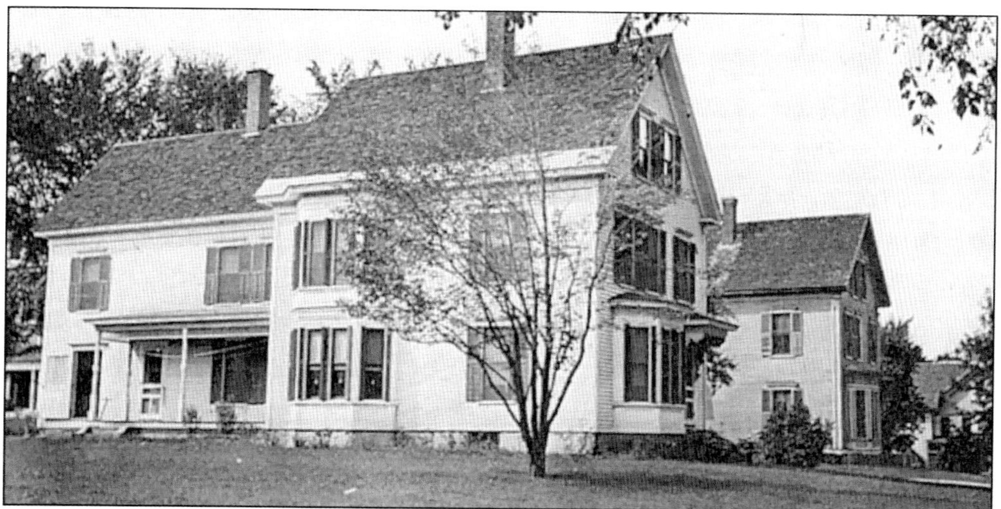

SMYTHE HOUSE, 1926. This men's dormitory was located on College Row, a street west of Mary Lyon Hall. It was later torn down to make way for Blair Hall. During its tenure, this hall was named Belknap Hall.

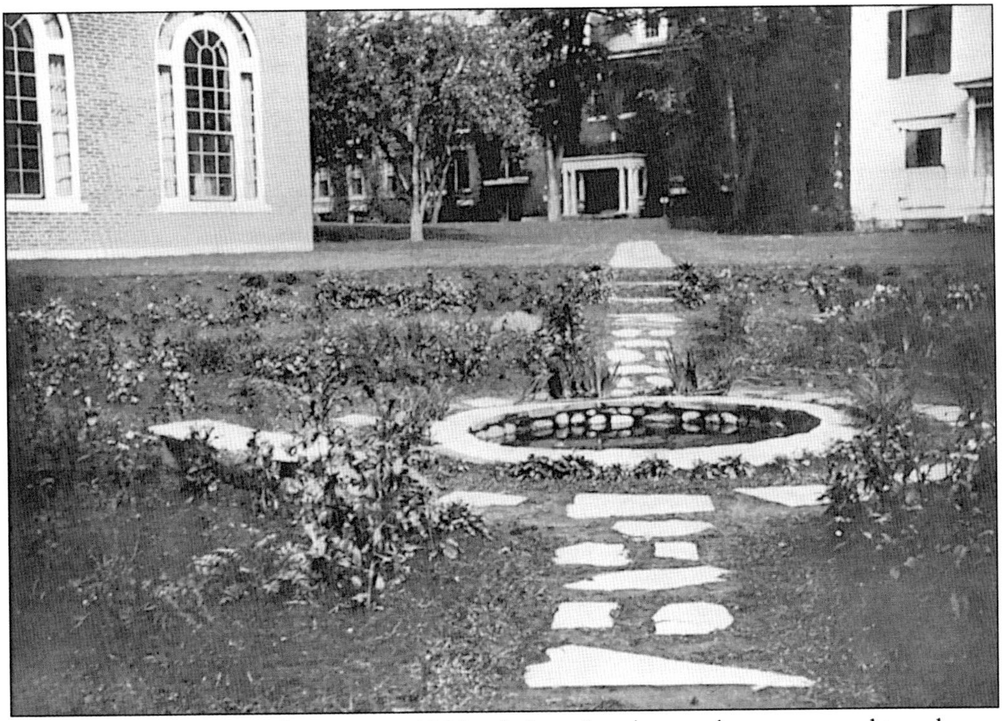

The Circular Sunken Garden, c. 1930s. A formal sunken garden was created to enhance the landscaping around Mary Lyon and Samuel Read Hall dormitories when Samuel Read Hall was remodeled in the early 1930s. Robert Boyd, who had graduated from the University of Massachusetts, was Dean of Men and Superintendent of Grounds at the time; thus, he used his expertise to design this beautiful garden.

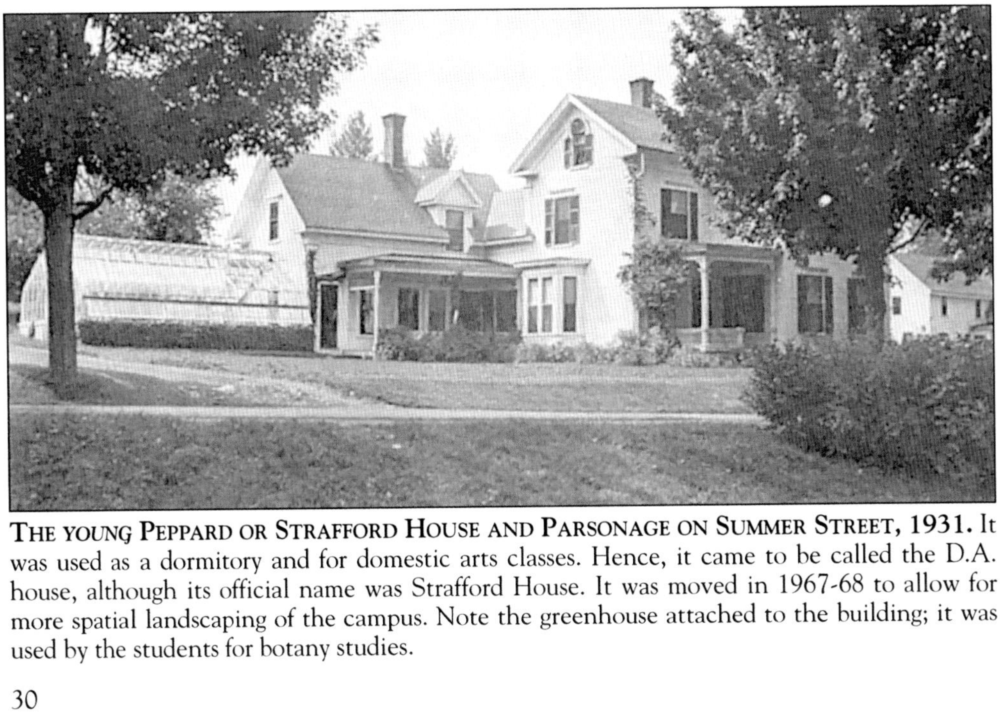

The young Peppard or Strafford House and Parsonage on Summer Street, 1931. It was used as a dormitory and for domestic arts classes. Hence, it came to be called the D.A. house, although its official name was Strafford House. It was moved in 1967-68 to allow for more spatial landscaping of the campus. Note the greenhouse attached to the building; it was used by the students for botany studies.

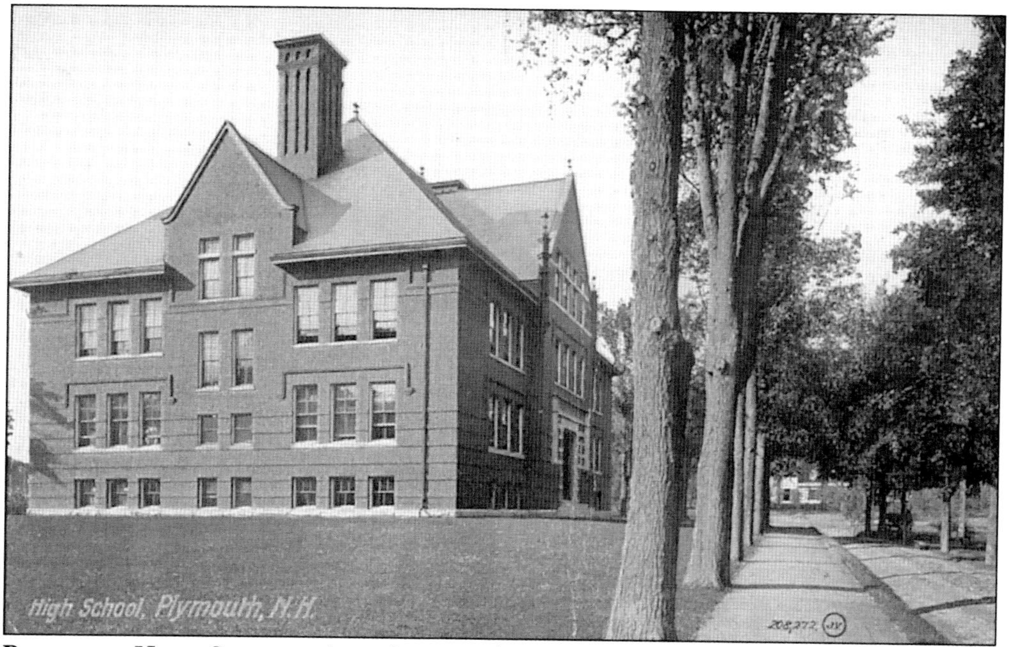

PLYMOUTH HIGH SCHOOL. According to Plymouth historians, the first high school was established in 1883 and met in Normal School facilities (Rounds Hall) and in a downtown business block until 1903. Later, it acquired its own building at the corner of Summer and High Streets. This building was dedicated in 1904.

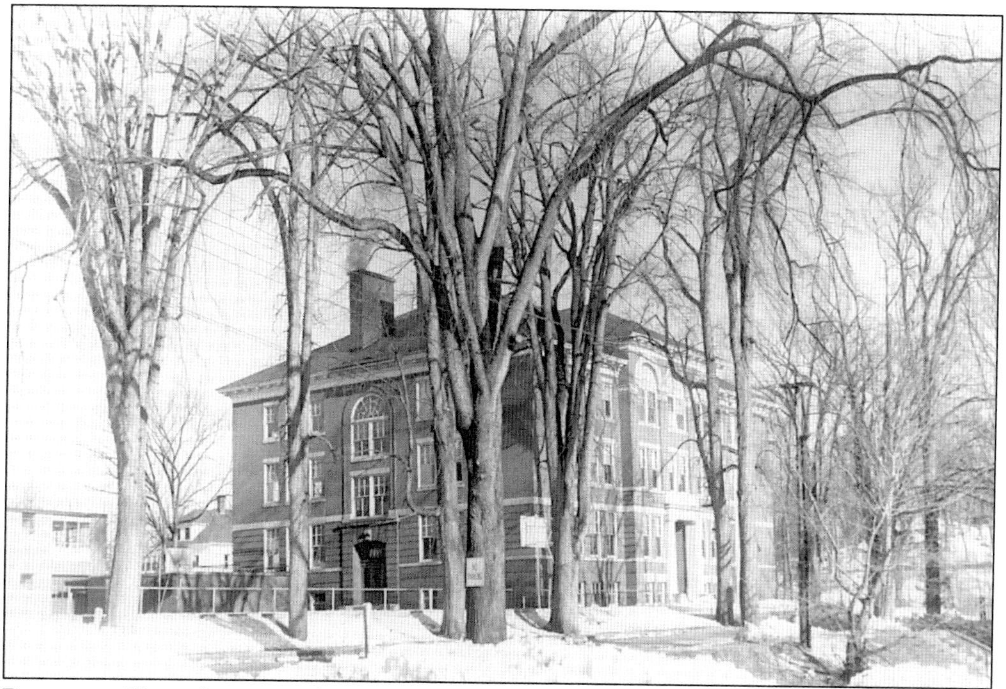

PLYMOUTH HIGH SCHOOL. The original building was lost to fire in 1914. It was replaced by a three-story building that was sold to Plymouth State College in 1970. In 1978, the high school was razed. Today, the sight is the Academic Common.

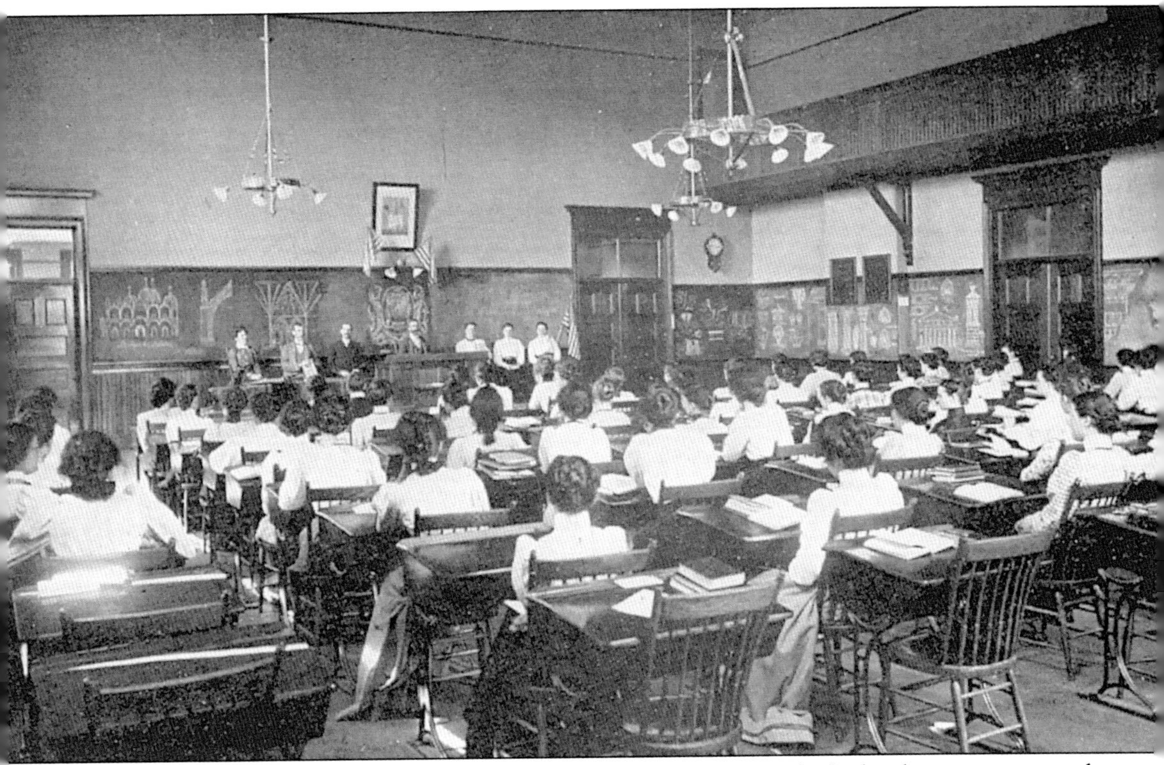

STUDENTS IN THE CLASSROOM. In 1883, the curriculum consisted of school organization and management, psychology, history and science of education, methods of teaching, practice in teaching, school law of New Hampshire, reading, composition, grammar, English literature with lectures three times weekly on American authors, arithmetic, bookkeeping, algebra, geometry, physics, chemistry, physiology, hygiene, mineralogy, botany, zoology, geography, history, civil government, writing, drawing, and singing. The course of study extended through two years; each year was divided into three terms respectively, of 12, 13, and 13 weeks.

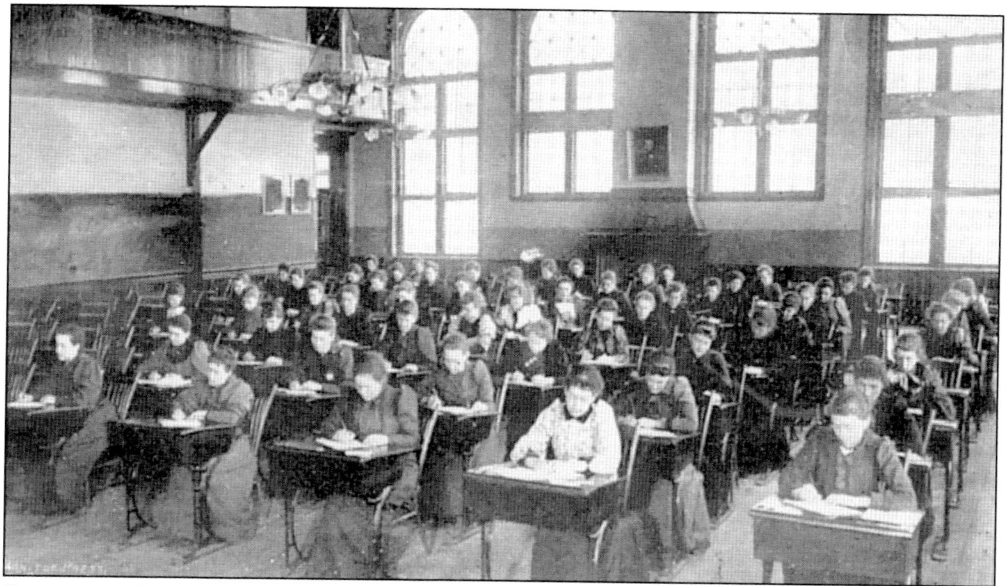

STUDENTS ATTENDING CLASS IN LIVERMORE HALL AT ROUNDS ASSEMBLY ROOM, 1899. During Dr. Silver's administration, the school saw a period of campus expansion and modernization—the opening of the new training school provided added space in Rounds Hall for additional instruction. Students were taught subjects that they would teach in the public schools. The students observed, participated, and taught in the model school or training school.

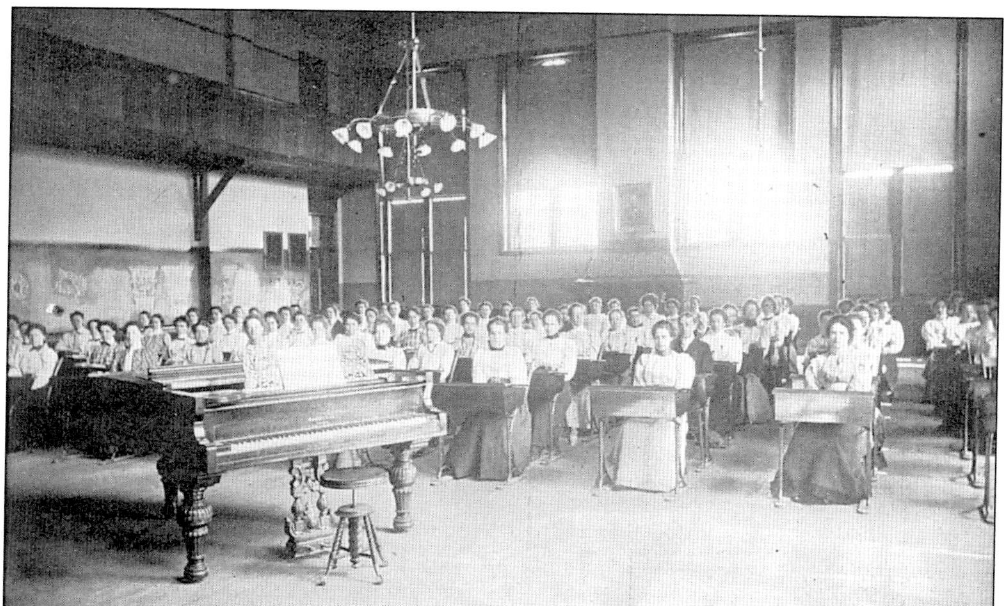

INTERIOR OF LIVERMORE HALL IN ROUNDS HALL, 1900–1901. This room was used for assemblies, music education, dramatics, and physical education.

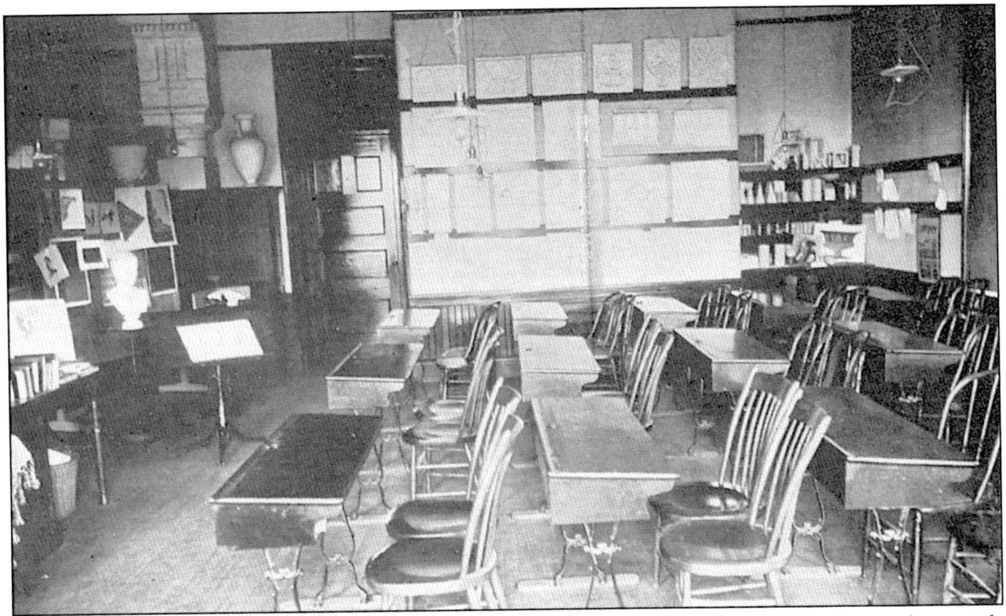

DRAWING ROOM, 1899. The course in drawing was introduced to familiarize the student with the work as taken up in all the grades of the public schools, to cultivate judgment and taste,; to train the eye and hand, and to enable the student as teacher to impart the same to others. No attempt was made to create artists, but to lead the student to see and express truth and beauty.

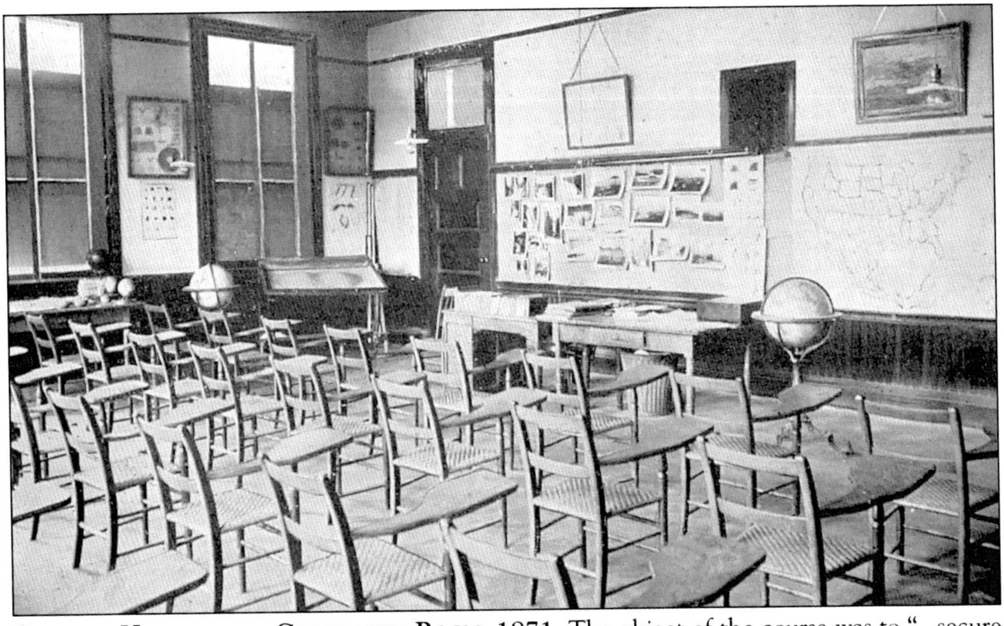

GENERAL HISTORY AND GEOGRAPHY ROOM, 1871. The object of the course was to "...secure proper methods of historical study, and the power to judge accurately the relative importance of facts and periods in history, and to gain a clear knowledge of the individual, social, and political life of our country. Connection of European and American history is made by means of a careful study of the early explorers and their influence on the colonization of America." —*NHNS Catalog and Curriculum Guide*.

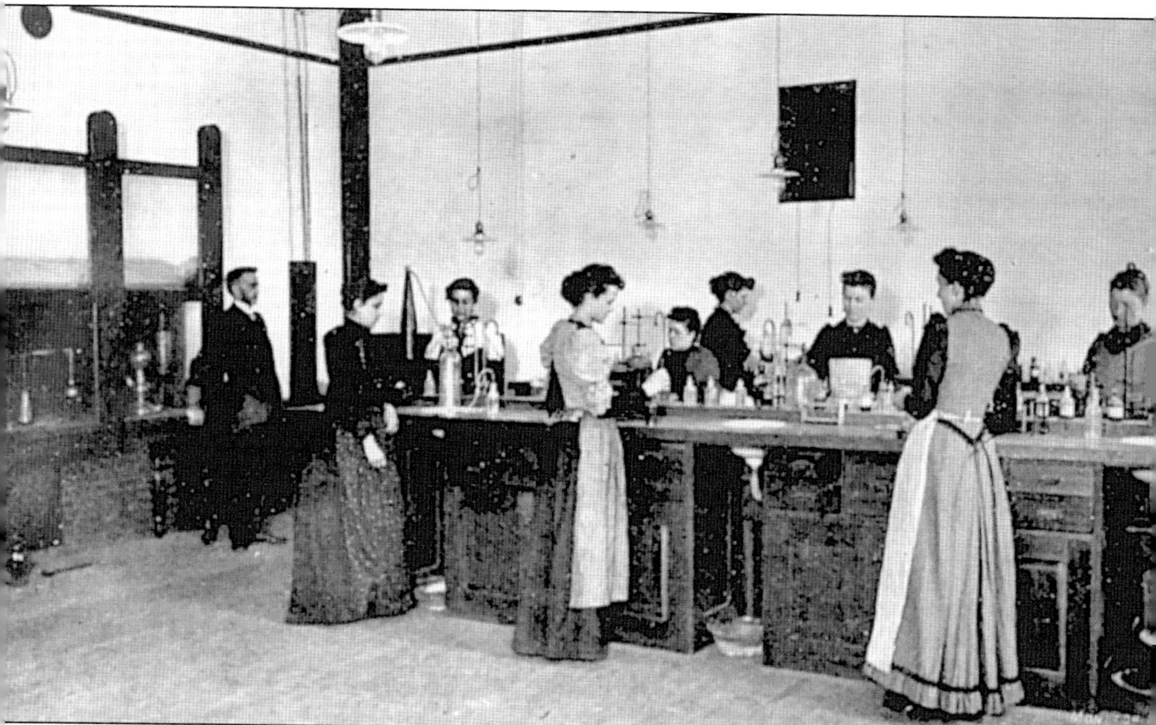

CHEMICAL LABORATORY, 1892–93. Here in Rounds Hall, these young ladies are seen at the laboratory bench in their typical Victorian dress with aprons. There were two courses in chemistry. The first included the most important principles of inorganic chemistry, while the second was spent in laboratory work in well-equipped laboratories. These exercises were intended to cultivate in the student the power to observe closely, experiment intelligently, reason logically, and judge impartially. She was expected to acquire these basic skills in manipulation and fundamental or typical facts—the study of which will lead to an understanding of laws and theories. Today, the Education Department has a classroom in the old lab.

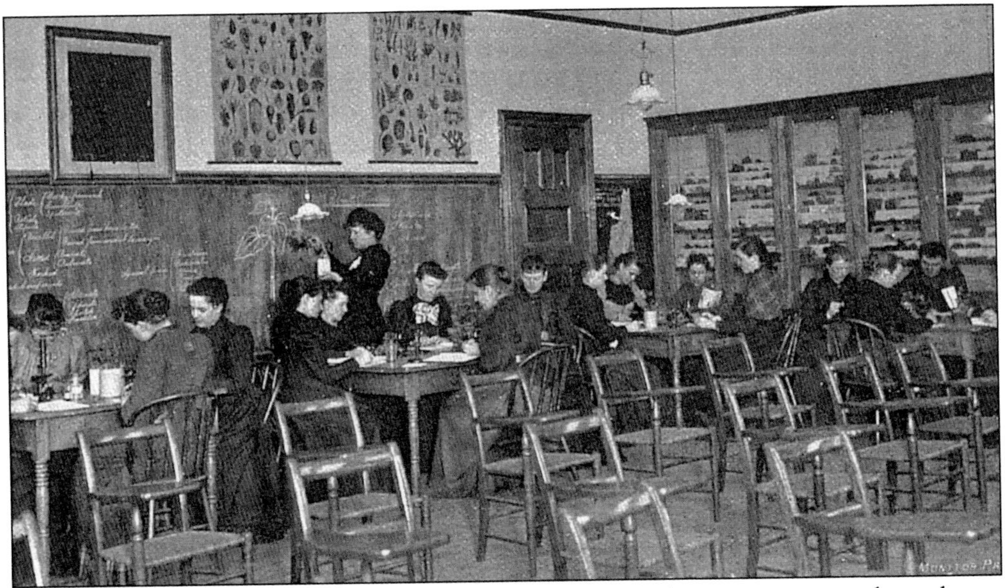

NATURAL HISTORY ROOM 107, 1892–93. Here, the young ladies are seen grouped together to make a floral calendar in which to make collections of pressed specimens and wood for a natural history class.

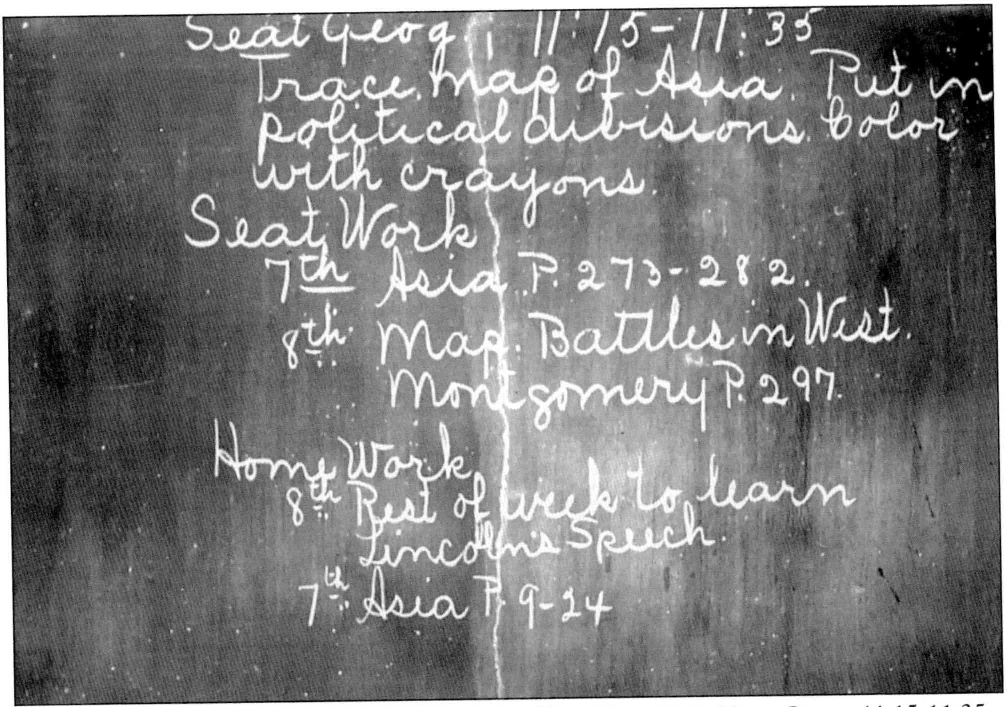

BOARD ASSIGNMENT GIVEN BY D.H. SAWYER, MAY 29, 1905. "Seat Geog., 11:15-11:35 - Trace map of Asia. Put in political divisions. Color with crayons. Seat Work 7th Asia. P. 273-282, 8th Map. Battles in West. Montgomery P. 297. HomeWork 8th Rest of week to learn Lincoln's Speech. 7th Asia P. 9-24." This board was found during the renovation of the classroom in 1998.

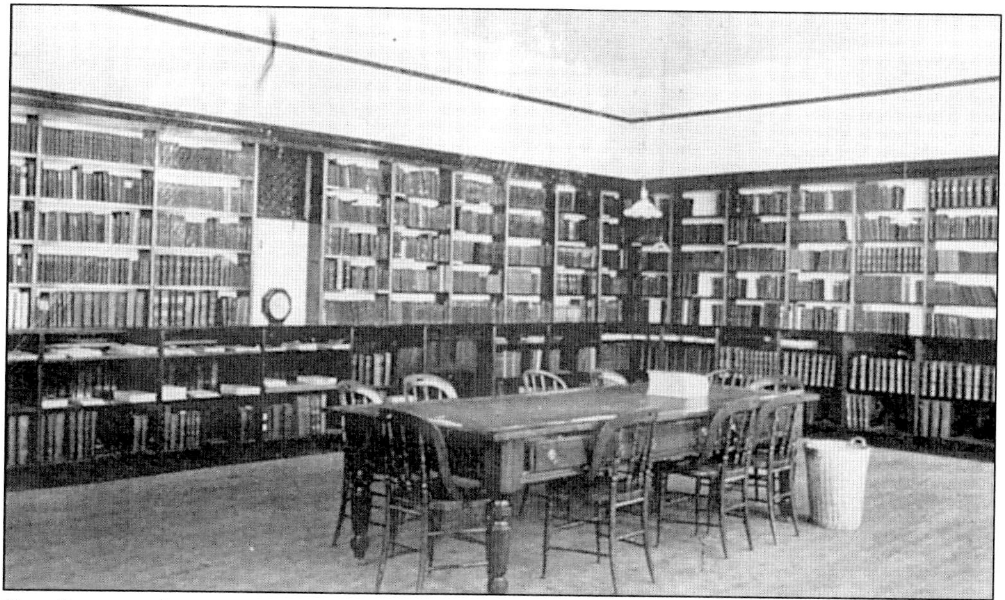

OLD LAMSON LIBRARY, 1897–98. A good general reference and professional library, which comprised several thousand volumes, was open daily to students for their use from 7 a.m. to 6 p.m. This reading room was well supplied with daily and weekly papers, pedagogical magazines, and leading profession journals of the time.

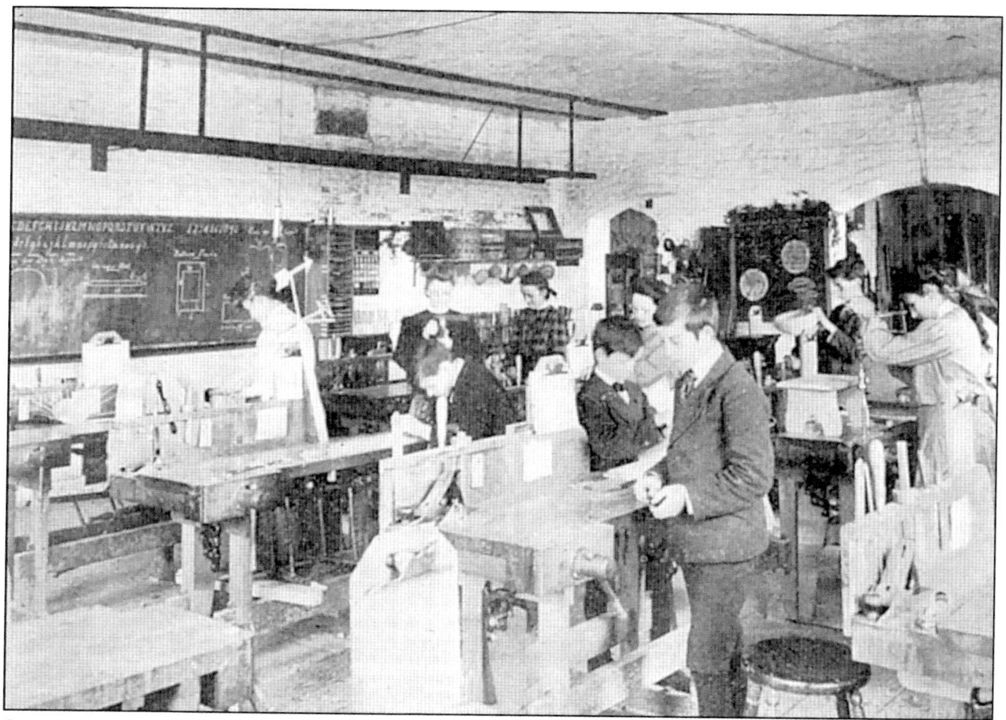

SLOYD ROOM, 1906–1907. Manual training was another innovation added in the curriculum.

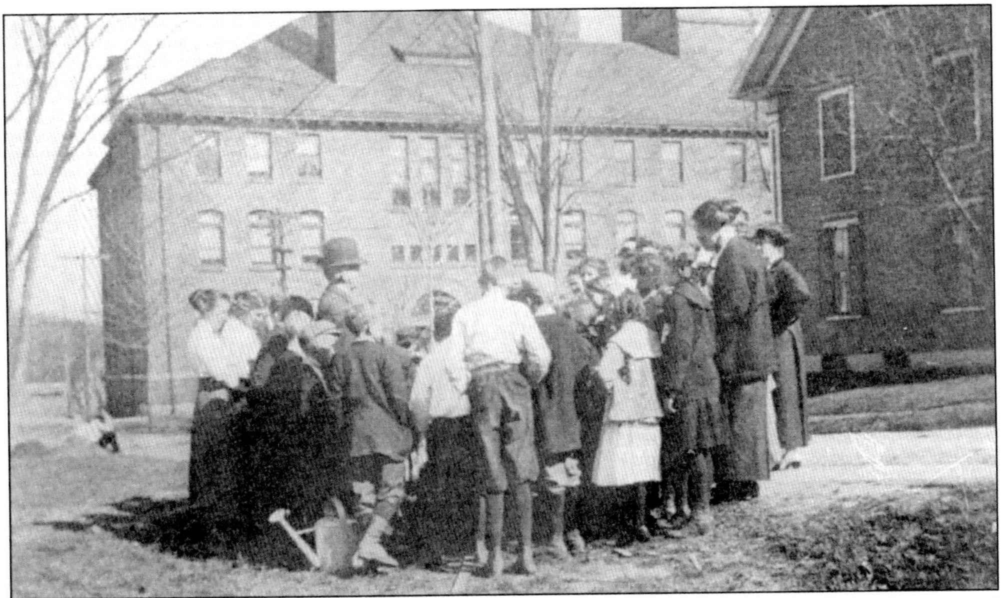

Dr. Lamson Planting a Tree, 1913–14. In 1903, revisions were made when physics and chemistry became electives; at that time, the natural sciences including, geography, nature study, elementary science, manual training, domestic economy (home economics), and gardening became included in the curriculum. In the background is Rounds Hall with the Ellen Reed House to the right.

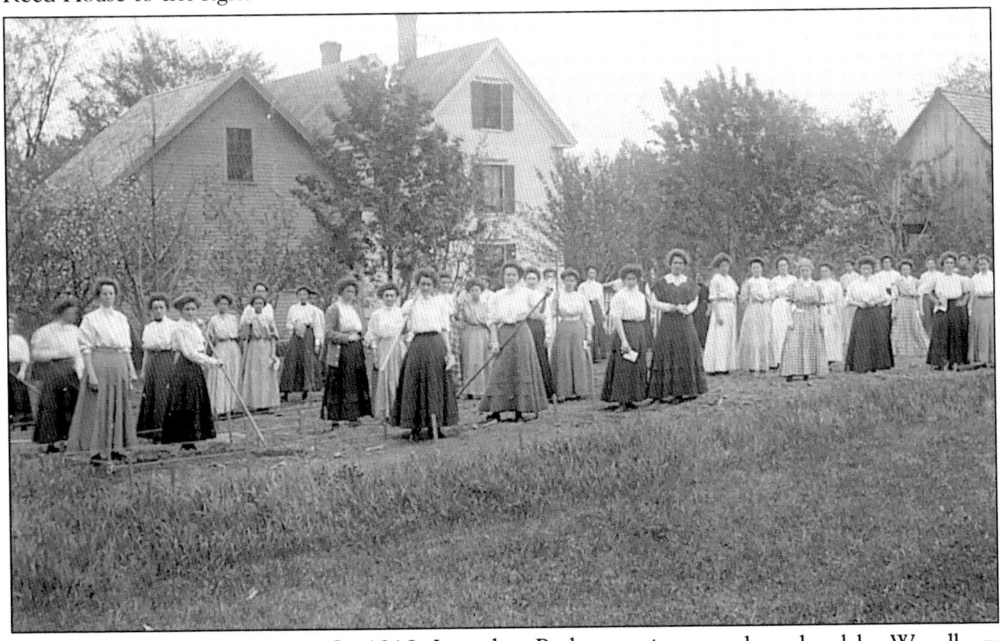

Normal Girls Gardening. In 1918, Langdon Park was given to the school by Woodbury Langdon, a citizen of Plymouth. This tract of land, approximately 20 acres located on the shores of the Baker River, was widely used for many years for nature study, recreation, and other varied college activities. The college also maintained a garden there for many years in which vegetables were grown for college use. Gardening was considered essential in making practical applications in the elementary school for the natural sciences.

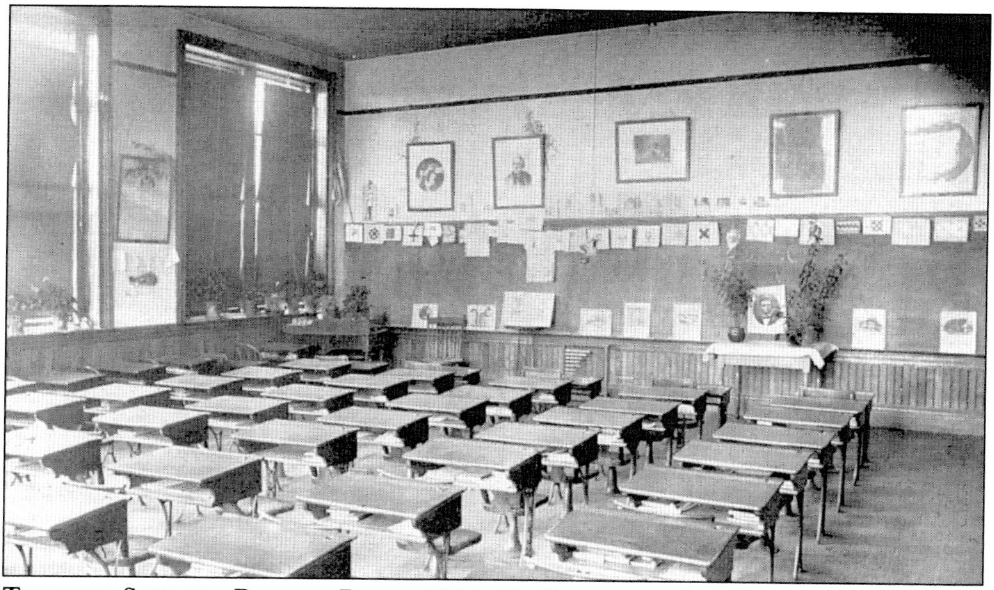

TRAINING SCHOOL—PRIMARY ROOM, 1896–97. Training in teaching was essential to the success of the normal school. This training school was the laboratory for individual work. As model schools, illustrating methods of school organization and management, they were designed to teach the characteristics of well-organized public schools objectively. As training schools, they were used for teaching the practical application of the principles and methods previously learned through observation and instruction.

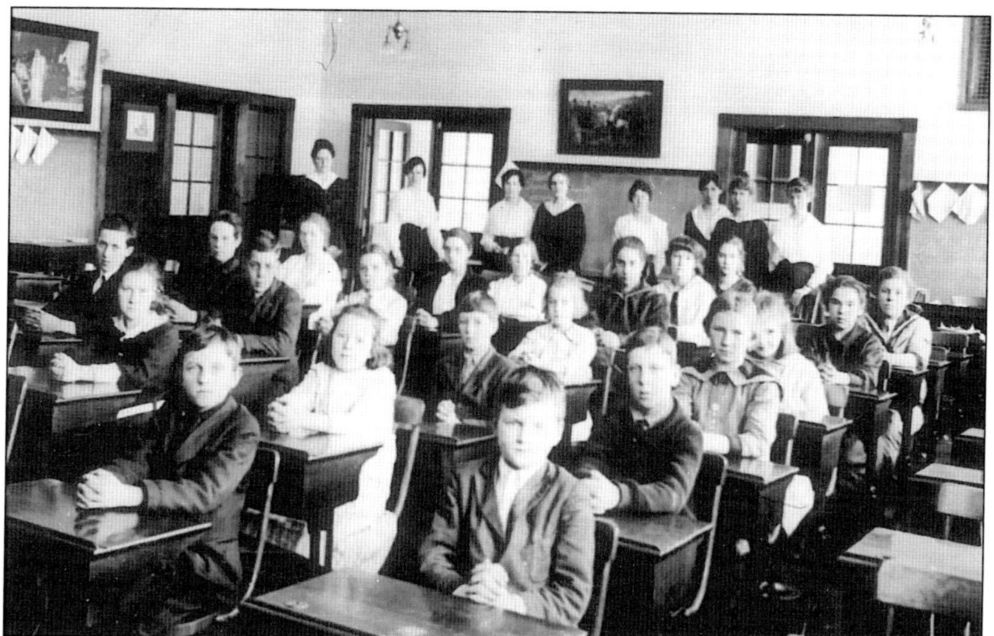

STUDENTS IN TRAINING SCHOOL WITH TEACHERS IN THE BACK OF THE ROOM. In 1910–1912, a curriculum was introduced for teachers of special subjects. This curriculum was the first three-year program. The first two years were the elementary curriculum, but the third year was devoted to advanced study in special subjects with practice teaching in the special field.

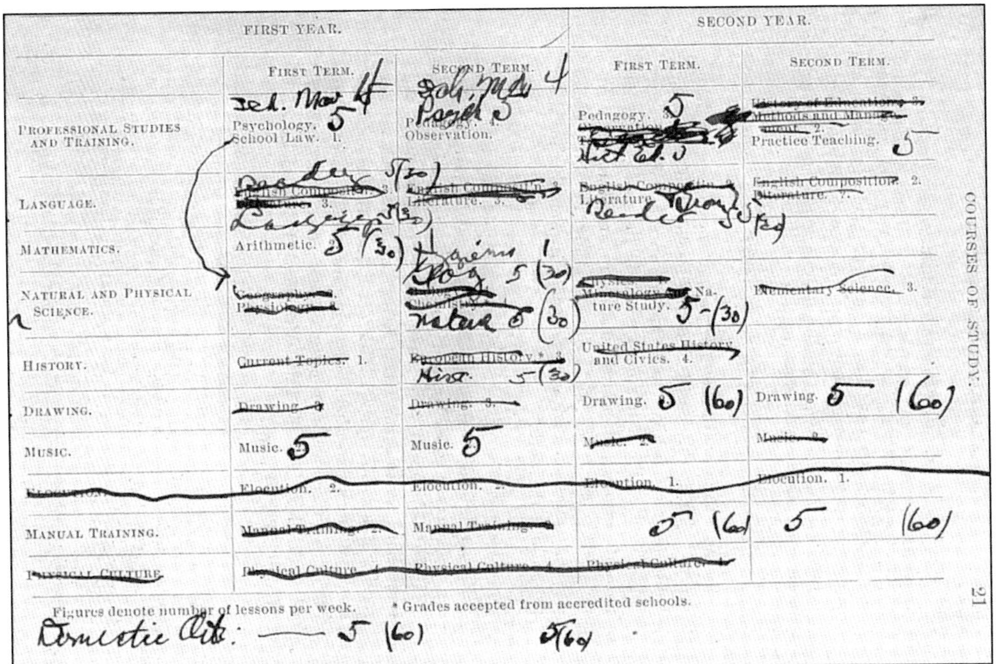

	FIRST YEAR. First Term.	FIRST YEAR. Second Term.	SECOND YEAR. First Term.	SECOND YEAR. Second Term.
PROFESSIONAL STUDIES AND TRAINING.	Psychology. 5 School Law. 1.	Pedagogy. 1. Observation.	Pedagogy. 3.	History of Education. 3. Methods and Management. 2. Practice Teaching. 5
LANGUAGE.	English Composition. 3. Literature. 3.	English Composition. 3. Literature. 3.	English Composition. 3. Literature. 3.	English Composition. 2. Literature. 2.
MATHEMATICS.	Arithmetic. 5			
NATURAL AND PHYSICAL SCIENCE.	Geography. 3. Physiology. 3.	Biology. 3. Chemistry. 3.	Physics. Mineralogy. 3. Nature Study.	Elementary Science. 3.
HISTORY.	Current Topics. 1.	European History.* 3.	United States History and Civics. 4.	
DRAWING.	Drawing. 3.	Drawing. 3.	Drawing. 5 (60)	Drawing. 5 (60)
MUSIC.	Music. 5	Music. 5	Music. 2.	Music. 2.
ELOCUTION.	Elocution. 2.	Elocution. 2.	Elocution. 1.	Elocution. 1.
MANUAL TRAINING.	Manual Training. 2.	Manual Training. 2.	5 (60)	5 (60)
PHYSICAL CULTURE.	Physical Culture. 4.	Physical Culture. 4.	Physical Culture. 4.	

Figures denote number of lessons per week. * Grades accepted from accredited schools.

COURSES OF STUDY. 21

COURSE OF INSTRUCTION, 1910. The development of skill in teaching is the practical aim and the immediate test of the character and value of the instruction given in the Normal School. Teachers were responsible for the methods of instruction in their respective branches used by pupil-teachers in the training schools and governed themselves in conjunction with the training school teachers concerning the planning of work and supervising of instruction. The essential elements in the qualifications of the teacher were personal character, scholarship, power of control, and skill in teaching. Fitness of character was demanded as a condition of admission to the normal school and its course of study was adapted to assure adequate scholarship.

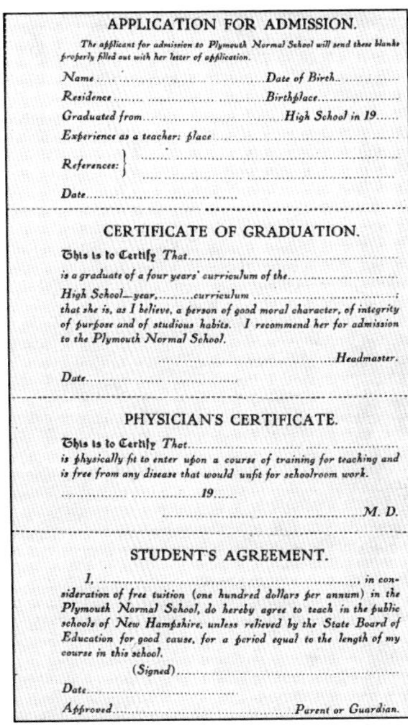

APPLICATION FOR ADMISSION.

The applicant for admission to Plymouth Normal School will send these blanks properly filled out with her letter of application.

Name .... *Date of Birth* ....
Residence .... *Birthplace* ....
Graduated from .... *High School in 19* ....
Experience as a teacher: place ....
References: ....
Date ....

CERTIFICATE OF GRADUATION.

This is to Certify *That* ....
is a graduate of a four years' curriculum of the ....
High School—year, ... *curriculum* ....;
that she is, as I believe, a person of good moral character, of integrity of purpose and of studious habits. I recommend her for admission to the Plymouth Normal School.
.... *Headmaster.*
Date ....

PHYSICIAN'S CERTIFICATE.

This is to Certify *That* ....
is physically fit to enter upon a course of training for teaching and is free from any disease that would unfit for schoolroom work.
.... *19* ....
.... *M. D.*

STUDENT'S AGREEMENT.

I, ..., *in consideration of free tuition (one hundred dollars per annum) in the Plymouth Normal School, do hereby agree to teach in the public schools of New Hampshire, unless relieved by the State Board of Education for good cause, for a period equal to the length of my course in this school.*
(Signed) ....
Date ....
Approved .... *Parent or Guardian.*

CERTIFICATES, 1920. In 1918, the program of studies in the various curricula were first set up in terms of credit hours, with 100 credits being required for graduation from the two-year elementary program and 120 semester hours for the three-year programs. This change represents another trend toward the college atmosphere and customs as opposed to the normal school. Graduates and students of colleges, scientific schools, and other normal schools would receive credit by a transfer of records; students received the diploma of this school when they accomplished the additional work needed for the completion of its course of study and training.

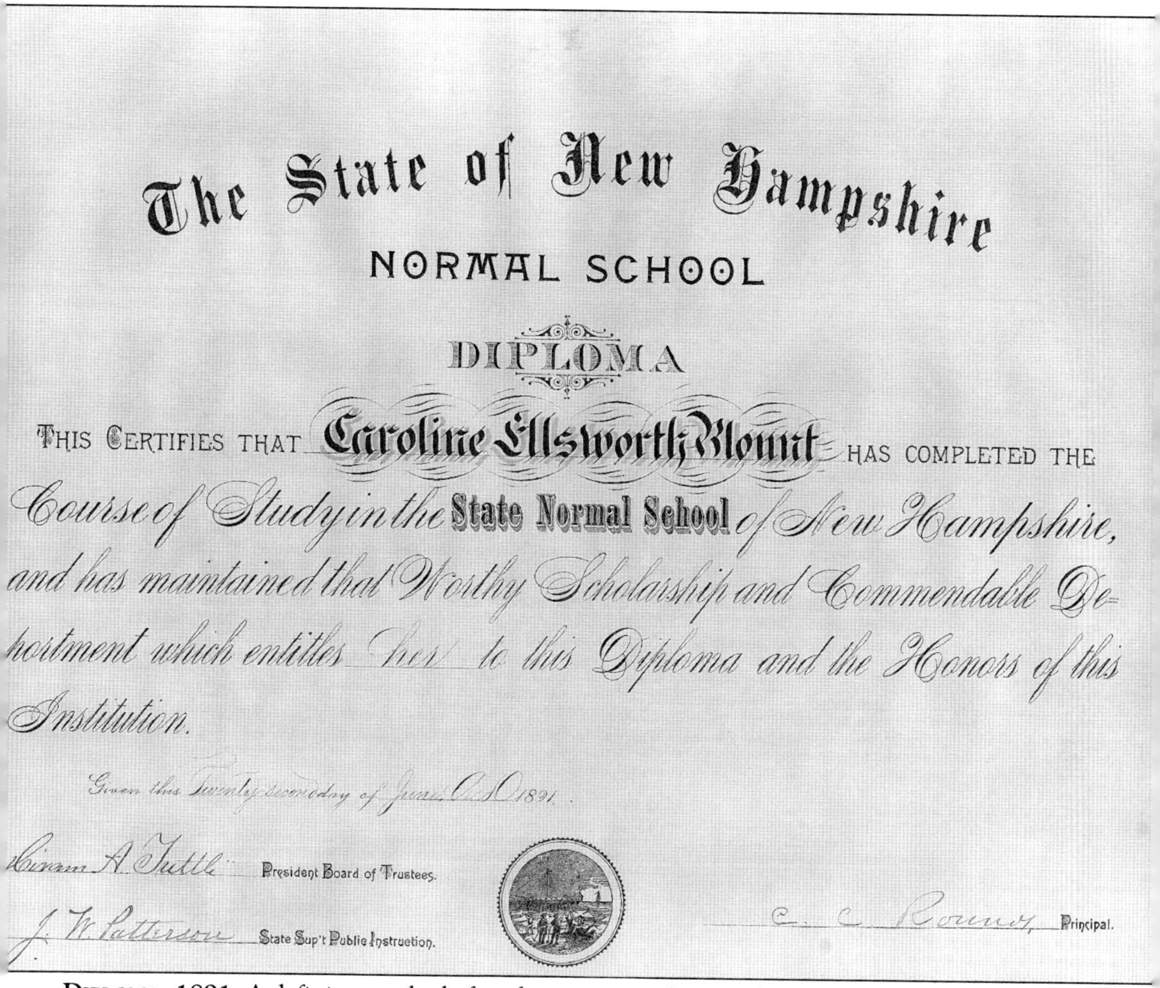

The State of New Hampshire

NORMAL SCHOOL

DIPLOMA

THIS CERTIFIES THAT Caroline Ellsworth Blount HAS COMPLETED THE Course of Study in the State Normal School of New Hampshire, and has maintained that Worthy Scholarship and Commendable Deportment which entitles her to this Diploma and the Honors of this Institution.

Given this Twenty second day of June A.D. 1891.

Hiram A. Tuttle President Board of Trustees.

J. W. Patterson State Sup't Public Instruction.

C. C. Rounds Principal.

DIPLOMA, 1891. A definite standard of proficiency in studies was demanded for promotion, but aside from this, it was not found necessary to make distinctions of scholarship. Faithful attention to duty for its own sake was the surest passport to the honors of the school. Students were graduated when they had satisfactorily completed the course of study and upon graduation they received a diploma. "This diploma is a certificate of admission to the profession, and is received throughout the United States as evidence of professional character."—*State Normal School*, 1891.

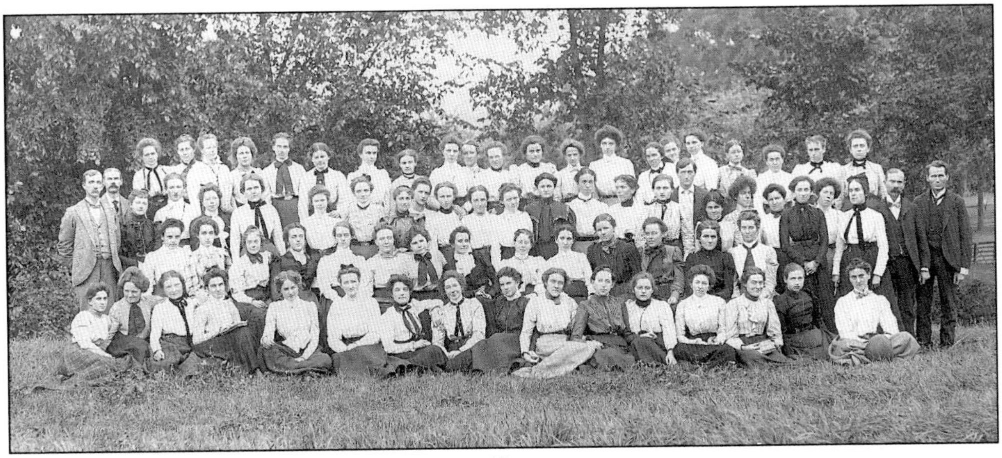

THE CLASS OF 1900 IN SEPTEMBER OF THAT YEAR.

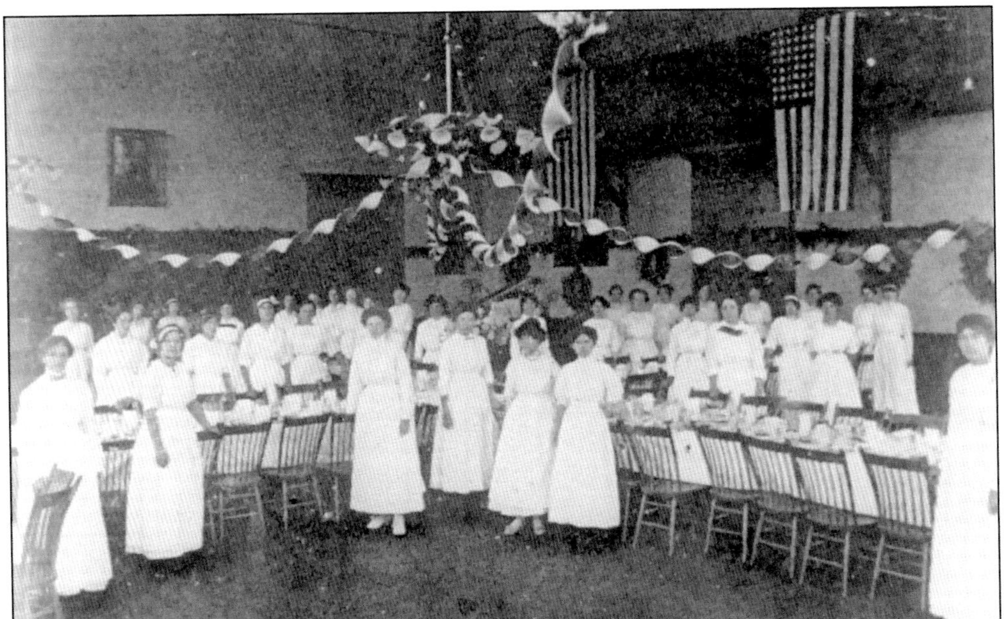

ALUMNI BANQUET IN THE ASSEMBLY ROOM IN ROUNDS HALL, C. 1890S. Here, the Junior class is seen serving their guests their own prepared meal.

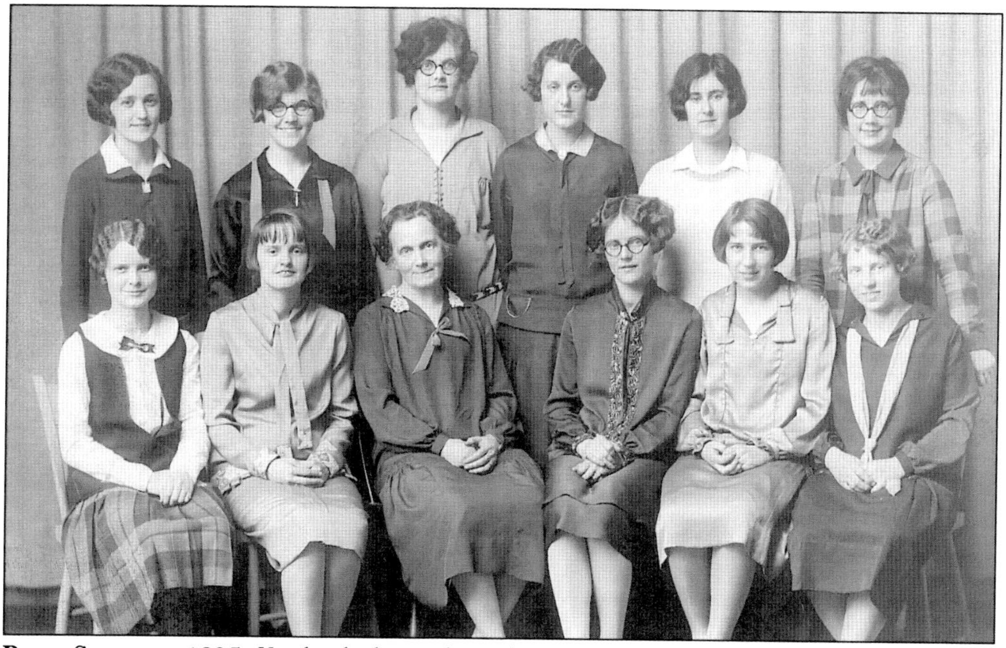

BOOK STAFF, C. 1935. Yearbooks have always been an important asset to school in order to record and preserve their legacy and heritage through the years. Seen here, from left to right, are as follows: (front row) T. Pease, L. Johnson, Mrs. Furlong, B. Hunt, S. Morrill, and R. Pearson; (back row) K. Sanborn, E. Ramburg, M. Allen, B. Cram, E. Ward, and D. Holman.

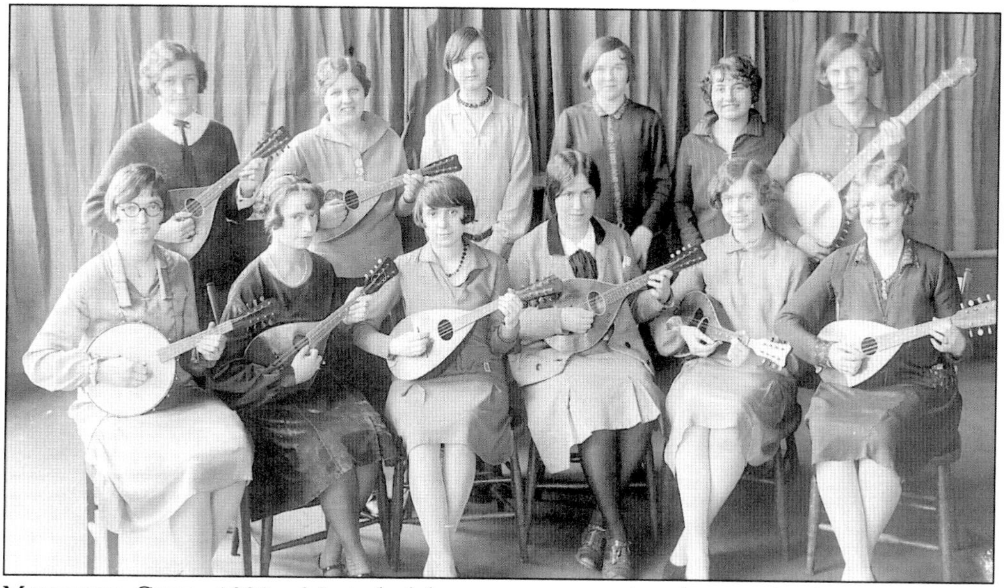

MANDOLIN CLUB, 1920S. Musical clubs were very popular; during school functions, each musical group would be asked to perform. This small enthusiastic group of girls constituted the mandolin club. Through regular rehearsals and serious practice a great deal of pleasure was attained by the participants. This group joined daily with the orchestra to furnish music for the chapel exercises. Seen here, from left to right, are as follows: (front row) R. Young, A. Harriman, M. Twombly, R. Abbott, E. Eastman, and B. Maiwald; (back row) K. Sanborn, L. Davis, E. Fiske, I. Boucher, D. Grevior, and H. Wheeler.

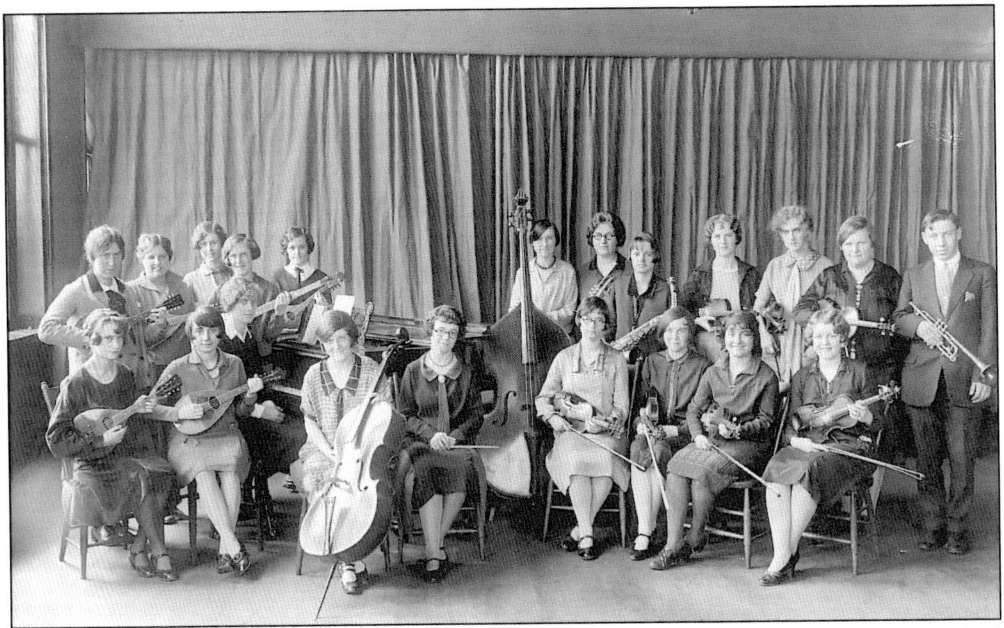

ORCHESTRA, 1930S. This popular musical group developed in-depth talents and furnished entertainment for school functions. Seen here, from left to right, are as follows: (front row) A. Harriman, M. Twombly, I. Langmard, A Mills, Miss Glasson, R. Young, I. Boucher, D. Grevoir, and B. Maiwald; (back row) R. Abbott, L Davis, E. Eastman, H.Wheeler, K. Sanborn, E. Fiskke, L. Shaft, L. Johnson, V. Pray, R. Luce, H. Smith, and F. Thompson.

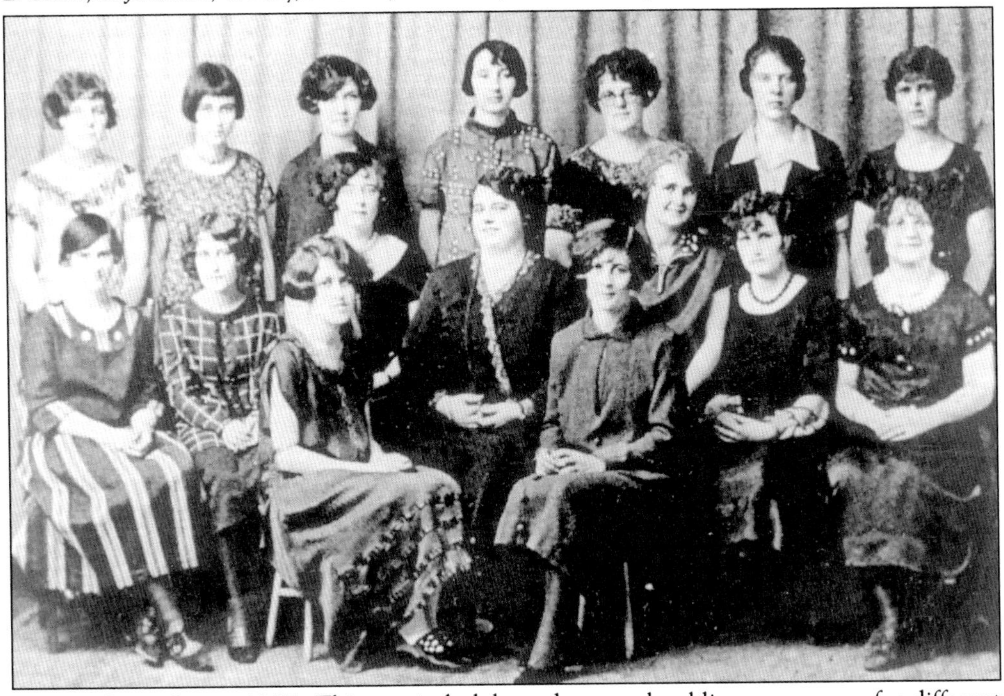

SENIOR GLEE CLUB, 1925. This musical club made several public appearances for different school occasions and frequently contributed to the entertainment in town and other nearby communities.

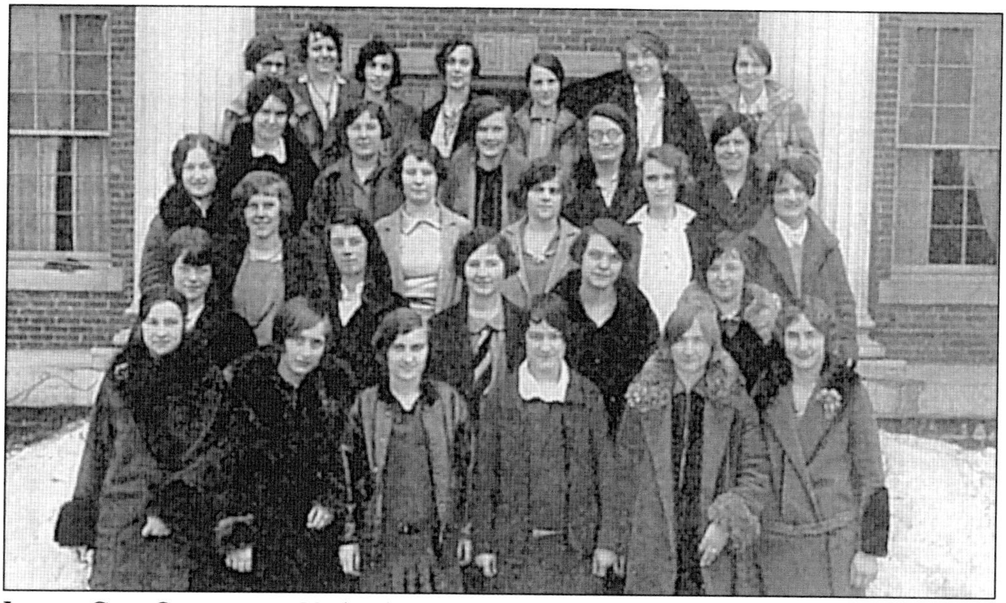

JUNIOR GLEE CLUB, 1928. Under the direction of Mrs. Schroeder, the Junior Glee Club, like the Senior club, made several public appearances for different school occasions. During this year, the performing groups entertained in the Livermore Hall (Music Hall) for the benefit of the flood sufferers of Plymouth and the surrounding towns.

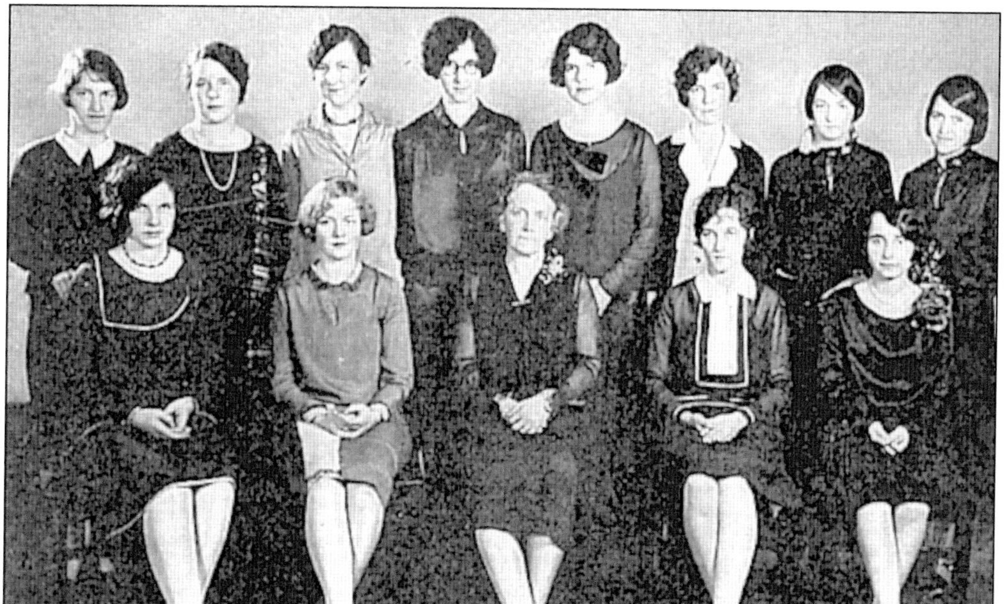

THE PAN-ATHENIAN CLUB, 1928. This club was a dramatic organization that consisted of students who were interested in the acting, the directing, and the producing of plays. The Christmas and Commencement pageants, which the club produced, were elaborately set, involving music and dramatics. For many years, these performances were held on the west lawn of Mary Lyon Hall. It is interesting to note that membership in the society was restricted to upperclassmen only. Officers included president Edna Smith, vice president Leone Whitcomb, and secretary Alice Ashley.

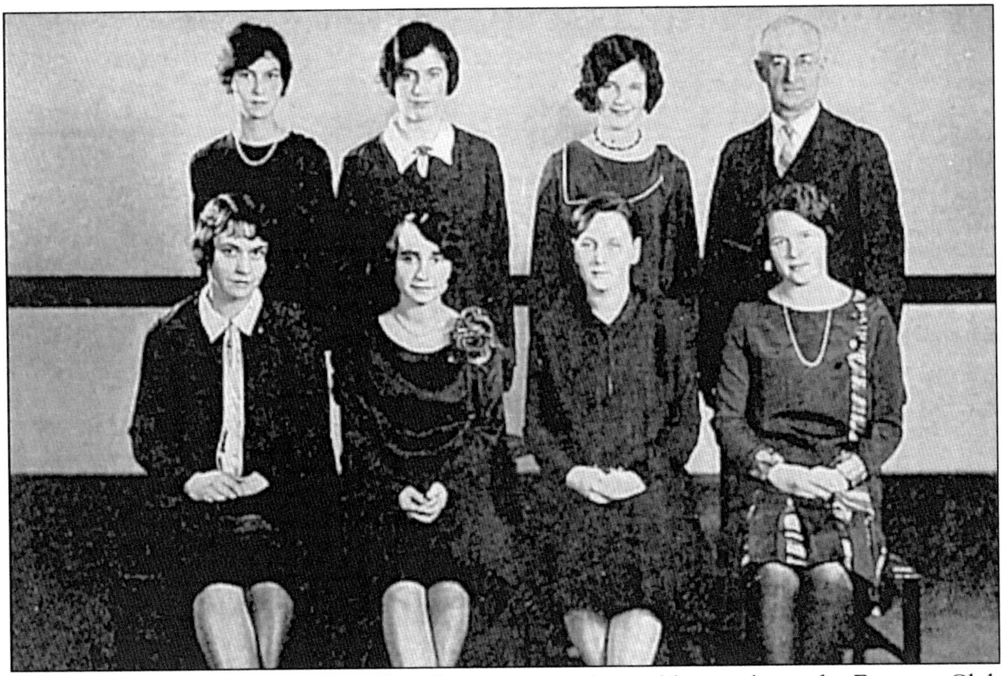

THE FORENSIC CLUB, 1928. For all students interested in public speaking, the Forensic Club extended this opportunity. This society was organized for the purpose of selecting eight girls who would prepare to uphold Plymouth in the annual Plymouth-Keene debate, as well as to allow all its members to exercise their skills in the regular bi-weekly meetings or in the occasional public debate. Officers included President Edna Smith, Vice President Dorothy Evans, Treasurer Ruby Swinnerton, Recording Secretary Nelliemae Connor, and Corresponding Secretary Edith Giles.

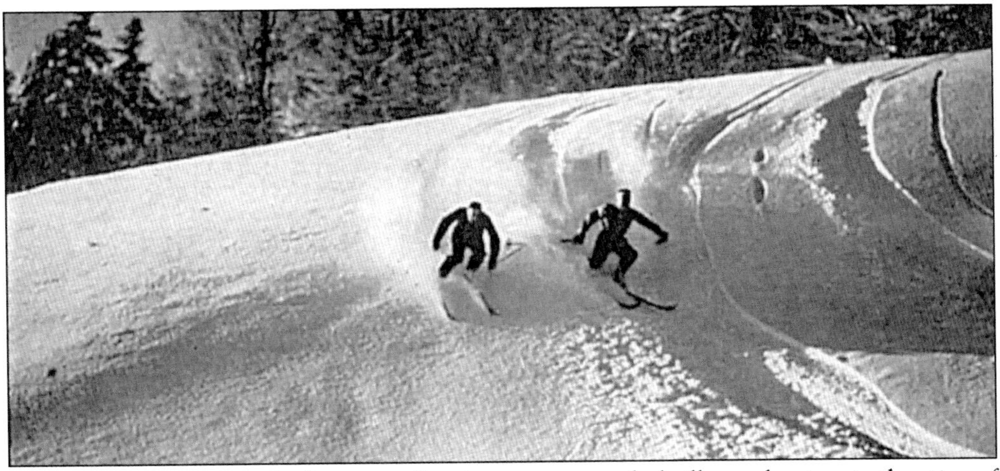

SKIING, 1937. "Action, rhythm, co-ordination, grace, speed, thrills, cool, crisp air, the sting of wind on your face as you race irresistibly down the well packed ski trail. Plymouth was one of the first New England towns to become 'ski-conscious.' Blessed with lovely surroundings, natural advantages, and an enterprising group of citizens, the town has rapidly become a winter sports center." "There are real possibilities for further development of winter sports at the Normal School. Langdon Park could become a winter time recreation center and advertise to the State that its teachers are well-rounded, active people." —Lillian Kenison '37.

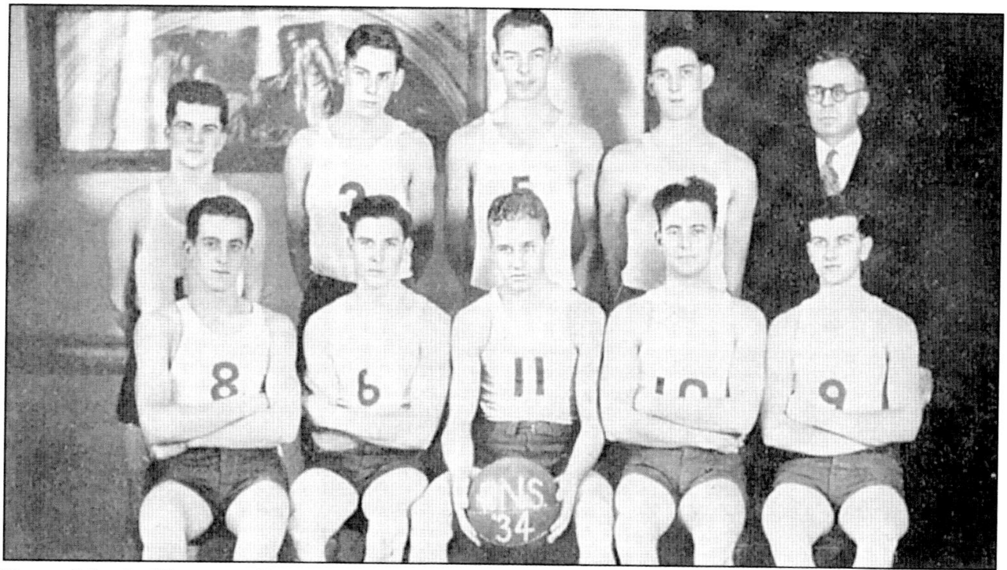

First Men's Varsity Basketball Team with Coach Luther Pollard, 1934. During the mid-1930s, a few male students appeared so that it was possible to have a men's basketball team in 1934. However, after World War II, a great influx of male students began attending the college.

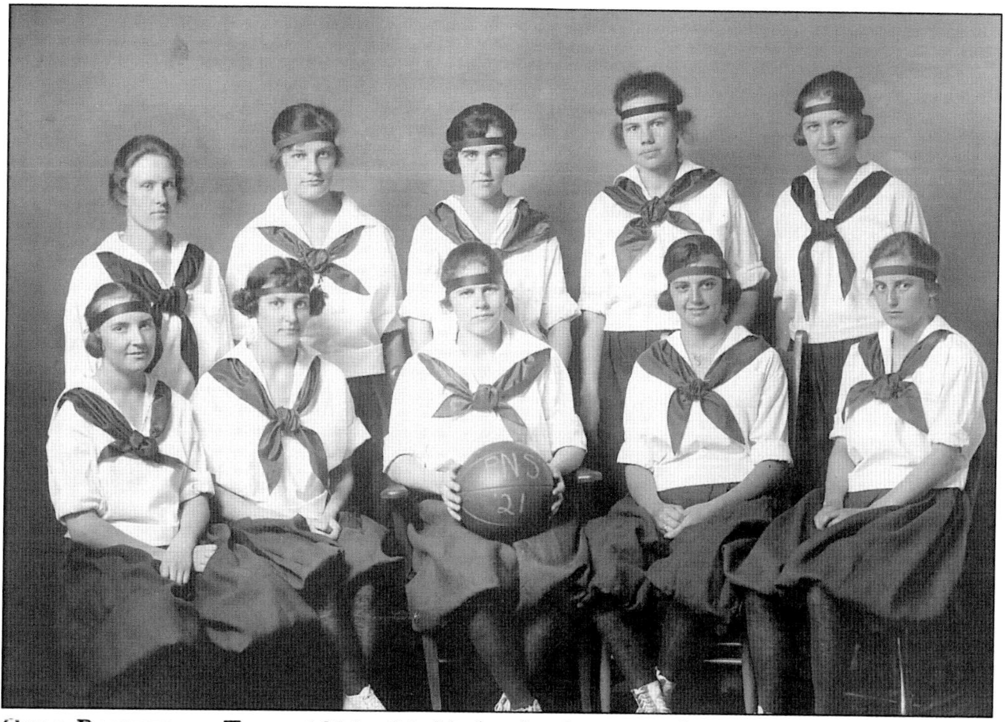

Girls Basketball Team, 1920—21. Under the direction of Miss Beatrice Hodgdon (for whom Hodgdon Married Students' Apartments was named), physical education played a prominent role in the college life of its students. Note: One of the sights on the campus was the gym costume of the women. Green blouses and green bloomers with long black stockings were the established garb of the time.

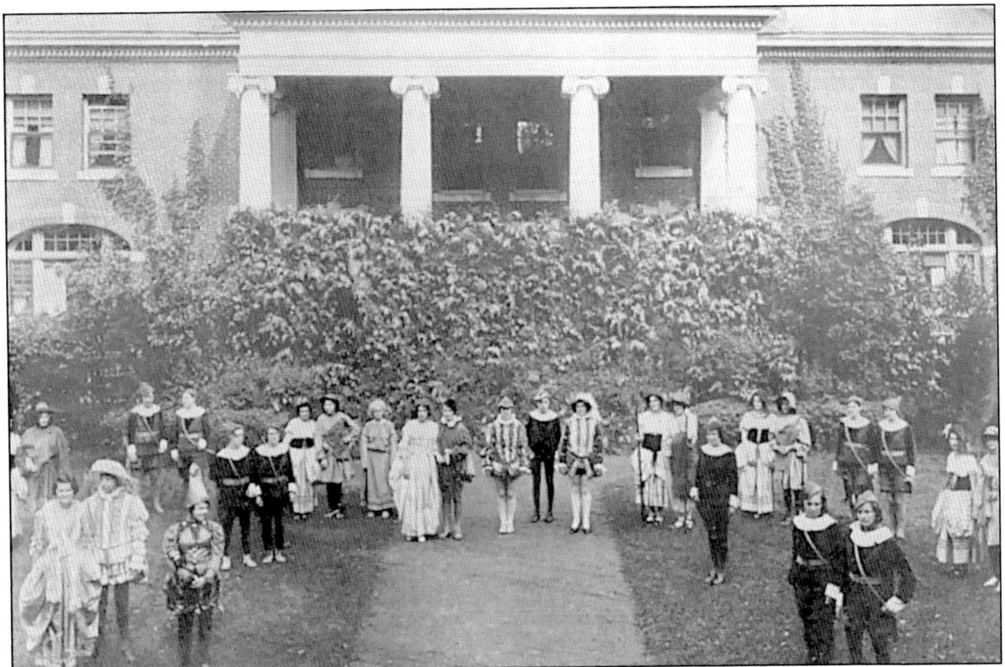

AS YOU LIKE IT IN FRONT OF MARY LYON HALL, 1932. For many years, there was a commencement pageant performed on the west lawn of Mary Lyon Hall. This event involved the presentation of one of Shakespeare's plays and included the music, physical education, and English students and faculty. During the middle 1930s, these presentations were discontinued.

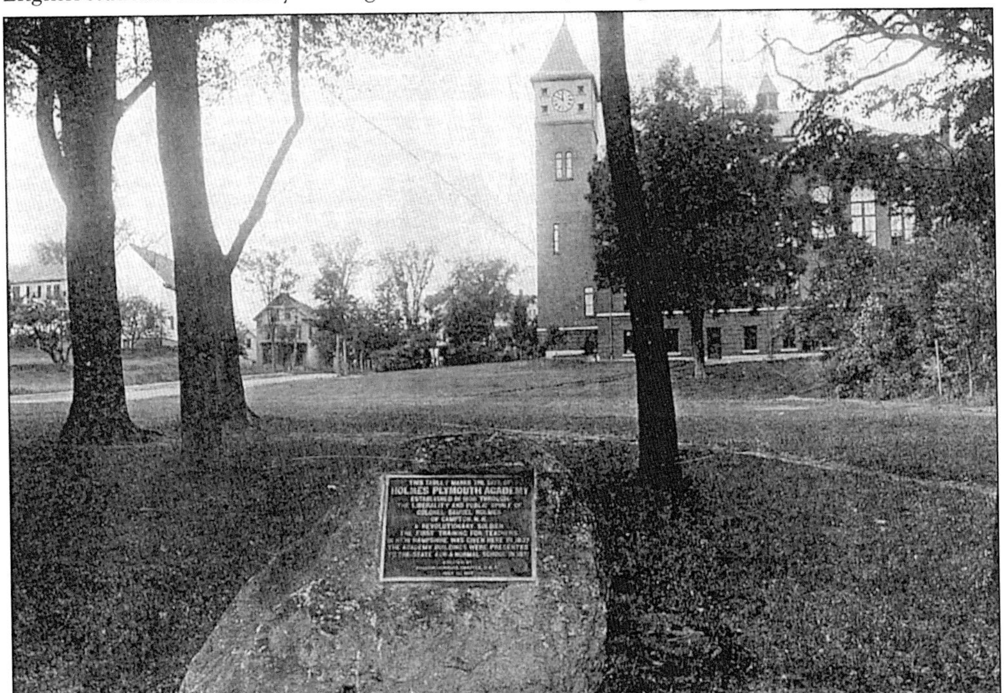

PLYMOUTH NORMAL SCHOOL, 1923. The site of the first training school for teachers in New Hampshire with Rounds Hall in the background.

Two

Plymouth Teachers College: 1939–1963

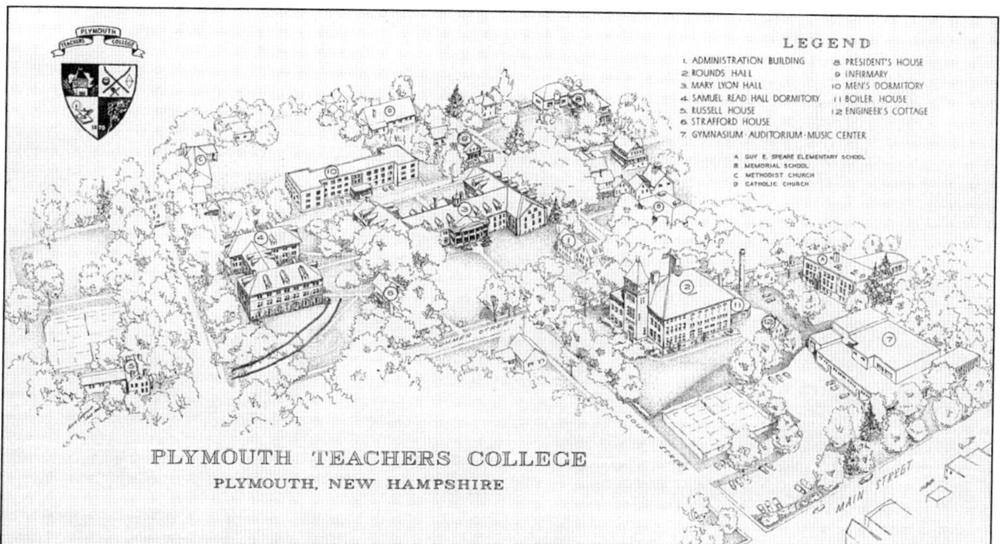

MAP OF PTC WITH LEGEND, 1960S.

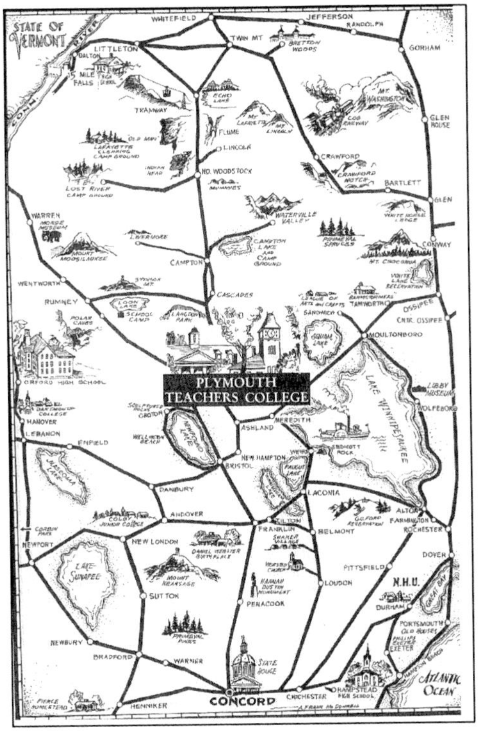

A MAP OF NEW HAMPSHIRE SHOWING THE PTC LOCATION, 1940.

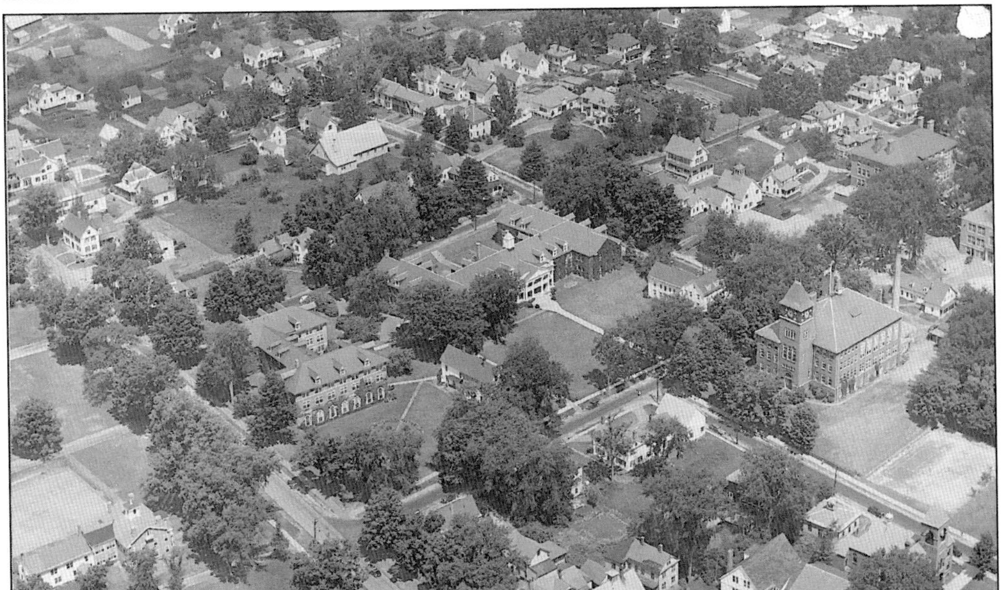

BIRD'S-EYE VIEW OF PTC, 1940S. The beauty of the college lies in the placement of the attractive and substantial buildings situated under graceful elms on gently sloping lawns. In 1939, by an act of the legislature, the name of the college was officially changed to Plymouth Teachers College. The college was one of the first teachers colleges in New England to gain accreditation by the American Association of Colleges for Teacher Education. Later, in 1954, the college was accredited by the New England Association of Colleges and Secondary Schools as a teacher-preparing institution.

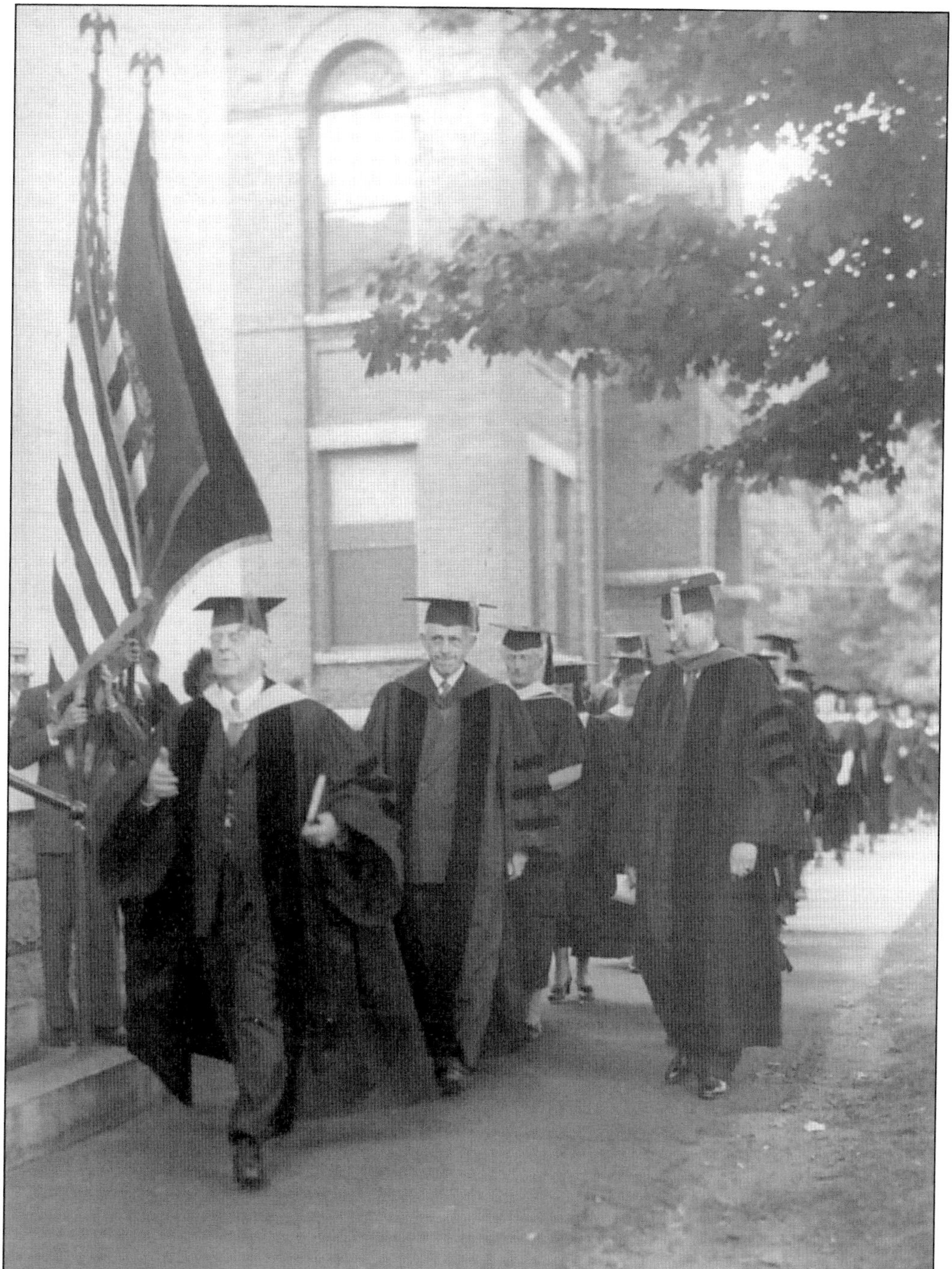

Parade Past the Congregational Church on Main Street, June, 1946. Pictured is Dr. Howard Jones beside Dr. Silver. Baccalaureate and commencement were memorable occasions under Dr. Silver's regime. The baccalaureate service was held in the old Methodist Church (before it burned); commencement was held in the town theater. The commencement procession began on campus, while the academic procession, headed by the flags and the college band led by Mr. Robert L. Boyd, marched down the hill for the exercises.

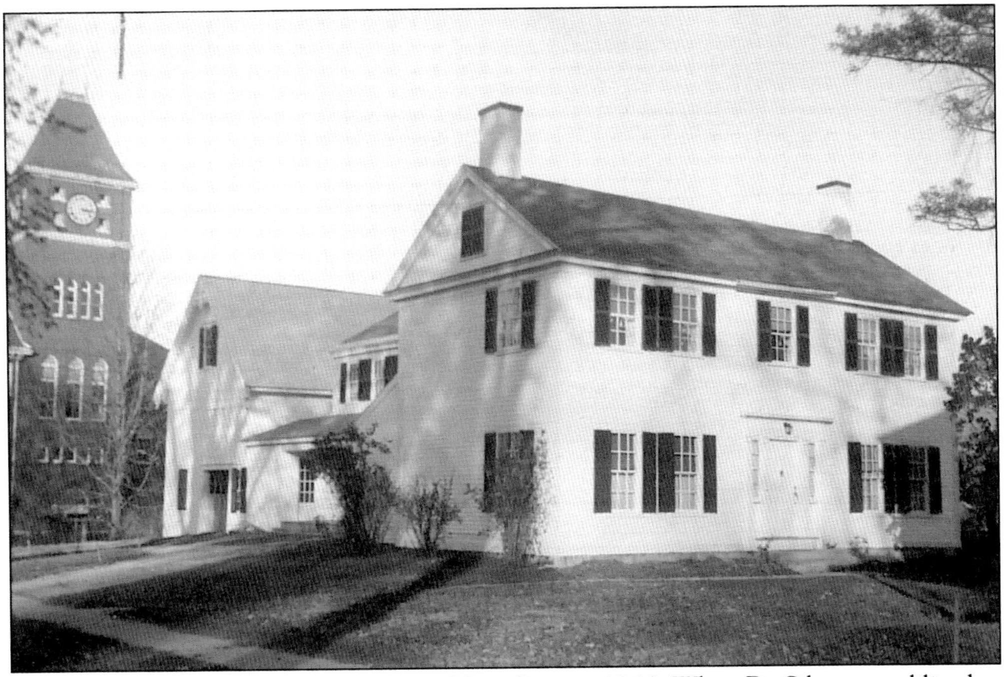

Caroline Leverett Home of Dr. and Mrs. Silver, 1946. When Dr. Silver was obliged to retire in 1946, and the new president and his family were ready to occupy the president's residence on School Street, Miss Shaw, secretary to the new president, welcomed Dr. and Mrs. Silver into her spacious Leverett Homestead.

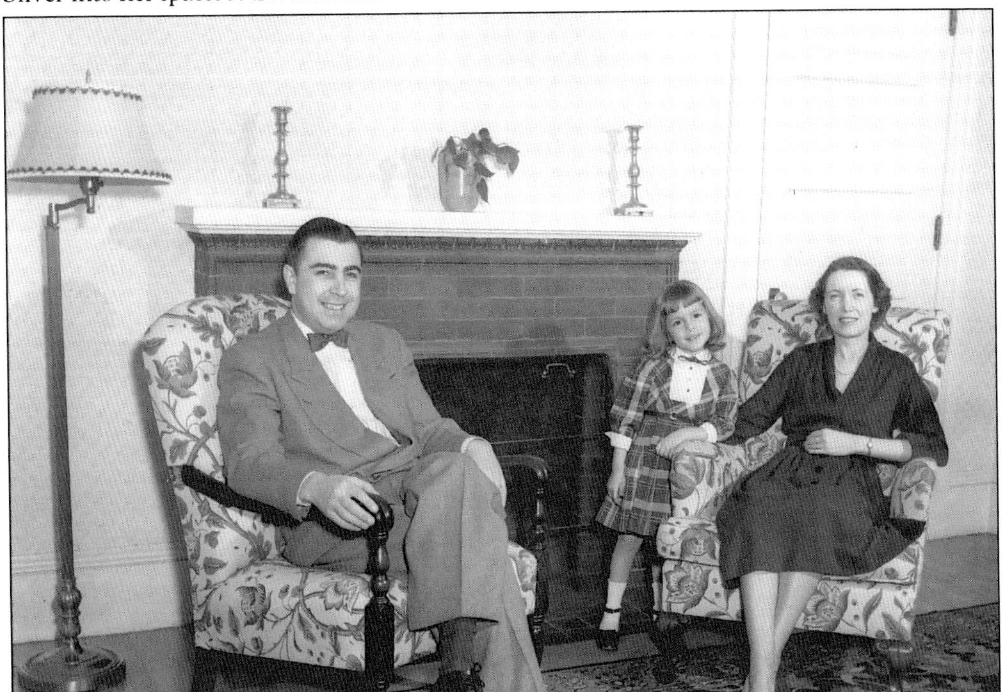

Dr. and Mrs. Harold Hyde and Their Daughter Mary Ann. In 1951, Dr. Harold Hyde became the 10th President of Plymouth Teachers College.

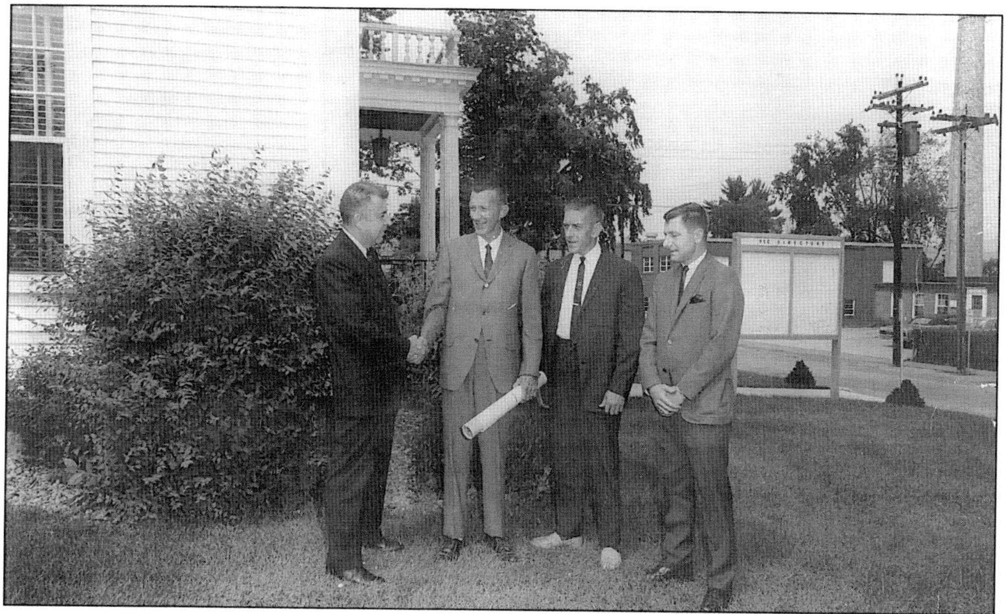

DR. HAROLD HYDE. Dr. Hyde stands in front of Ellen Reed House Administration Building with, from left to right, Lionel deLacey, Bruce Ryan '49, and Alumni Director Chuck Bailey as Bailey presents an alumni gift to Dr. Hyde. Across the street to the right is the Howard Hutchins Maintenance Shop.

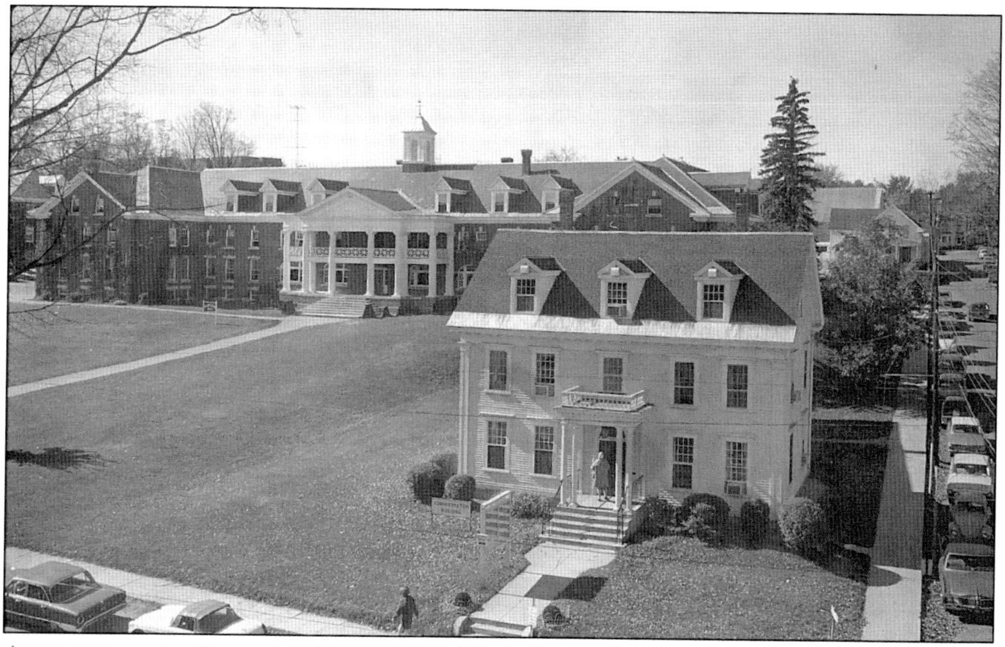

ADMINISTRATION BUILDING (ELLEN REED HOUSE), 1950. In 1934, this house (Calley House) became the offices of the president, dean, and registrar; other administrative offices were also located in this building. In 1974, it was remodeled and called the Faculty Office Building PSC #24. In 1976, it was renamed the Ellen Reed House. Today, this is the home of the English Department faculty offices. In the background is Mary Lyon Hall.

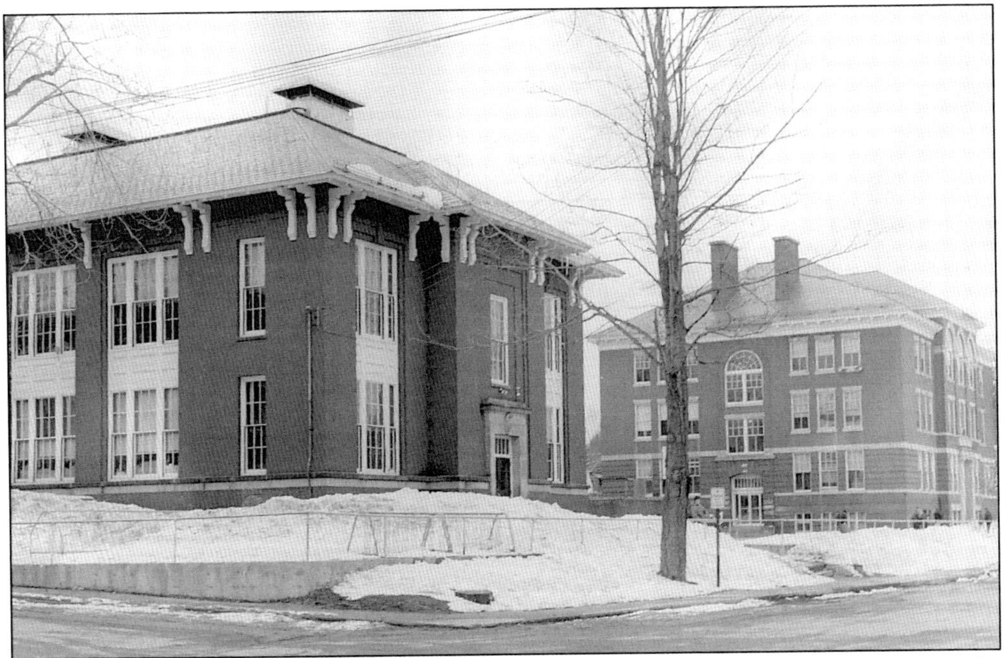

Memorial Hall with the Plymouth High School in back to the right, 1950s. In 1950, the town completely remodeled the old model school, which had been closed since 1939, and dedicated it "The Memorial School" in honor of the Plymouth's war veterans. This edifice housed a cafeteria, library, workrooms, and additional classrooms, which enabled grades to be divided for more efficient instruction. In the background is Plymouth High School before it was razed in 1970.

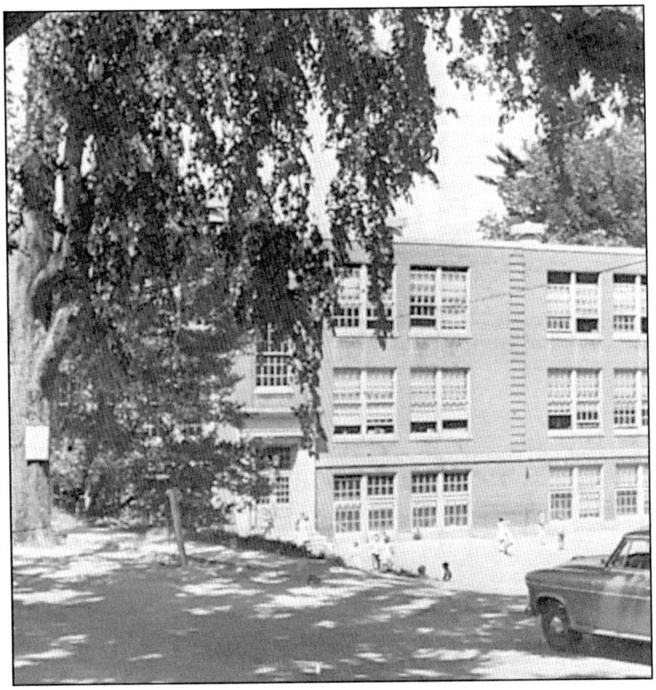

Guy E. Speare School Elementary School, 1962. Originally this building was built as a WORK PROJECTS ADMINISTRATION project and opened in 1939. In 1967, an agreement was made to purchase the land and building from the Plymouth School District by the University System of New Hampshire. In 1972, it was renovated to house the college administration. Note the children playing in the playground on the back side of the building when it was used as the public elementary school and gymnasium for the town of Plymouth, New Hampshire.

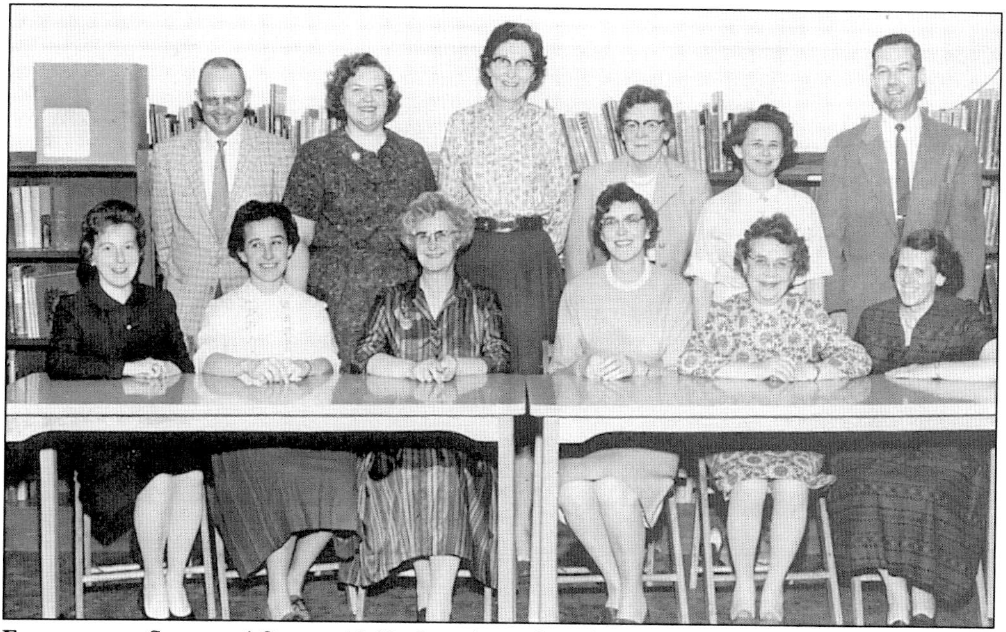

Elementary Schools' Staff, 1962. Seen here, from left to right, are as follows: (front row) Ms. R. Miller, Ms. L. Drew, Mrs. D. Wilkins, Mrs. E. Bowie, Mrs. E. Batchelder, and Ms. M. Rand; (back row) Mr. M. Bownes (principal), Ms. G. Cunningham, Ms. A. Baston, Mrs. C. Noyes, Mrs. E. Hall, and Mr. B. Ames.

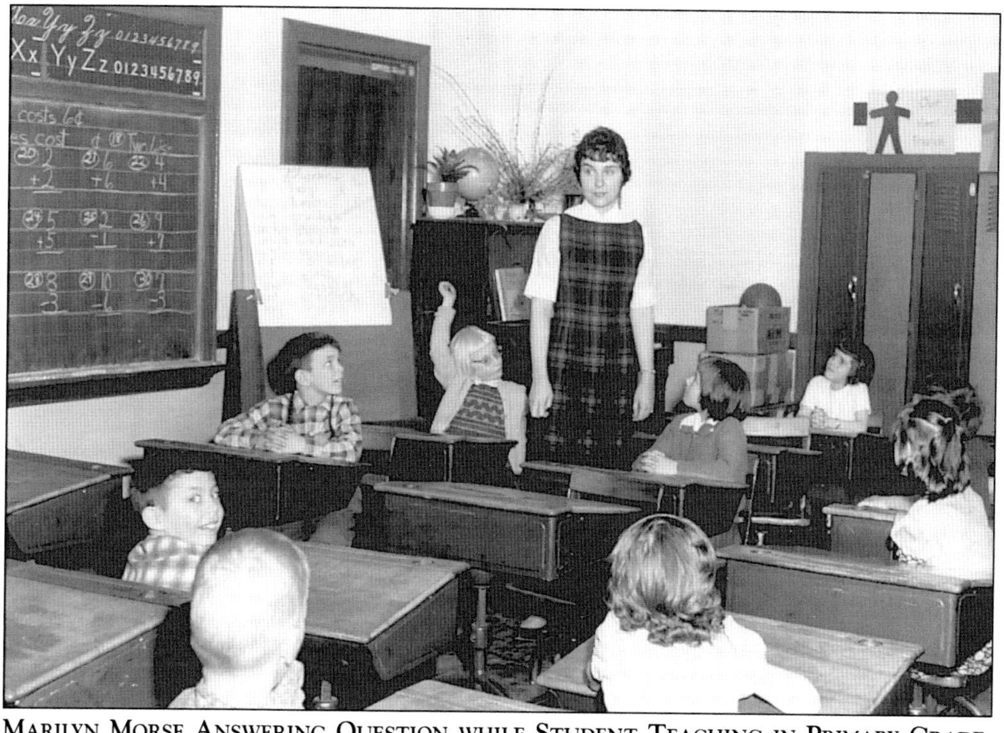

Marilyn Morse Answering Question while Student Teaching in Primary Grade, Plymouth, 1940s. In all programs, there came to be an emphasis on a liberal arts education in order to prepare the teacher with a rich and many-sided personality.

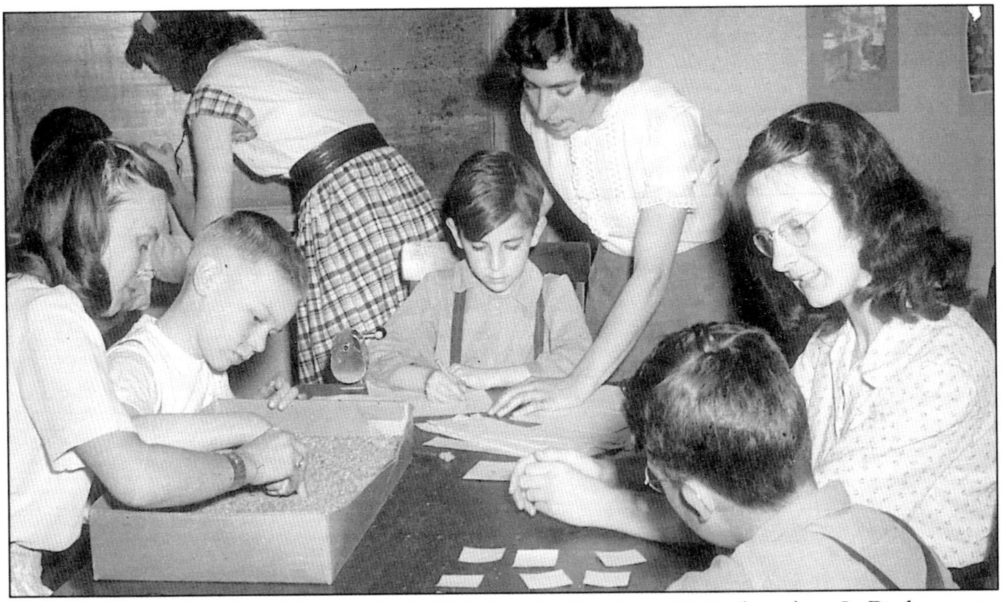

LANGUAGE ARTS CLASS, 1948–49. J. Blakeley, L. Harrison, C. Raftopolus, S. Dodge assist elementary students in their studies. In 1951, a dual elementary-secondary curriculum was introduced. This program prepared teachers for the upper elementary grades and secondary schools.

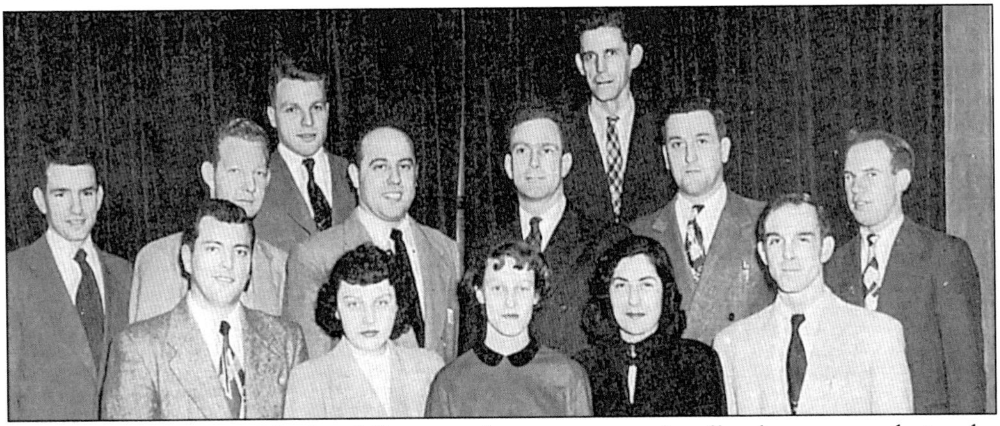

GRADUATE STUDENTS. The first full-year graduate program to be offered on campus during the regular year in the New Hampshire Teachers Colleges was inaugurated at Plymouth Teachers College in September 1950. In 1948, the State Board of Education authorized the teachers colleges at PSC and Keene State College (KSC) and the State Department of Education to offer a Master of Education degree. The program was designed primarily for graduates of liberal arts colleges and secondary teacher preparation curricula who wished to prepare for elementary teaching. The graduate program had undergone several changes during the Hyde administration. Gradually the state department withdrew from participation, by then the programs at PSC and KSC seemed strong enough to function by themselves, so the Master's degree ceased to be granted jointly by the two institutions. Under the direction of Dr. Richard Seltzer, the graduate requirements were more prescribed and more professional and content courses were required. Seen here, from left to right, are as follows: (front row) R. Martens, B. Martens, J. Saunders, E. Aronoff, and C. Dustin; (middle row) R. Bissonette, C. Rolfe, A. Juris, R. Fuller, B. Macey, and R. Covey; (back row) C. Smith Jr. and B. Thompson.

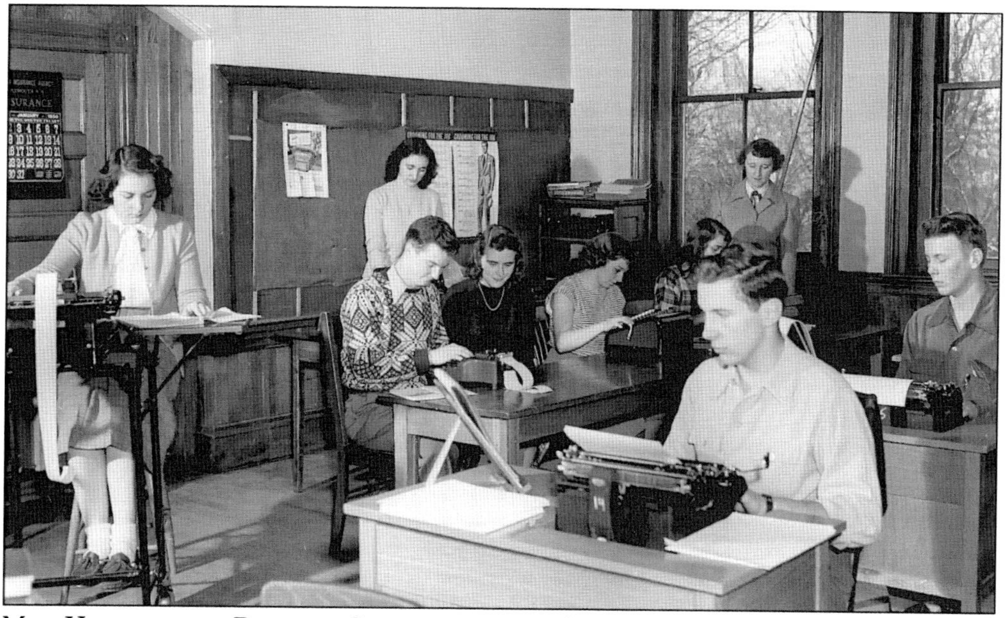

MISS HORACE WITH BUSINESS CLASS, C. 1940S. There were many internal changes in the elementary program that stressed less emphasis on methodology and more on content. There came to be a common general education core for all students regardless of curriculum. With the change from a three-year elementary curriculum to a four-year, elementary graduates also received the Bachelor of Education degree; Plymouth Normal School had become a teachers' college, a fact legalized by the legislature in 1939 when it voted formally to change the name to Plymouth Teachers College.

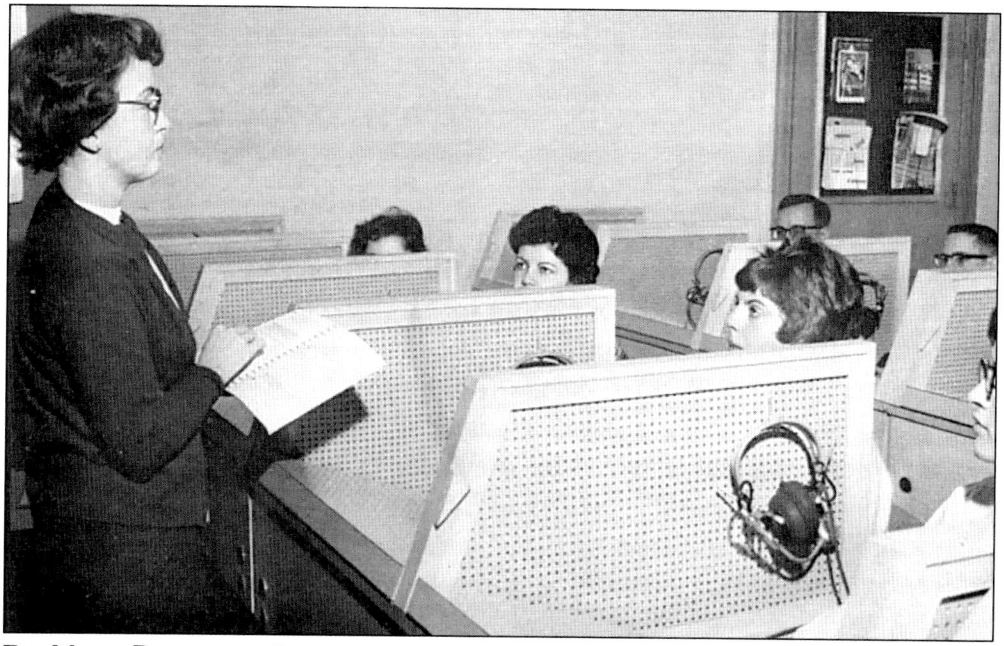

DR. MADIE BARRETT IN LANGUAGE LABORATORY, C. 1950S. A popular method of teaching language arts was via individual compartments for listening to and recitation of individual recordings.

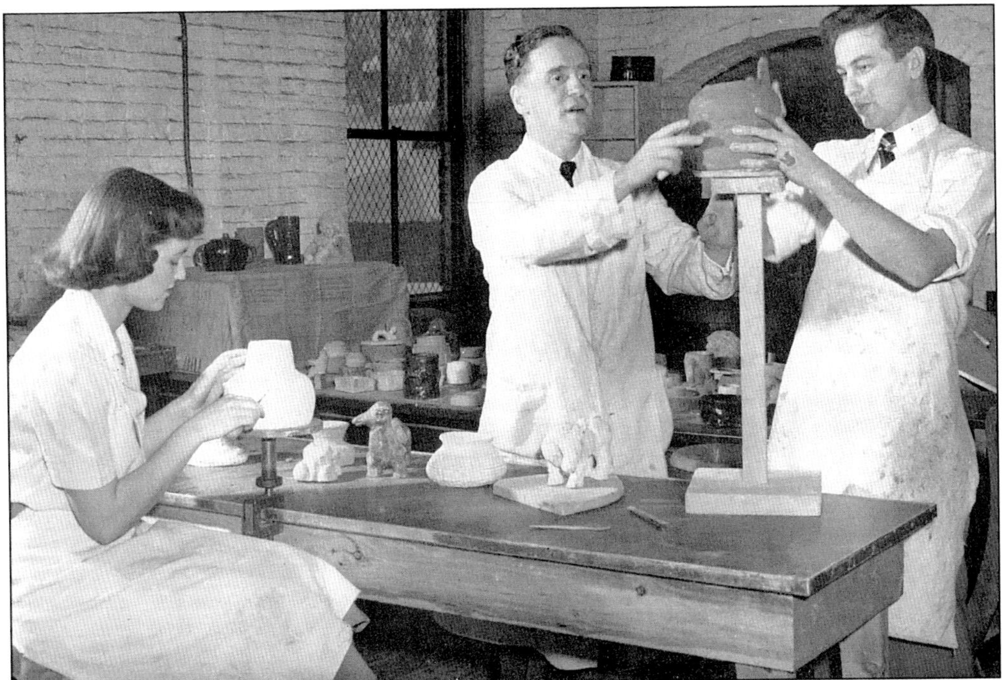

ART CLASS, 1950. Mr. Karl Drerup inspired artistic endeavor in the art room located in the basement of Rounds Hall. At this time, art was considered an elective; however, it later became a major program in the curriculum.

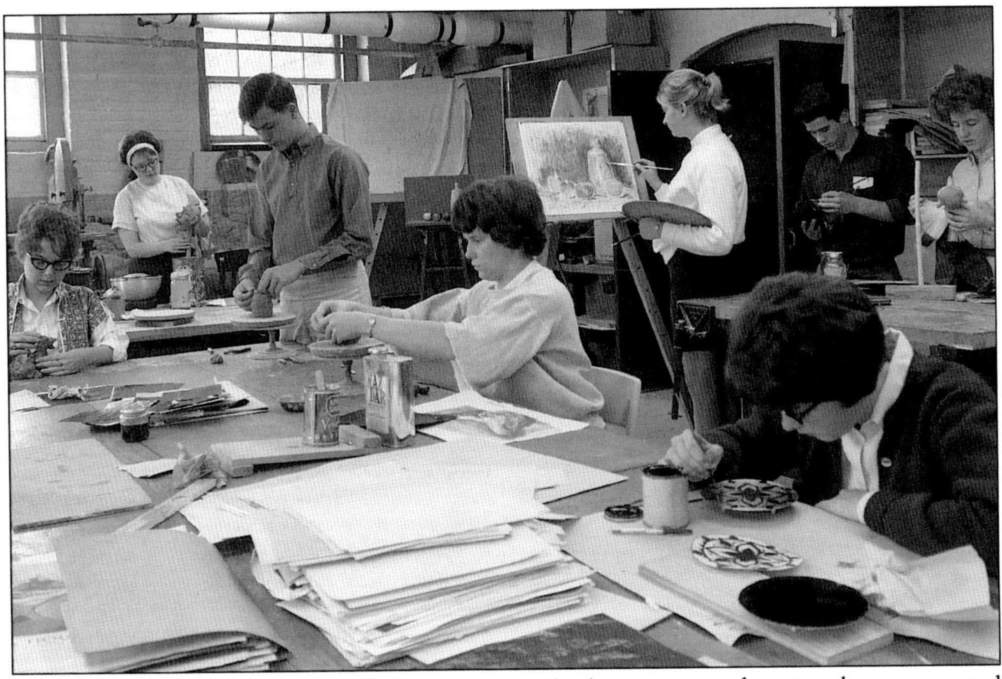

ART CLASS IN THE BASEMENT OF ROUNDS HALL. This basement area has since been converted into offices for the Education Department; the Art Department moved to Hyde Hall in 1976 and has since moved to the Draper Maynard Building on Main Street.

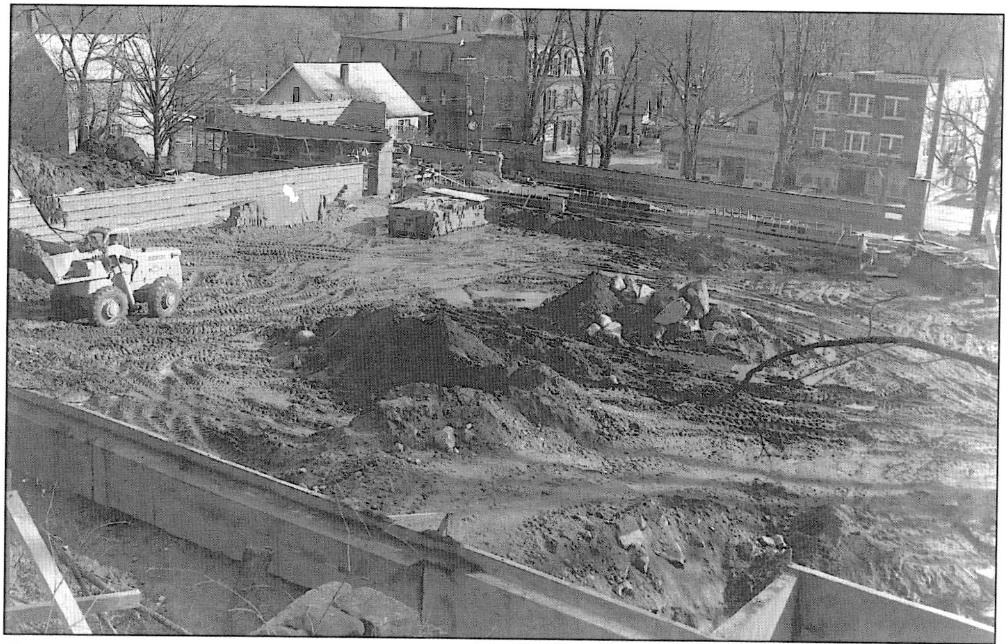

THE SILVER AUDITORIUM-GYMNASIUM UNDER CONSTRUCTION, 1955. With the increased enrollment in physical education and music, the school was quickly outgrowing its facilities, i.e. the gymnasium in the Guy E. Speare School, the gymnasium in the basement of Mary Lyon Hall, and the Livermore Hall in Rounds Hall. Thus, a new home was necessary to accommodate these expanding programs; this need resulted in the Silver Auditorium-Gymnasium.

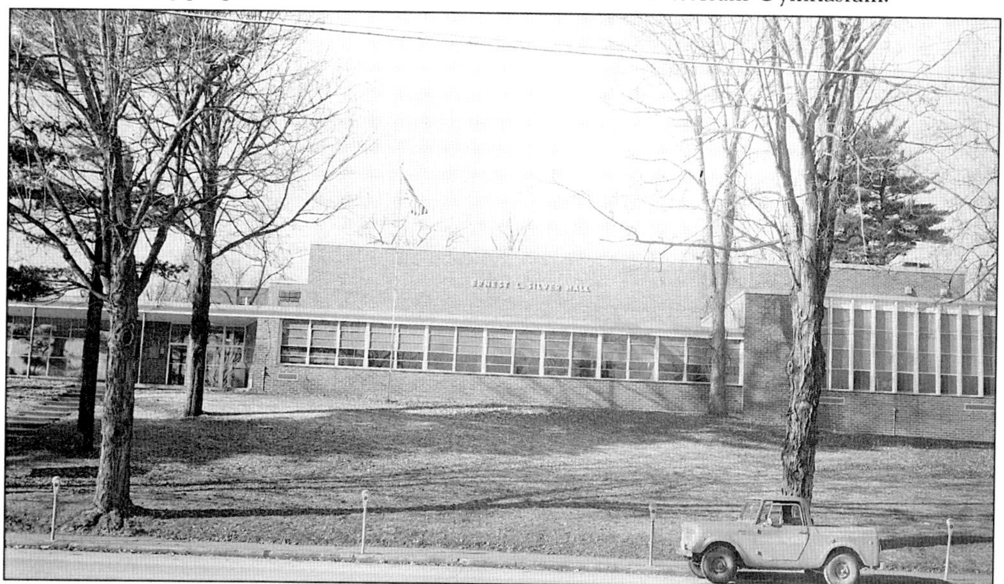

THE ERNEST L. SILVER AUDITORIUM-GYMNASIUM. In 1955, this new facility was constructed on the Ritter (Sargent) property on Main Street. The corner stone of this house, in which the abolitionist Nathaniel Rogers lived and wrote and in which Nathaniel Hawthorne had been entertained, is preserved in the new building. In 1959, it was rededicated as the Ernest L. Silver Hall, and, in 1969, new additions were created with music performance modules. New lighting and theatre type seating was added to the structure in 1976.

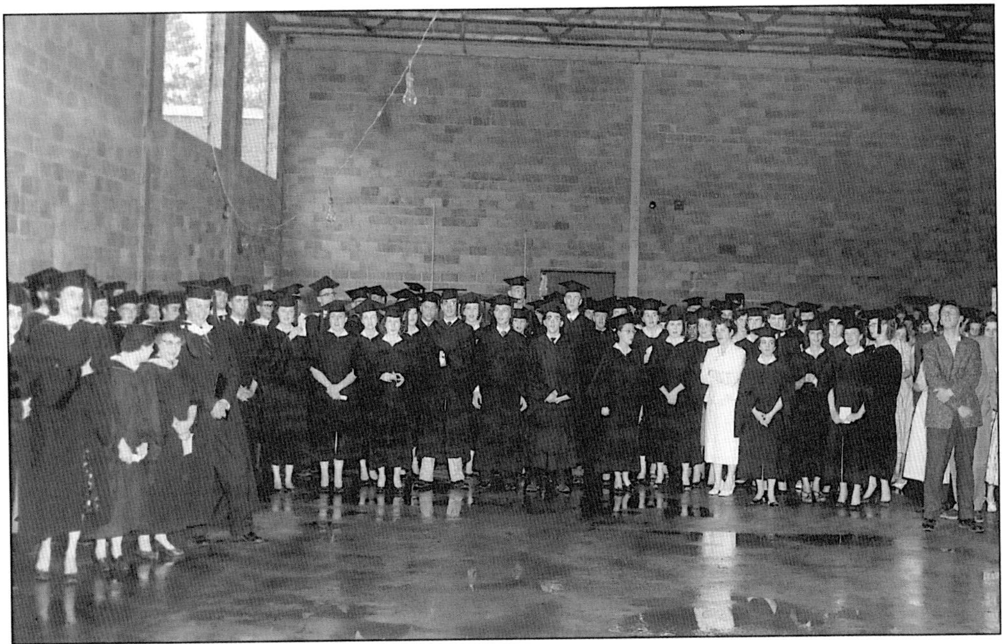

CLASS OF 1956 IN THE UNFINISHED SILVER HALL FOR OFFICIAL TASSEL-TURNING CEREMONY. Here, Dr. Hyde confirmed degrees to the graduating students.

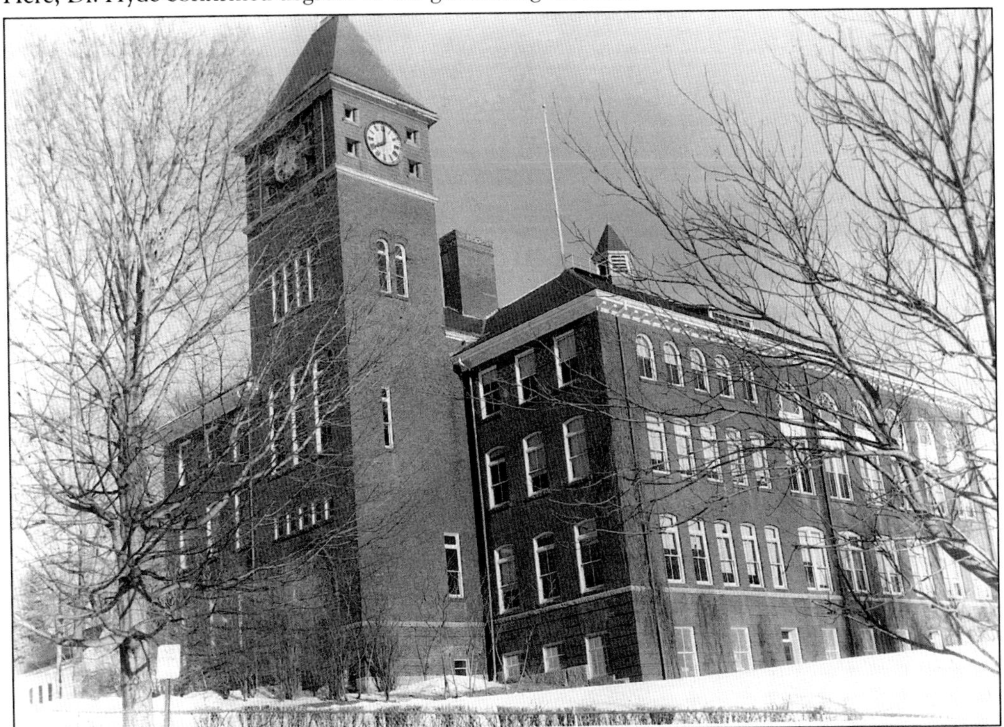

ROUNDS HALL. In 1958, the old Livermore Hall was divided into two floors to make room for more classroom space. On the top floor, the business education department with classroom laboratories, library, and offices was installed. On the lower floor, classrooms and office space were built. This renovation was completed in 1958.

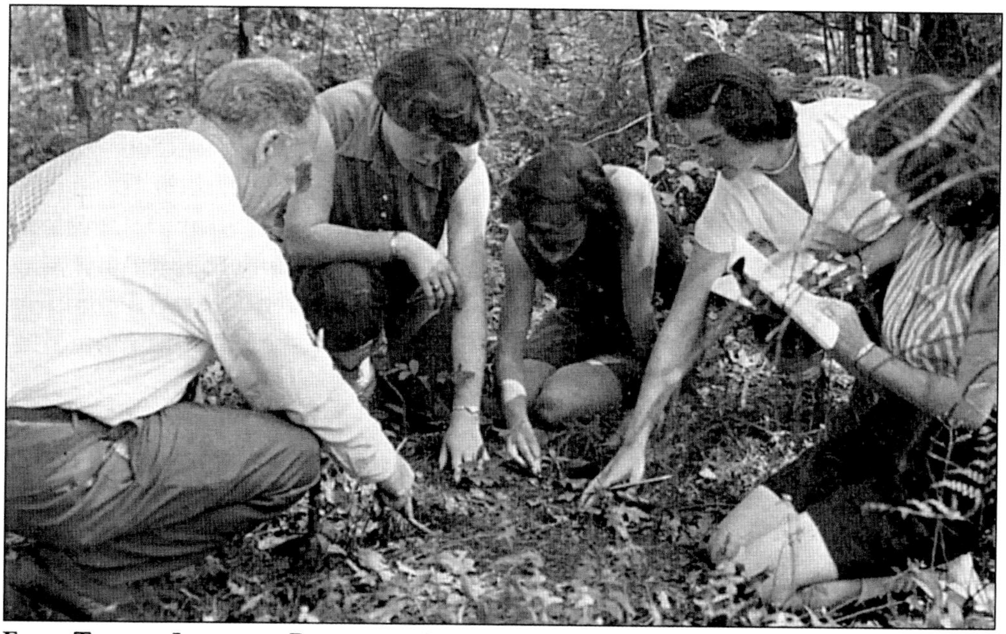

Field Trip to Langdon Park with Mr. Boyd. Mr. Woodbury Langdon, a public-spirited citizen of Plymouth, deeded to the Normal School a tract of land covering several acres, for purposes of instruction and recreation. The natural beauty of the winding river and wooded slope make it eminently desirable as a park. "The splendid outlook upon the mountains and valleys all around, particularly up the Baker River valley, is charming." —*State Normal School Catalogue*, 1939. During the winter, snowshoeing, skating, skiing, and tobogganing were favorite sports. In warmer months, tennis, baseball, soccer, bowling on the green, and other games provided exercise and fun. Inside recreation included dancing, bowling, and billiards.

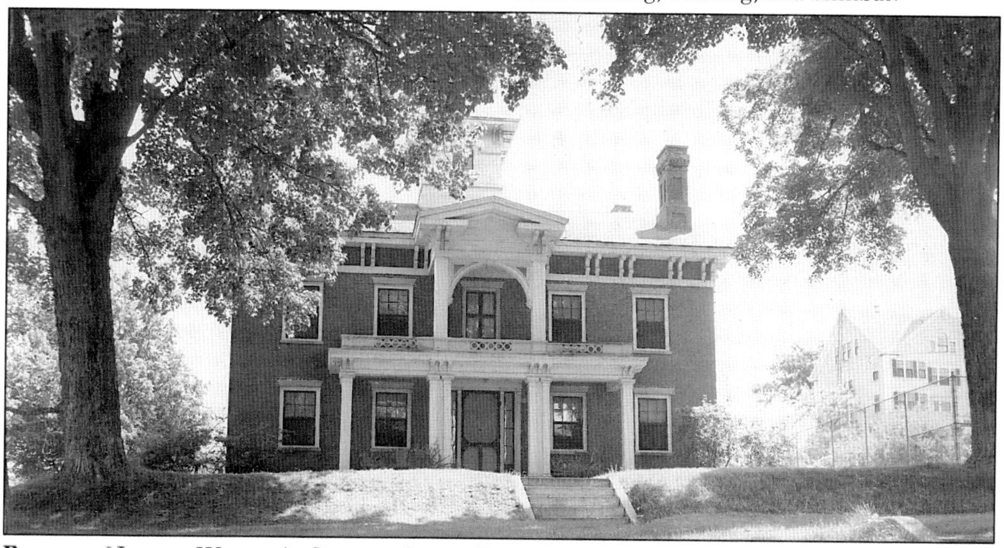

Russell House, Women's Senior Class Dormitory, 1959. "Each day at two minutes of eight finds Russell House a scene of great commotion. It is those Training School seniors collecting books and papers, putting that straggly hair in place and adjusting that crooked seam. One minute to one minute and a half later finds these people madly dashing to the site of the day's activities." —Marion Finnigan '40 and Deborah Stone '40

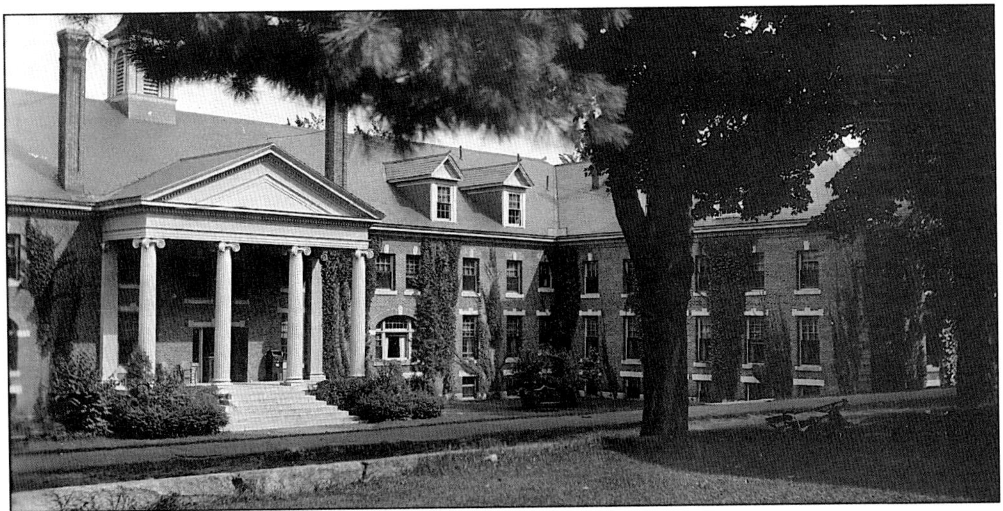

Mary Lyon Hall—West Side, 1963. The college dormitories serve as centers of community life on the campus. The lobbies and game rooms provide recreational opportunities leading to the development of those friendships that are an integral part of college life. Single and double rooms are provided and furnished with single beds, study tables, chairs, bureaus, and chests of drawers. Students not living in the dormitories are required to live in homes approved by the college. All students not living in their own homes are subject to the regulations and supervision of the college.

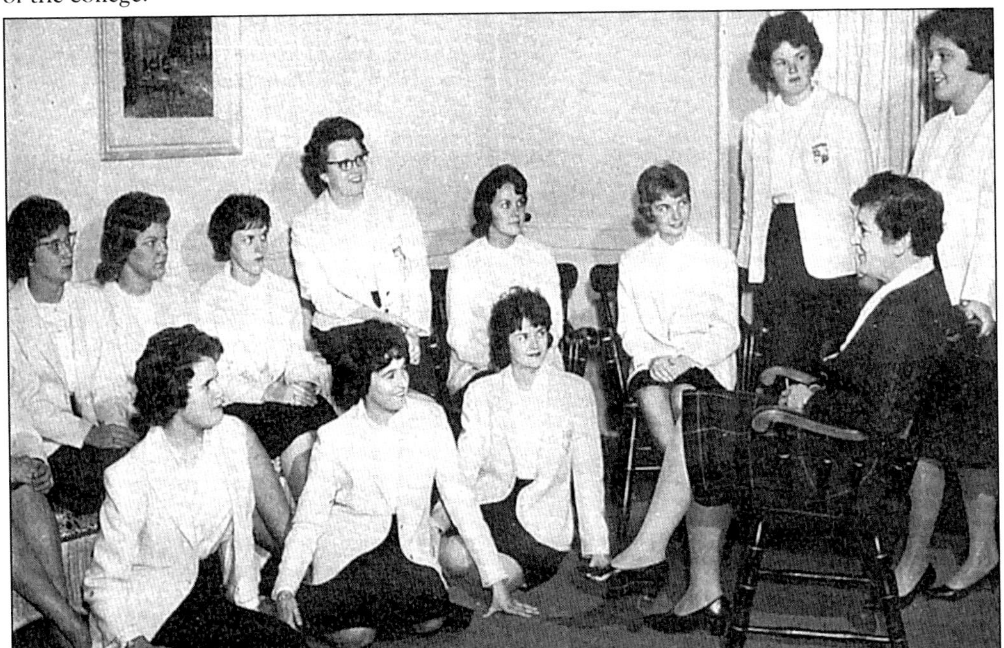

Mary Lyon Hall House Committee, 1963. All regulations regarding dormitory living approved by the president are formulated and directed by the students' house committees with the cooperation and assistance of the deans and the dormitory supervisors. Seen here, from left to right, are as follows: (front row) E. Pike, J. Perry, J. Hatfield, and Mrs. Kent (dormitory supervisor); (back row) C. McCollough. M. Decato, J. Campbell, C. Davis, C. Saunders, A. Holden, J. Hanover, and S. Bradbury.

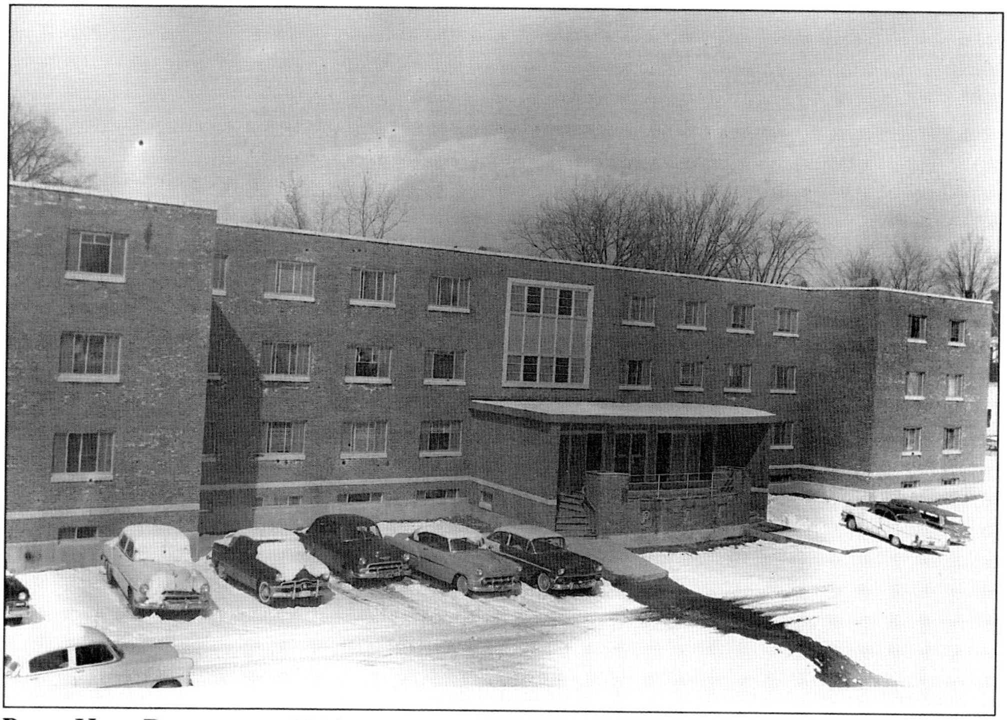

BLAIR HALL DORMITORY, 1960.

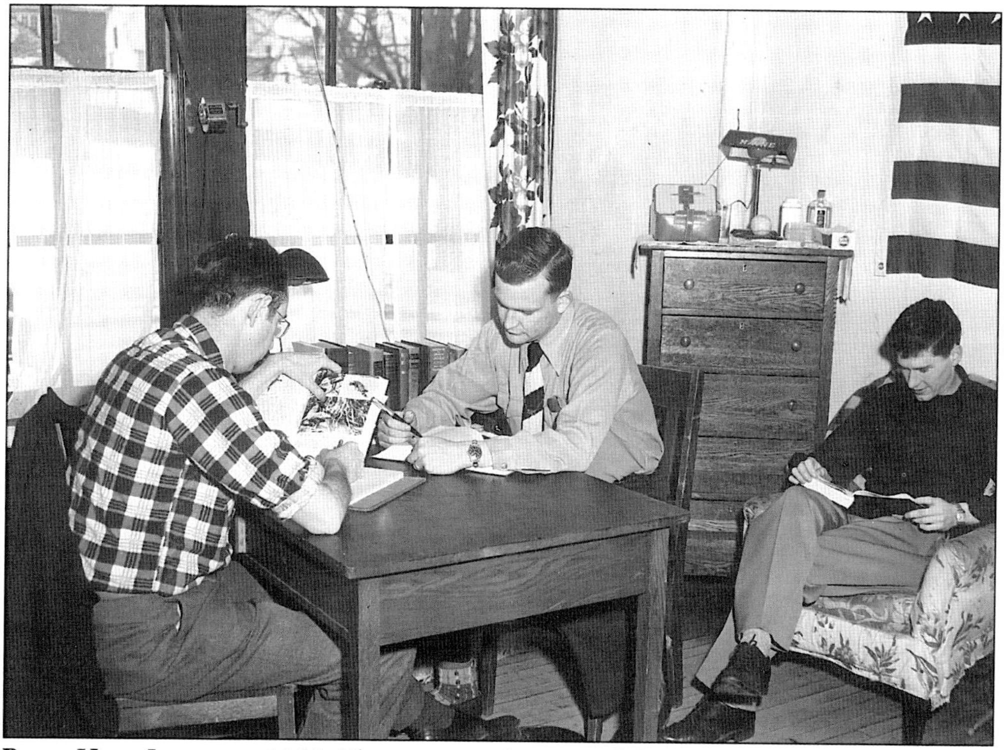

BLAIR HALL INTERIOR, 1961. This is a typical setting of the men's dormitory rooms as they appeared during the 1940s and 1950s.

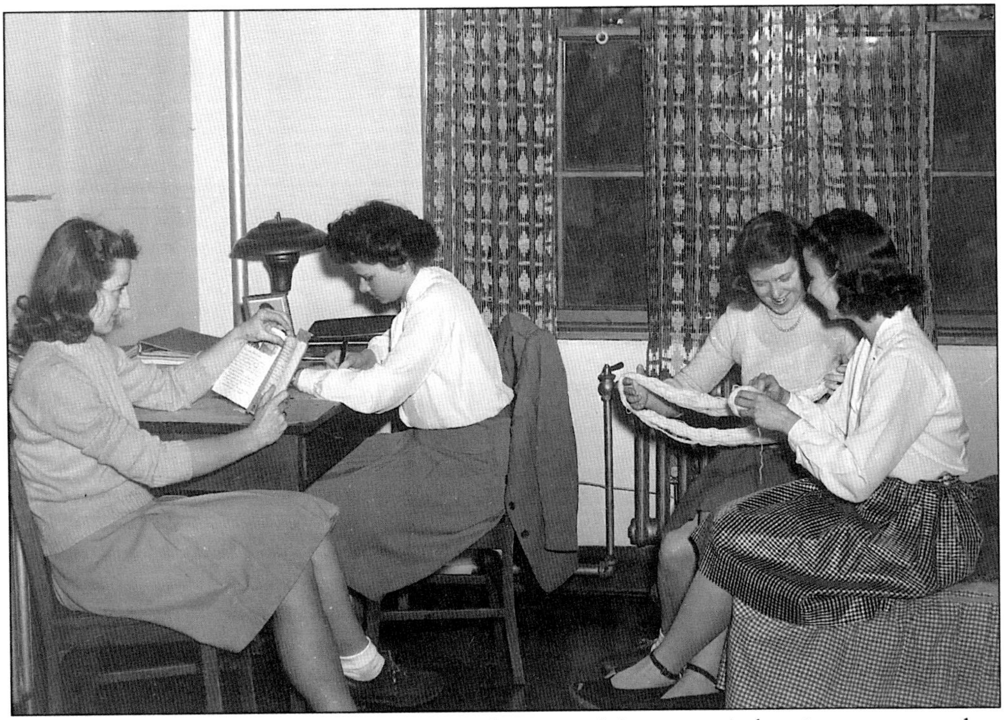

DORMITORY INTERIOR, 1942. This is a typical setting of the women's dormitory rooms as they appeared during the 1940s and 1950s.

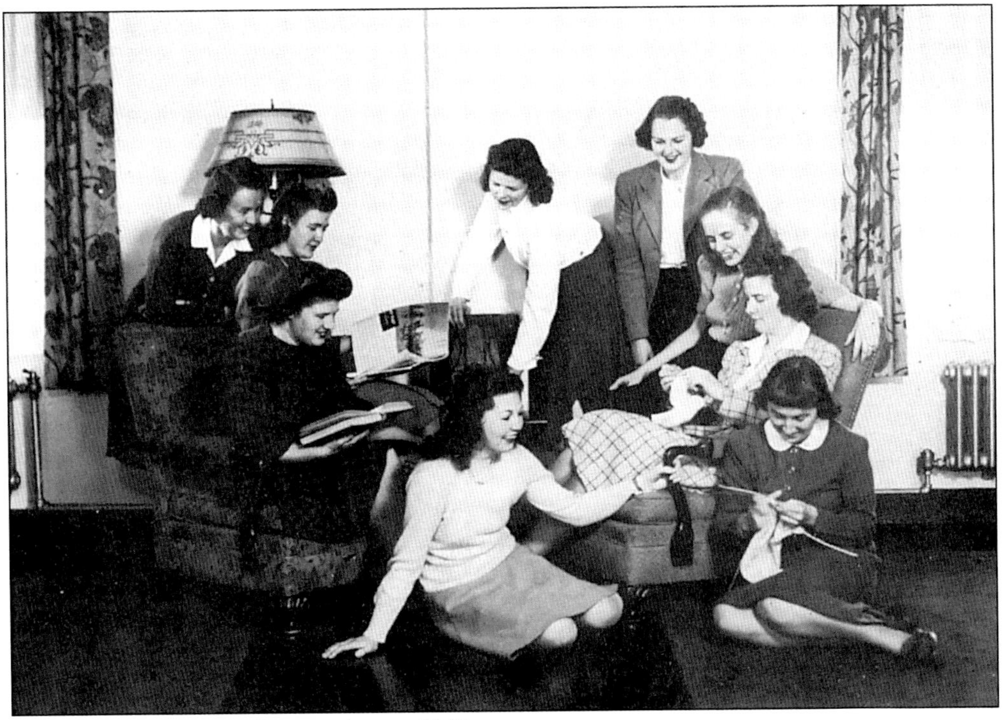

DORMITORY INTERIOR SOCIAL AREA, 1942.

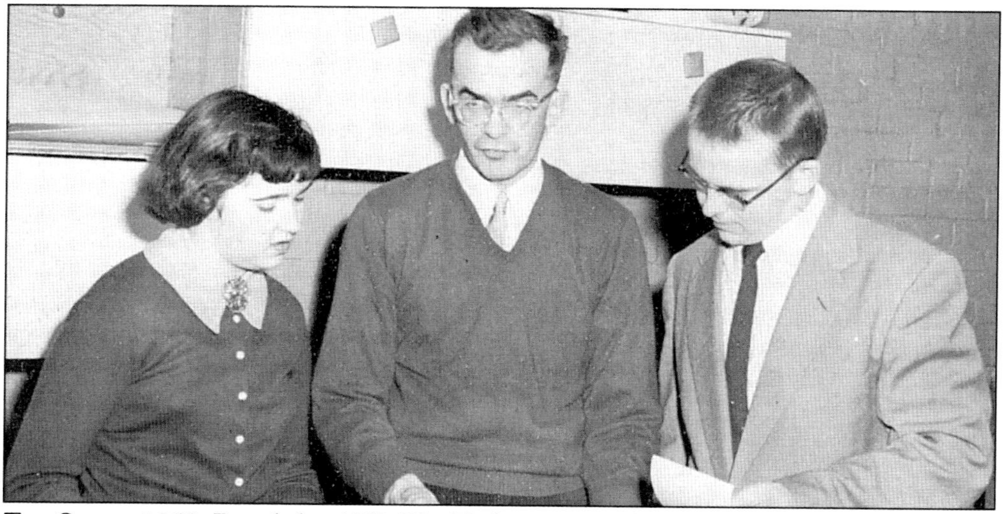

THE CLOCK, 1959. Founded in 1952, *The Clock* represents the journalistic efforts of our college newspaper staff. It covers the activities of the college, some educational features, and literary works. News was also submitted by members of the college who wished to contribute articles. Today, *The Clock* is a visible and healthy entity heading into the 21st century. Pictured, from left to right, are editor G. Jenney; Eric Potter; and assistant editor Arthur Slade.

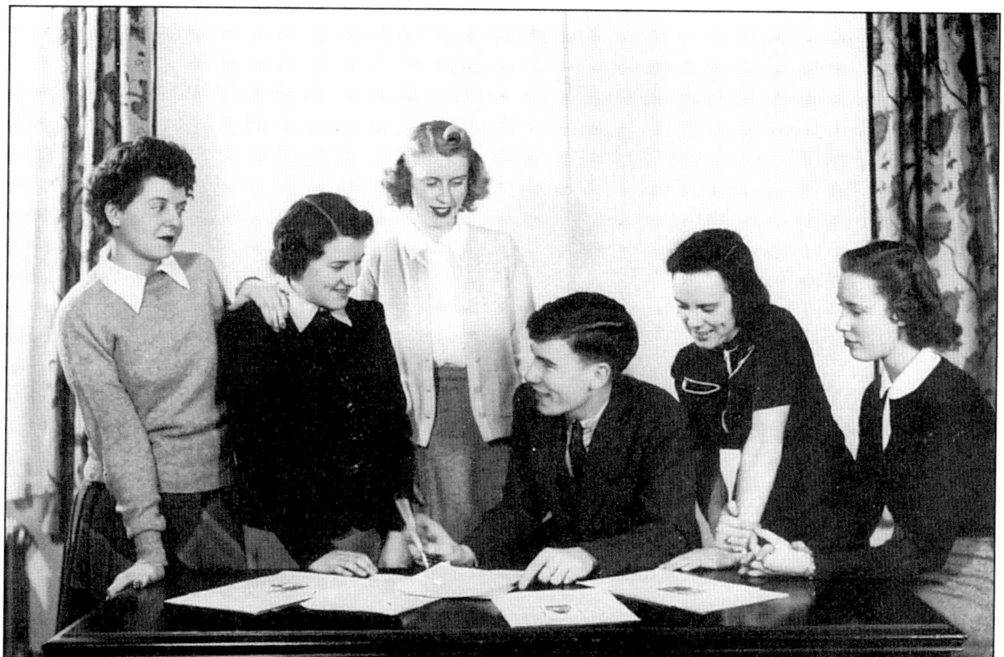

THE PROSPECT, 1941. In the years 1908–1909, *The Prospect*, a self-supporting paper published four times a year and edited by a student board, was first mentioned. Some of Robert Frost's writings first appeared in this literary paper. In 1940, this paper was issued weekly. *The Prospect* and the yearbook first named *The Conning Tower*, in 1928, all provided opportunity for fellowship and learning. Staff shown here, from left to right, are R. Rushlow, A. Whittemore, Prof. Norton Bagley, M. Garland, and F. Caswell.

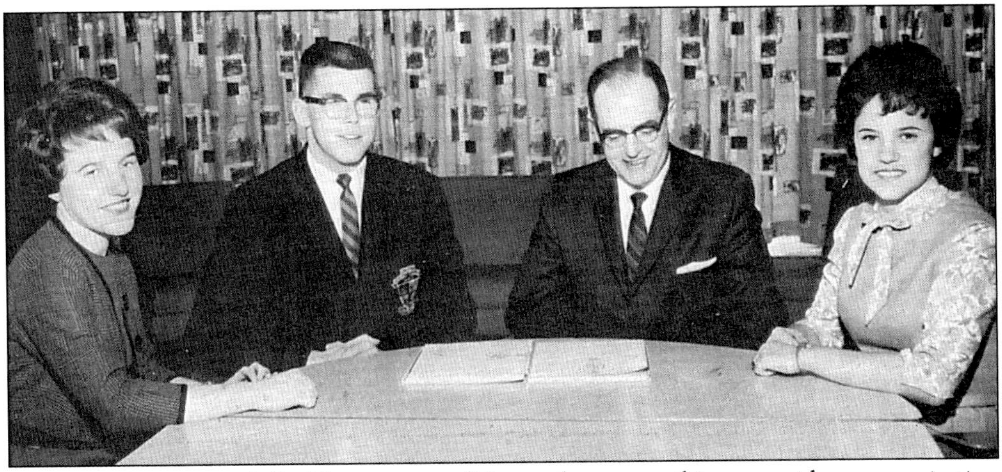

STUDENT COUNCIL, 1963. The purposes of the student council is to provide an organization through which the various responsibilities and activities of the student body may be handled; to increase the appreciation of individual responsibility; to enact and enforce regulations which promote high and intelligent standards for personal conduct; and to form a body for the expression of student and faculty opinion regarding matters of general interest in the college. Later, the student council was transformed into the student senate, which, after consultation with the administration and faculty, acts as the governing body; it has been very influential in changing student life at Plymouth. Officers seen here, from left to right, are P. Cummings, J. Connors, Dean Hartman (advisor), and L. Pollard.

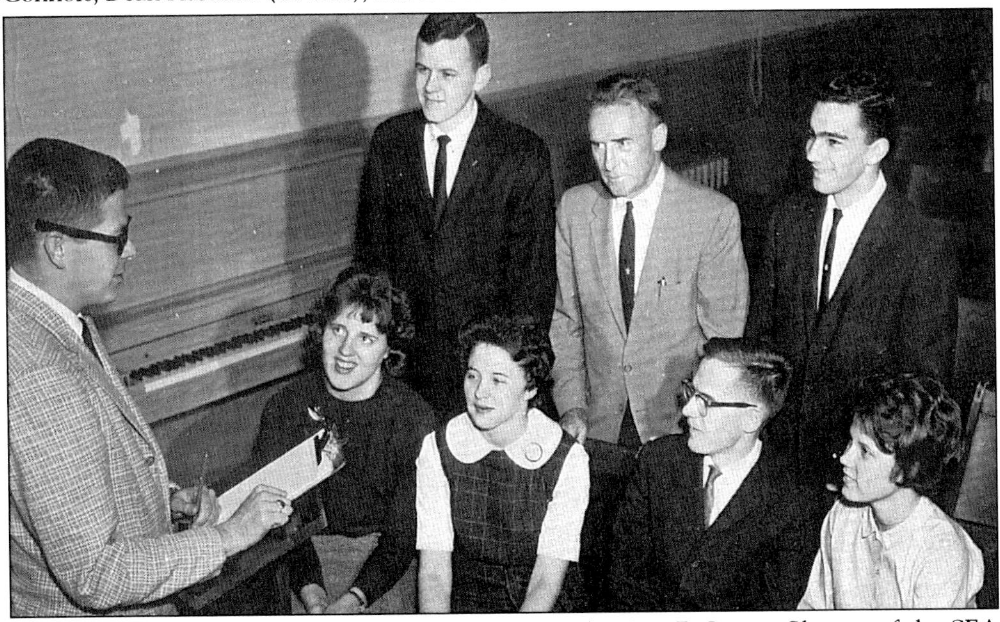

STUDENT EDUCATION ASSOCIATION (SEA), 1963. The Guy E. Speare Chapter of the SEA served the campus as a professional organization. In 1963, the club functioned to acquaint the students with some of the problems and situations in the field of education. At the SEA meetings, the club presented films, speakers, and panels on topics pertaining to phases of the teaching profession. Seen here, from right to left, are as follows: (presiding) Don Chase; (front row) G. Gordon, J. Langmead, L. Wood, and B. Brewd. (back row) L. Coffin, Dr. Osgood (advisor), and J. Wagner.

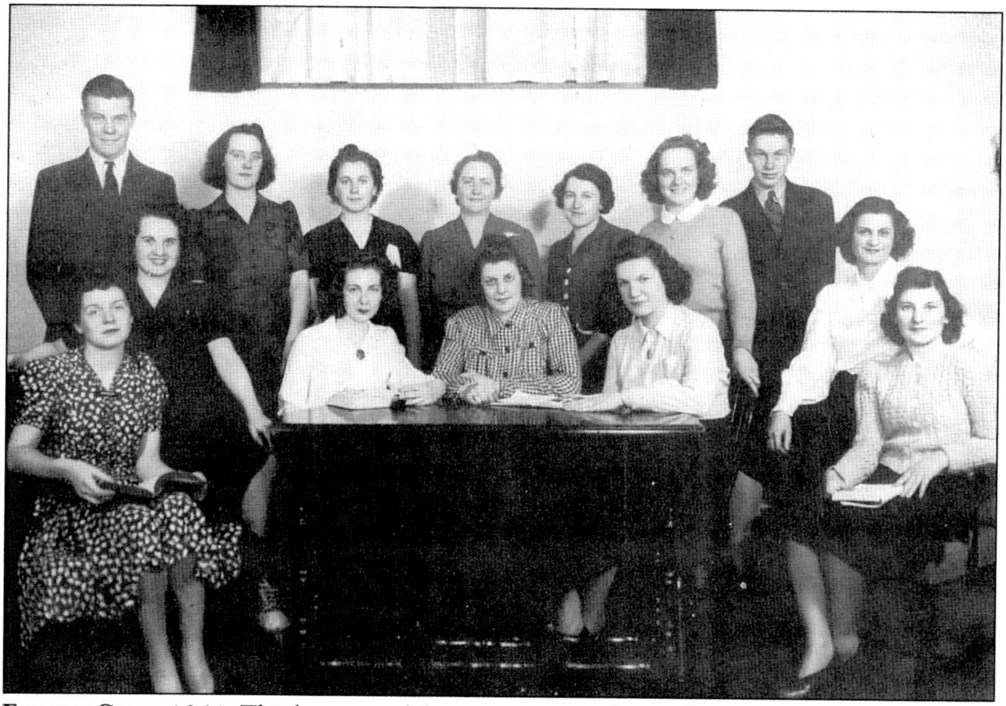

FRENCH CLUB, 1941. This language club was very active during the 1940s. Seen here, from left to right, are as follows: (sitting) R. Rushlow, L. Demers, E. Roy, S. Huckins, A. Whiteneck, R. Cannistraro, and H. Mallis; (standing) E. Connor, B. Carr. C. Mitton, Ms. Lindahl, A. Whittemore, E. Miller, and H. Vittum.

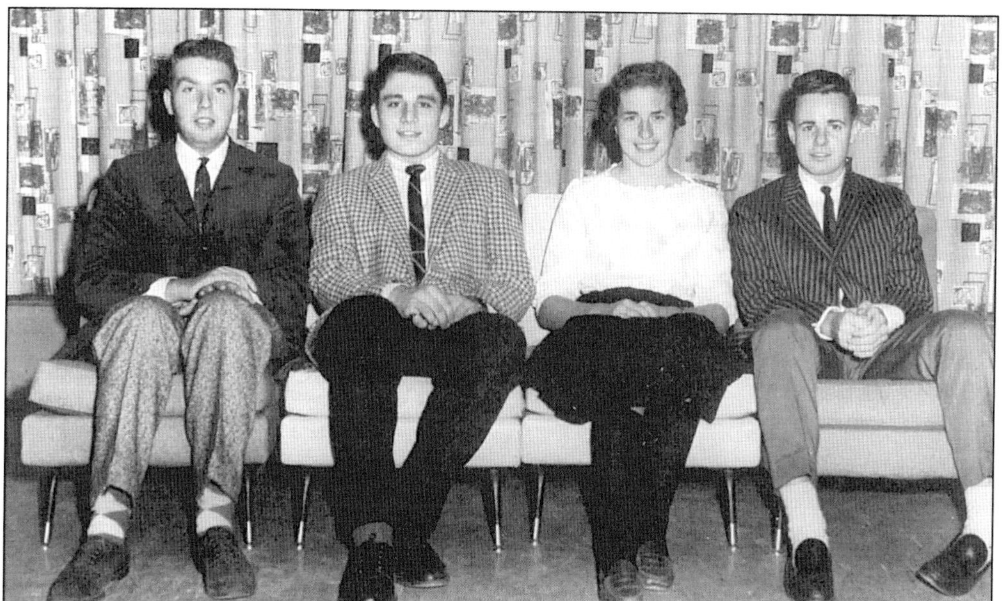

FRENCH AND SPANISH CLUB, 1960. At Plymouth Teachers College the student of language is expected to acquire a working knowledge of the various aspects of both French and Spanish. The object of the language department is to prepare teachers who will promote the idea of tolerance through the study of foreign languages, customs, and traditions.

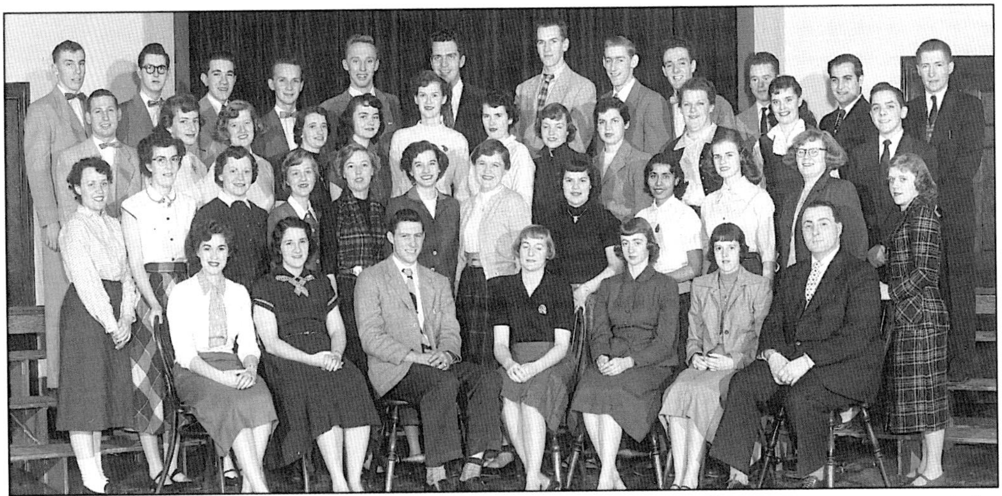

THE PLYMOUTH PLAYERS, 1954. In January 1952, the college and community witnessed the birth of a new dramatic club. In every college, there are a few who receive a stimulus from the smell of greasepaint; the Plymouth Players is made up of such individuals. All students were encouraged to increase their appreciation and knowledge of drama by attendance and participation in plays and their production. Under the direction of Roi White, the Plymouth Players introduced a new era in dramatics at the college, and soon became well known throughout the state for the quality of their performances. Seen here, from left to right, are as follows: (first row) D. Moffitt, H. Hamel, E. Bourey, O. Chayer, J. Burnham, C. Shaw, and Mr. White (advisor); (second row) A. Welch, P. Woodard, O. Blodgett, L. Avery, J. Temperley, A. Bourey, M. Turner, L. Viger, D. Pestonji, B. Albert, E. Anderson, and R. Seaver; (third row) G. LeClair, C. Chandler, E. Brown, I. Pare, B. Bryant, J. Buffum, J. Harrison, J. Homer, B. McNiff, T. Huggins, F. Kelley, and D. DesRoches; (fourth row) R. Blakslee, H. Peaslee, R. Blanchette, R. Murphy, R. Holden, M. James, E. Finnegan, R. Jackson, L. Gauthier, F. Ramsay, L. Rousseau, and R. Knowles.

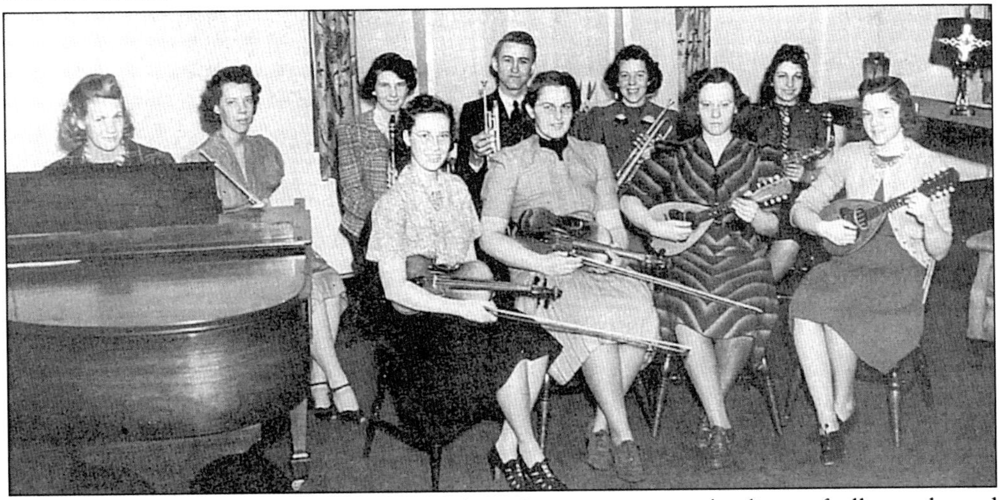

ORCHESTRA, 1940. As an important and vital experience in the lives of all people and especially for those who plan to teach, varied music organizations provide enjoyment and opportunity for participation. Seen here, from left to right, are as follows: (front row) F. Caswell, P. Agle, H. Thomas, and M. Finnigan; (back row) P. Stickney, R. deRochemont, E. White, B. Little, D. Wormstead, and F. Hikel.

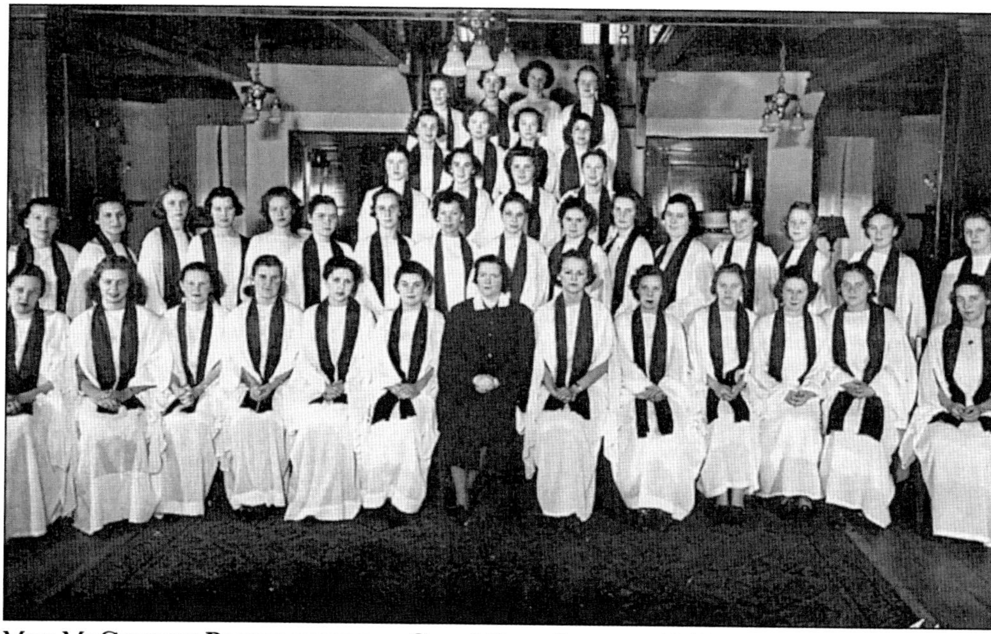

MISS MCGUNIGLE POSING WITH THE GIRLS' GLEE CLUB, C. 1940S.

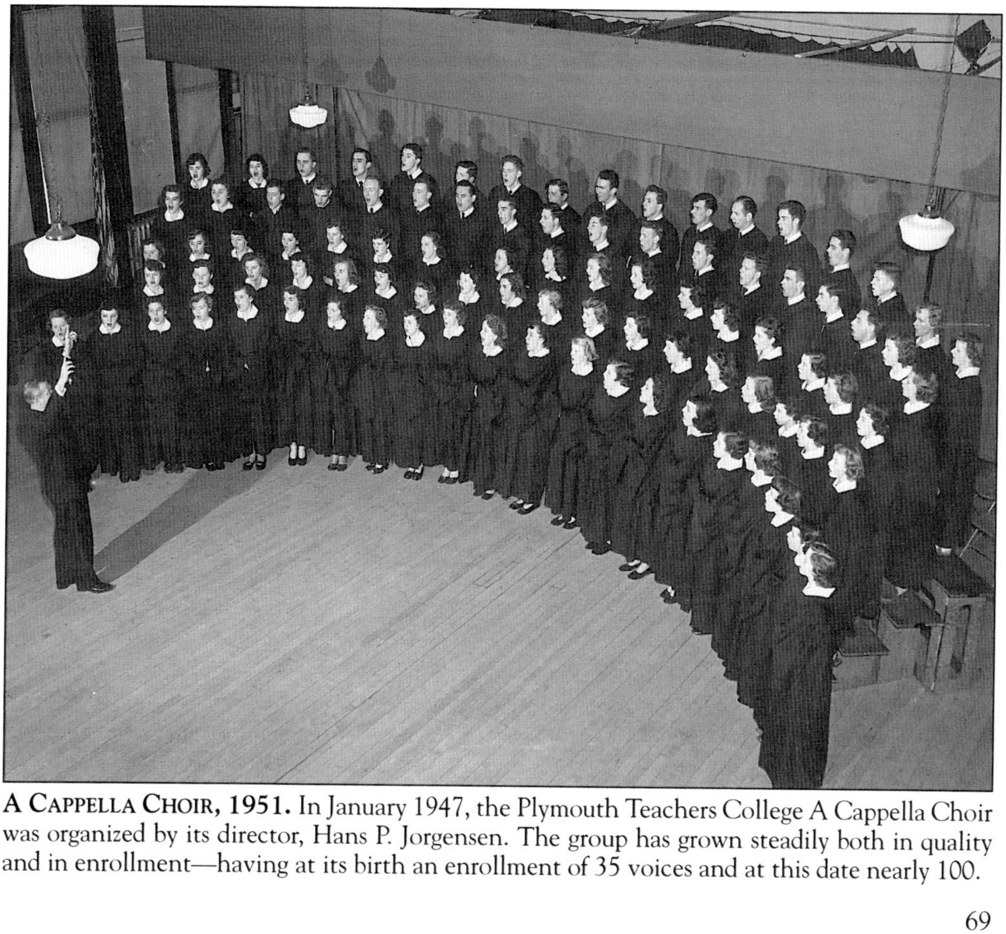

A CAPPELLA CHOIR, 1951. In January 1947, the Plymouth Teachers College A Cappella Choir was organized by its director, Hans P. Jorgensen. The group has grown steadily both in quality and in enrollment—having at its birth an enrollment of 35 voices and at this date nearly 100.

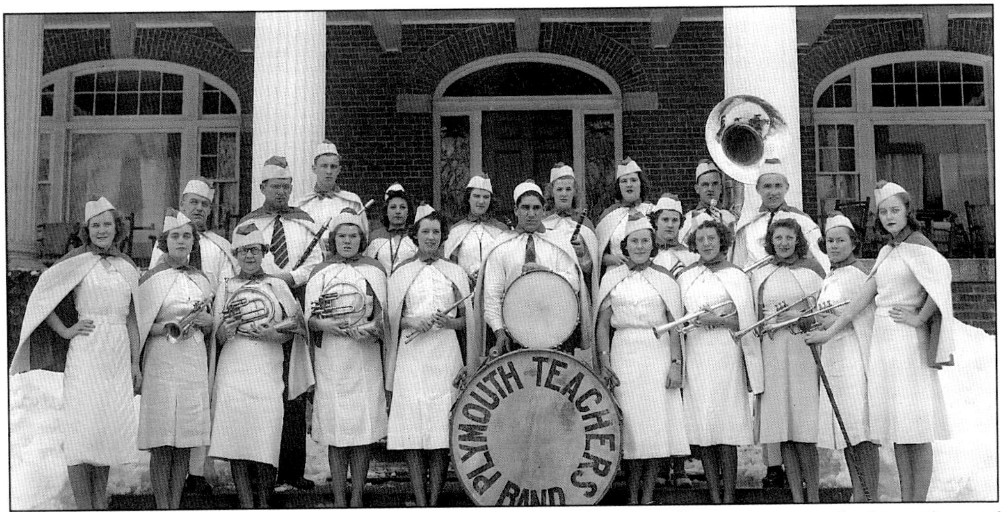

PTC BAND, 1940. The PTC band, directed by Mr. Robert Boyd, was composed of members of the student body and interested townspeople. This organization added spirit and enthusiasm by playing at basketball games, band concerts, and the annual commencement activities. Seen here, from left to right, are as follows: (front row) B. Millar, D. Newling, R. Bozarth, P. Pushee, M. Colby, T. Cassarino, R. Dennis, D. Wormstead, E. Smith, R. Theuner, and C. Lewis; (back row) Mr. Robert Boyd (director), R. Ernst, M. Leonard, F. Hikel, V. Griffin, P. Stickney, A. Huntress, B. Little, C. Gay.

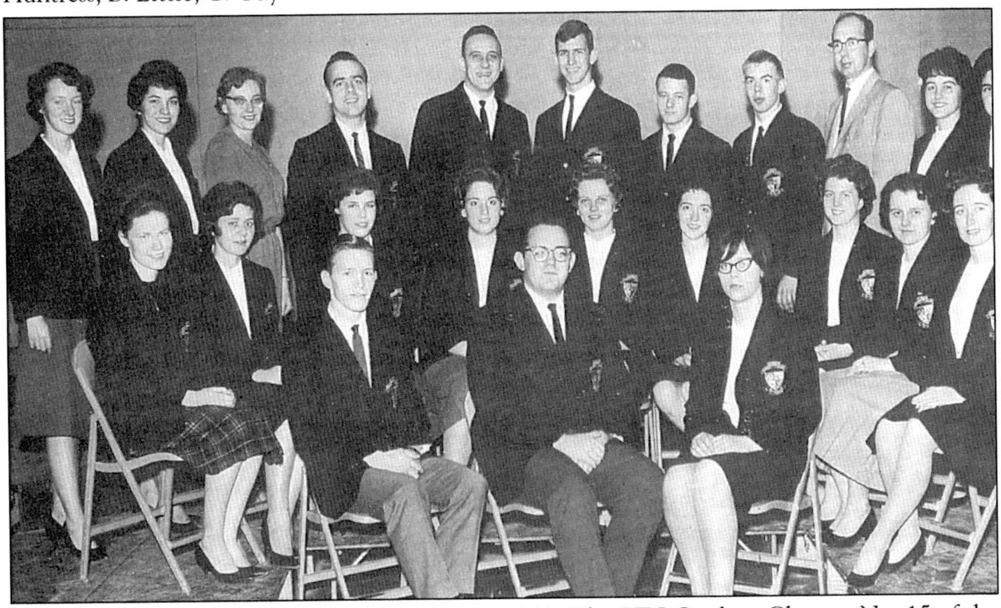

MUSIC EDUCATORS NATIONAL CONFERENCE, 1963. The PTC Student Chapter No. 15 of the Music Educators National Conference is a professional organization for music majors and minors. The group aims to foster better music on campus and provide for professional programs and projects for the students in the music department. Seen here, from left to right, are as follows: (front row) B. Lauterbach, L. Beck, and B. Butterfield; (second row) V. O'Hara, P. Grant, C. Roberts, S. Steele, M. Taylor, D. Dickinson, L. Grumman, J. Murdock, and N. Stephenson; (third row) L. Cook, A. Schenk, Carol Belmain, D. Downes, L. Cormier, D. Brown, J. Healy, D. Bigelow, Prof. Walter Smith (director), J. Perry, and H. Narkiewicz.

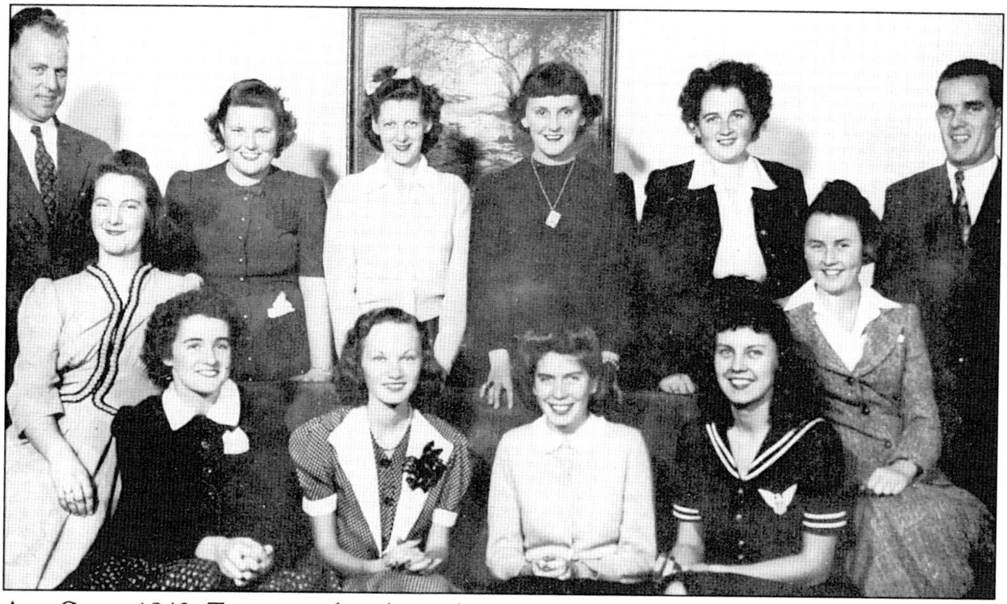

ART CLUB, 1942. To express their love of art and its language, the club became very active. Seen here, from left to right, are as follows: (front row) Mr. Stevenson, M. Nelson, E. Tapply, R. Cavaric, E. Page, and C. Gay; (sitting) R. Vittum, E. Page, H. Wittig, L. Richardson, J. Ryan, and A. Harrison.

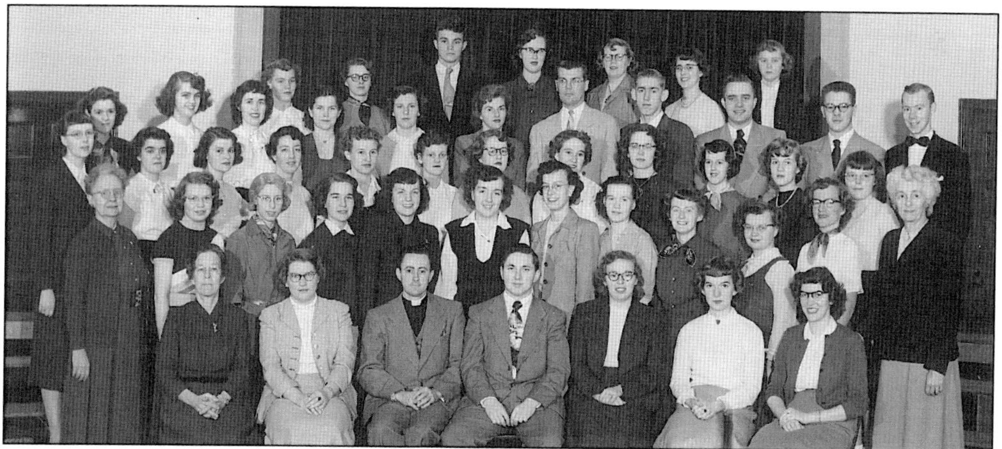

CHRISTIAN ASSOCIATION, 1952. The Christian Association was organized for the purpose of fellowship for both students and faculty who are united in the desire to understand the Christian faith and live the Christian life. Since its inception in October 1945, the club has continued to grow so that by this date it is one of the largest organizations on campus and has the highest percentage of faculty-student membership of any club in college. Seen here, from left to right, are as follows: (sitting) Miss Waugh (advisor), Miss Storer (advisor), Reverend Sprague (advisor), R. Thompson, A. Wright, J. MacKenzie, and J. Demag; (second row) Miss Bozarth, R. Bennett, P. Battis, N. Heath, J. Homer, H. Bridgeo, E. Corbett, M. Hanchett, J. Larrabee, M. Polhemus, M. Joy, and Mrs. Leslie; (third row) R. Dietzel, L. MacNeill, R. Eaton, A. Nihan, P. Fellows, C. Fowle, S. Ayer, F. Brooks, N. Nevers, C. Shaw, L. Avery, and B. Spaulding; (fourth row) F. Purington, M. Stratton, N. Thompson, M. Jewell, R. Kelly, P. Wynott, H. Fernald, R. Jackson, P. Magoon, D. Elsemore, and G. Low; (fifth row) B. Ashley, E. Hayward, R. Martel, J. Heald, E. Anderson, A. Woodward, and E. Stewart.

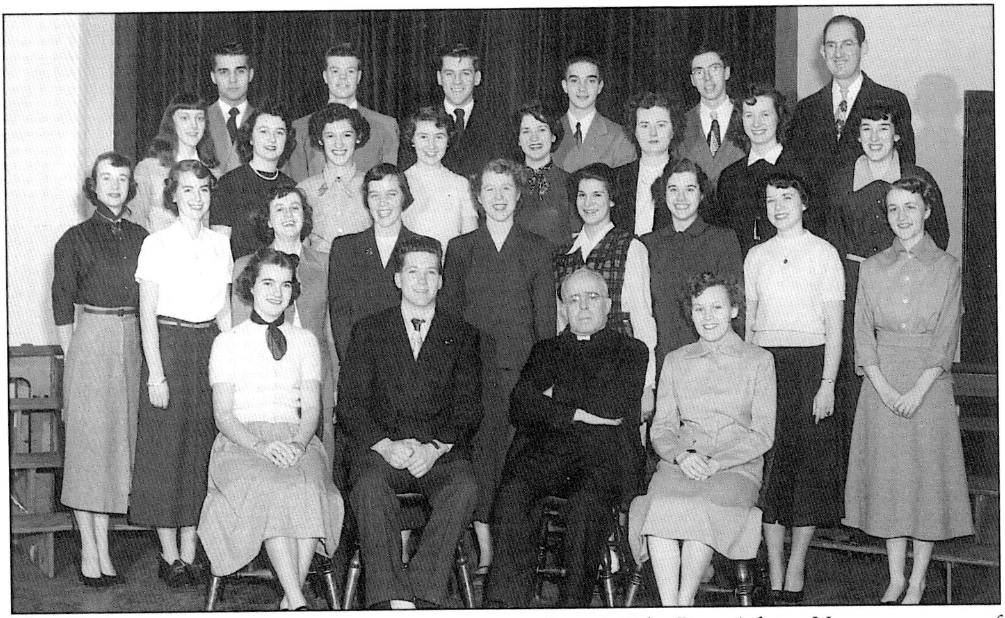

SETON CLUB, 1952. The Seton Club was organized in 1940 by Rev. Adrien Verrette, pastor of St. Matthew's Church. Its two-fold purpose was to enable the Catholic students of the college to further their knowledge of Christian Doctrine and to prepare them for spiritual and moral ideals in their teaching careers. The club was named after Mother Elizabeth Seton who, from her saintly works beginning in 1809, is now acknowledged as the "Mother of Many Daughters." Shown here, from left to right, are as follows: (sitting) B. Callaghan, R. Connors, Fr. Verrette, and K. Marcotte; (second row) K. Dow, J. Robinson, L. Ouelette, H. Reardon, M. Paris, E. Cannistraro, A. Bowers, J. Corrette, and L. Carey: (third row) H. Doyle, D. Roy, N. Bergeron, M. Welch, B. Armstrong, C. Barrette, M. Flanagan, and P. Doucette; (fourth row) A. Adams, E. Hanson, I. Clark, R. Simoneau, R. MacDougall, and A. MacDonald.

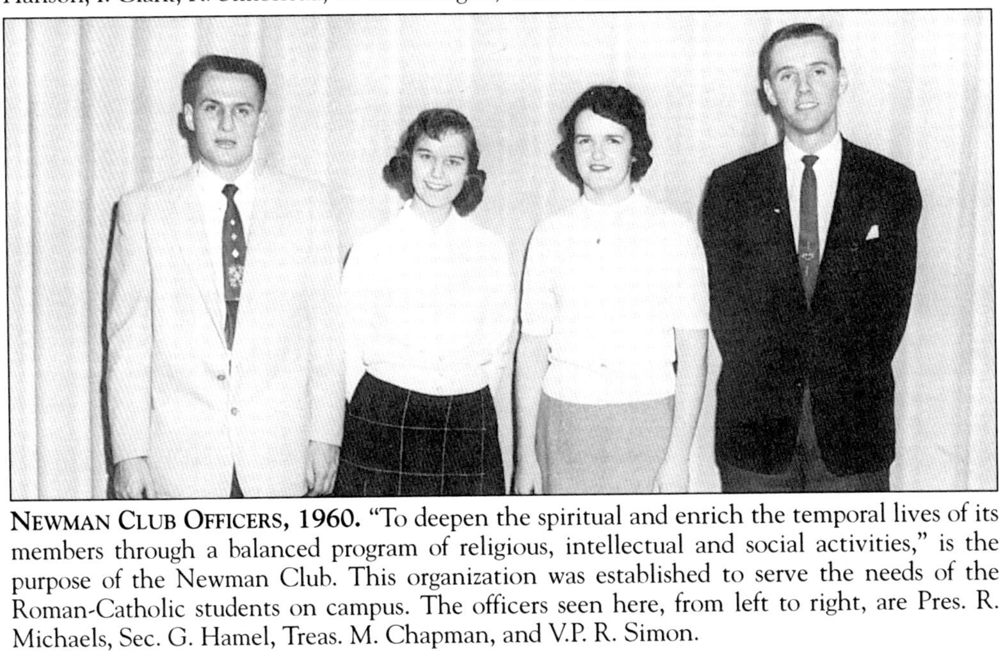

NEWMAN CLUB OFFICERS, 1960. "To deepen the spiritual and enrich the temporal lives of its members through a balanced program of religious, intellectual and social activities," is the purpose of the Newman Club. This organization was established to serve the needs of the Roman-Catholic students on campus. The officers seen here, from left to right, are Pres. R. Michaels, Sec. G. Hamel, Treas. M. Chapman, and V.P. R. Simon.

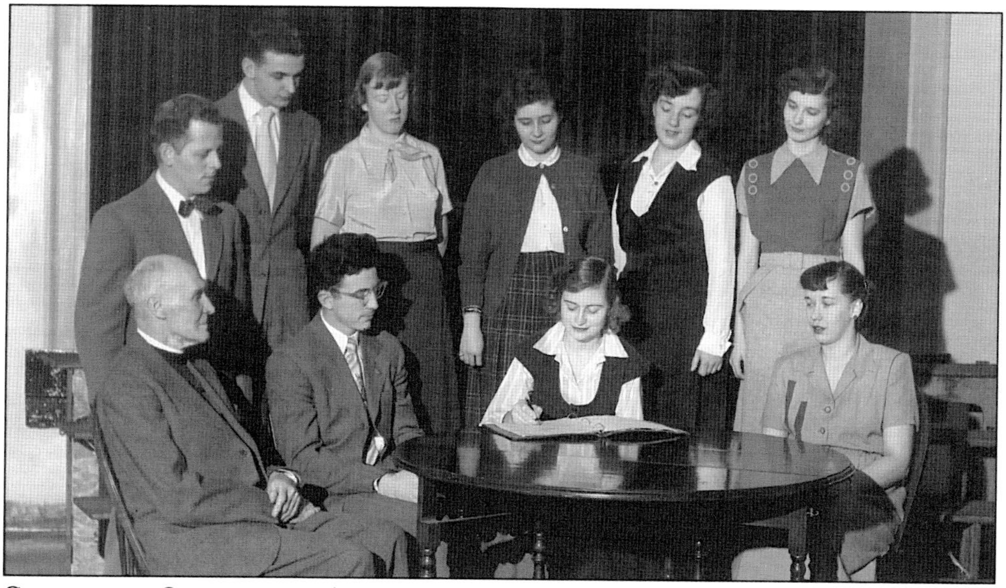

CANTERBURY CLUB, 1952. The Canterbury Club was organized in March 1948 under the supervision of Rev. Randall C. Gidding of the University New Hampshire. The prime purpose of this club was to provide the Episcopal student with the opportunity to share the enriching experience of a church-home away from his or her parish. Seen here, from left to right, are as follows: (sitting) Reverend Haight (advisor), E. Clark, L. Powell, and J. Boutwell; (standing) C. Pinkham, R. Gordon, C. Allison, J. Root, H. Bridgeo, and C.Hodder.

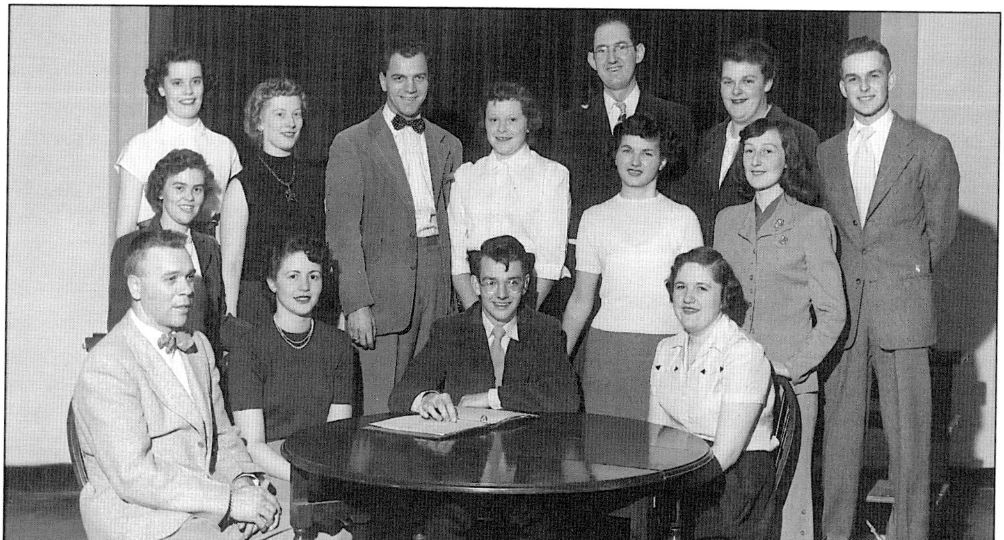

SCIENCE CLUB, 1952. The major project of the Science Club was the sponsorship of a science fair, which was held on campus. High schools from the Lakes-North Country Region were invited to exhibit their projects in the field of Physics, Chemistry, Biology, and General Science. The purpose of the science fair was to create and develop an active interest in science among high school students in this region of New Hampshire. Seen here, from left to right, are as follows: (front row) Mr. Kenney (advisor) L. Nichol, E. Desmond ,and M. Turner; (middle row) D. Bailey, D. Slack, J. Currier, O. Blodgett, G. Hiler, and P. Sinclair; (back row) F. Kelley, A. MacDonald, T. Huggins, and R. Gordon.

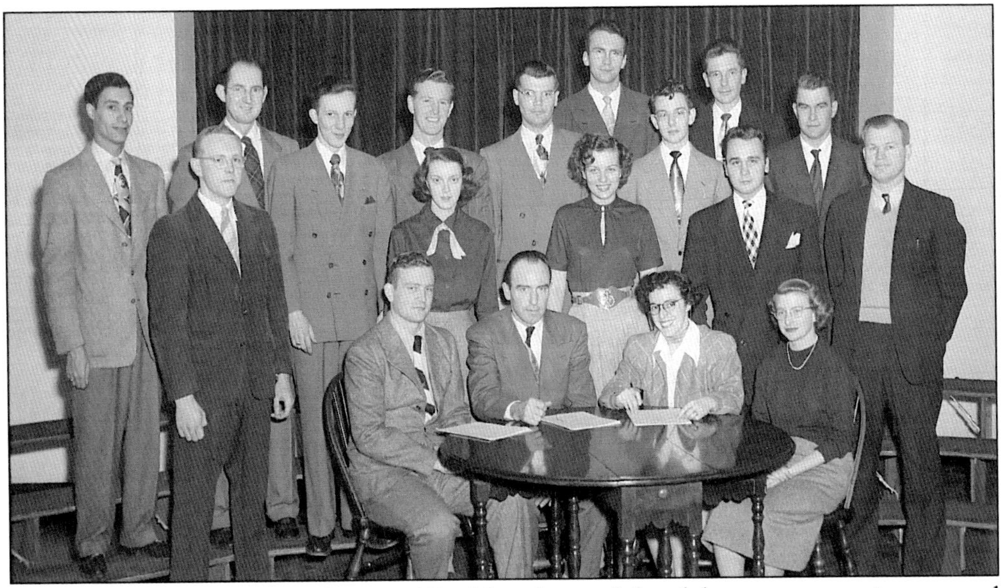

INTERNATIONAL RELATIONS CLUB, 1951. The object of the club was to create interest and understanding in world affairs. Through panel discussions, speakers, and films, interesting and educational programs were held at each meeting. Plans that year were being formulated for a model United Nations Assembly to be held on campus. Seen here, from left to right, are as follows: (seated) W. Pollard, J. O'Brien, E. Osgood, and D. Seguin; (second row) E. Blake, H. Doyle, J. Bowdoin, C. Potter, and Mr. Kenney (advisor); (third row) M. LaPlante, A. MacDonald, L. DeLacey, L. Metivier, H. Fernald, E. Desmond, and R. Osgood; (fourth row) J. Vares and W. Morris.

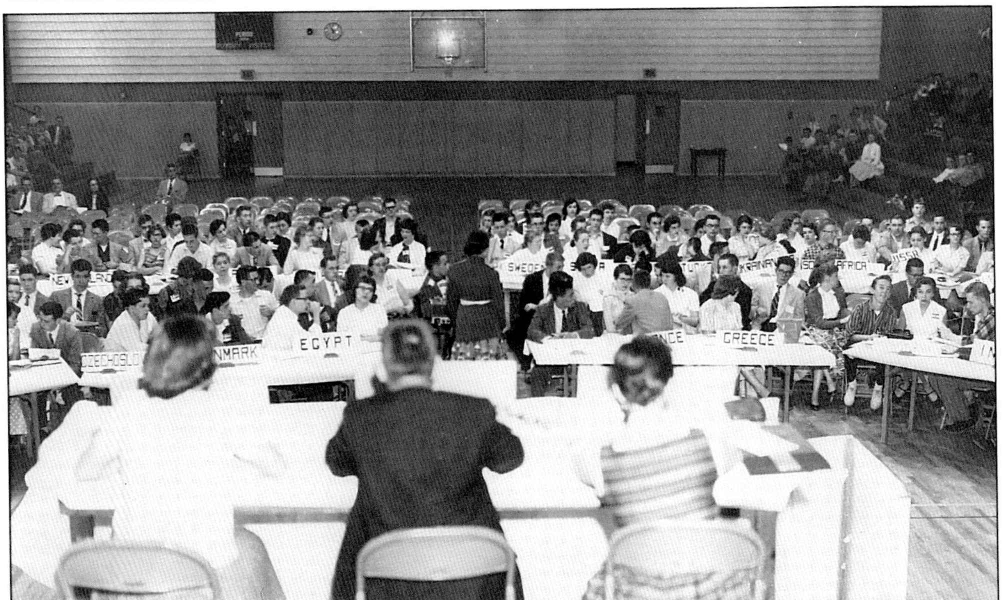

UNITED NATIONS MODEL GENERAL ASSEMBLY. This assembly was held for many years under the direction of Mr. James Hogan. Juniors and Seniors from high schools throughout the state, New England, and Canada were invited to participate as delegates from member countries in the U.N.

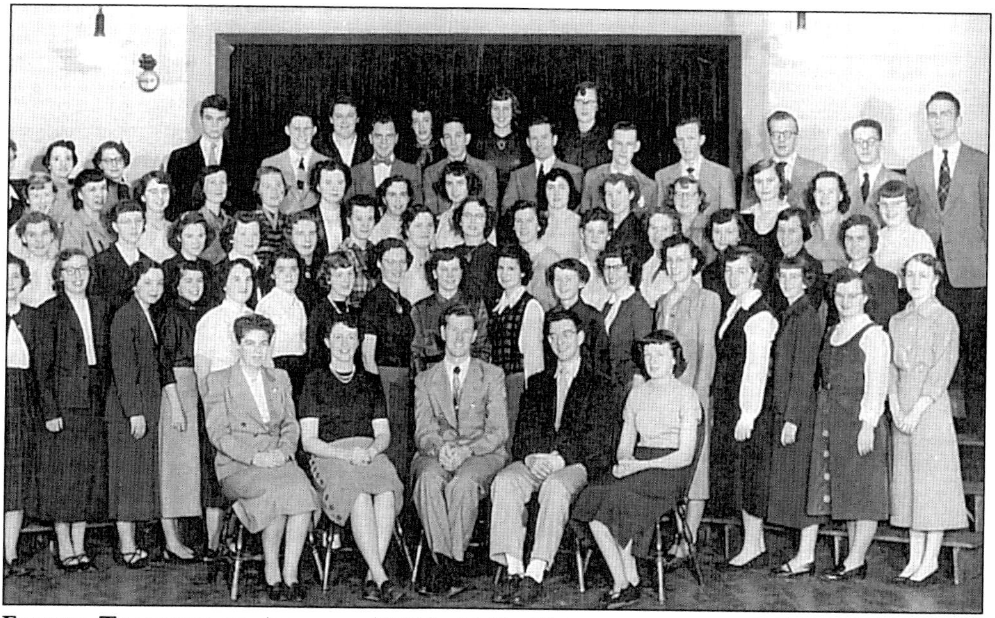

FUTURE TEACHERS OF AMERICA (FTA), 1952. This organization, which came to PSC in 1947, was the largest on campus. The FTA is a branch of the National Education Association; the FTA chapter strives to foster professional growth among the educators of tomorrow.

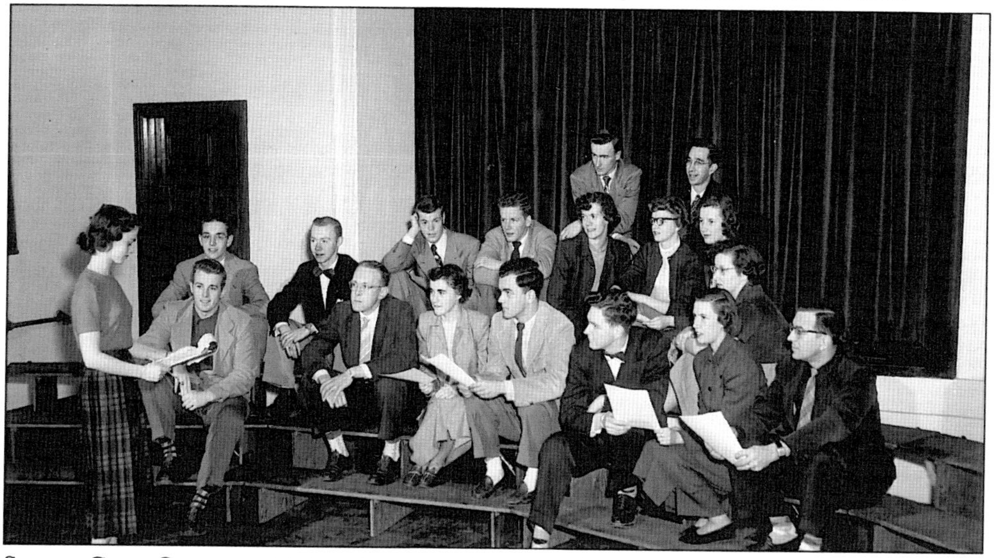

SOCIAL CLUB COUNCIL, 1951. The Council consisted of all class presidents, officers directly elected by the student body, two faculty advisors, and other members appointed by the president of the Social Club. All the students of the college belong .to the Social Club; their suggestions and cooperation is welcomed by the council as it plans and conducts the various social activities of the college year. The council sponsored such major events as the Halloween and Christmas banquets, the Winter Carnival, the Formals, and the informal weekend social programs. Seen here, from left to right, are as follows: (standing) D. Hussey (president); (front row) D. Day, E. Blake, M. Glass, J. Currier, R. Fish, J. Blake, and Dr. Bouchard (advisor); (middle row) E. Desmond, G. Low, E. Hanson, S. Tinker, J. Howe, A. Jette, M. Flanagan, and I. Jones; (back row) E. Beals and R. Hathaway.

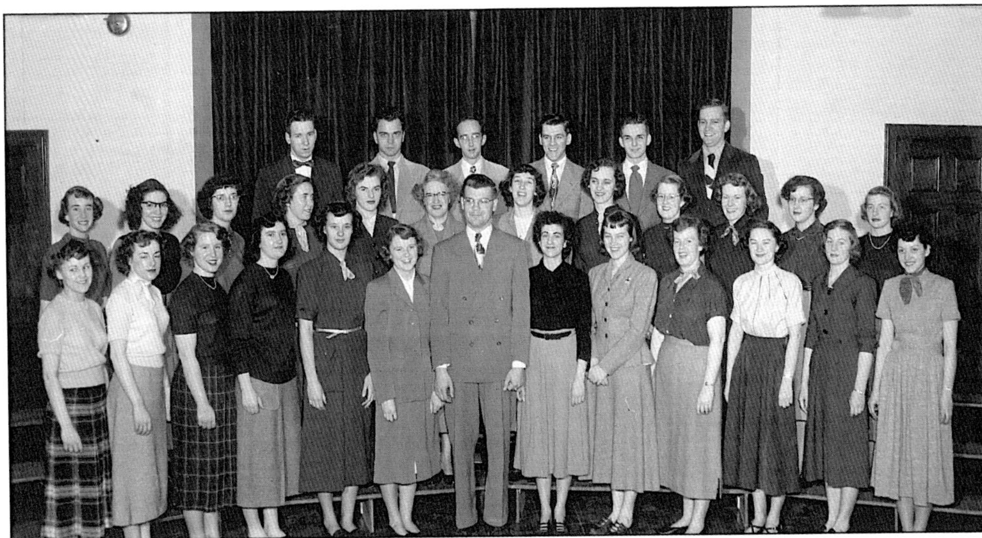

OUTING CLUB, 1951. This club, as its name suggests, is maintained for the purpose of promoting outdoor activities. An important event of its sponsorship is Mountain Day at which time the entire college community took a day off from classes to go mountain climbing. In addition, the Outing Club had charge of the snow sculpturing and skiing events at the annual Winter Carnival. Its program also includes other seasonal activities. Seen here, from left to right, are as follows: (front row) K. Marcotte, V. Corbeil, M. Paris, J. Janelle, P. Szopa, M. Head, H. Fernald, E. Samaha, B. Pettes, K. Gass, M. Miltimore, O. Chayer, and Miclon; (middle row) K. Dow, J. Demag, M. Dolliver, E. Crombie, P. Wynott, Miss Alder (advisor); P. Doucette, J. Champagne, S. Ayer, H. Davis, I. Jones, and D. Seguin; (back row) E. Cail, J. Currier, T. MacDonald, I. Clark, R. Gordon, and W. Polard.

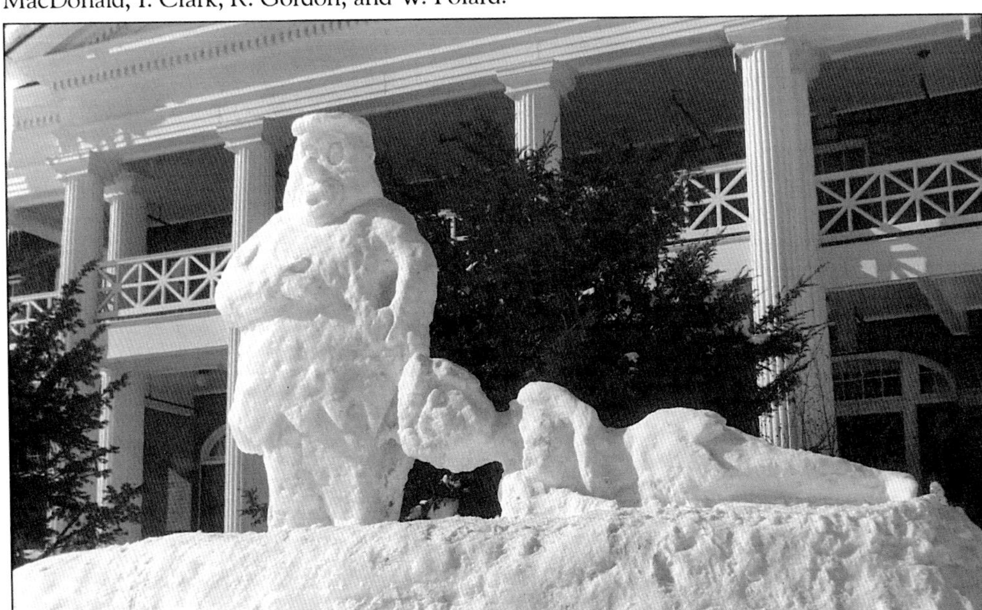

OUTING CLUB SCULPTURES IN FRONT OF MARY LYON HALL, 1963. This 1963 theme of the Winter Carnival was "*Bedrock, home of the Flintstones.*" The winning sculpture, Fred and Wilma Flintstone, was by the Junior Class.

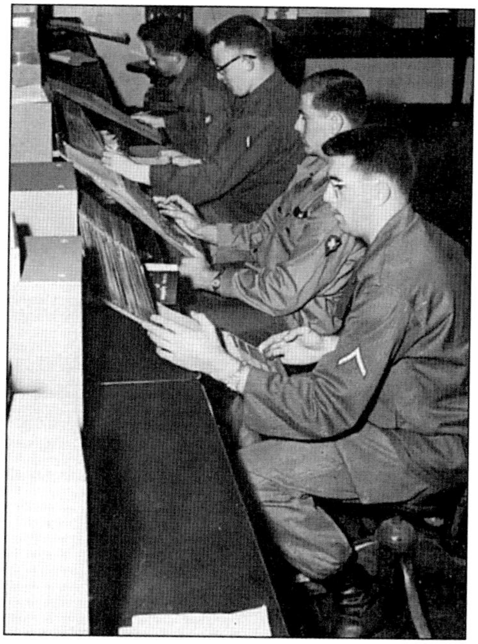

The 395 Engineer Company Learning How to Record Stock Items, 1959. This year marked the fifth and final year of Plymouth Teachers College's active U.S. Army Reserve Unit. This small unit, which was never more than 50 men, was composed almost entirely of college students; however, some of the members were graduates of PTC and others were people living in the surrounding area. At the time of disbanding, the unit had about 35 men engaged in training. However, with the new pentatomic division, this proved too small for efficient operation. The 395th Engineer Company had a training schedule that coincided with the college "year," thus allowing service-obligated students to relieve themselves of a portion of their draft responsibilities conveniently.

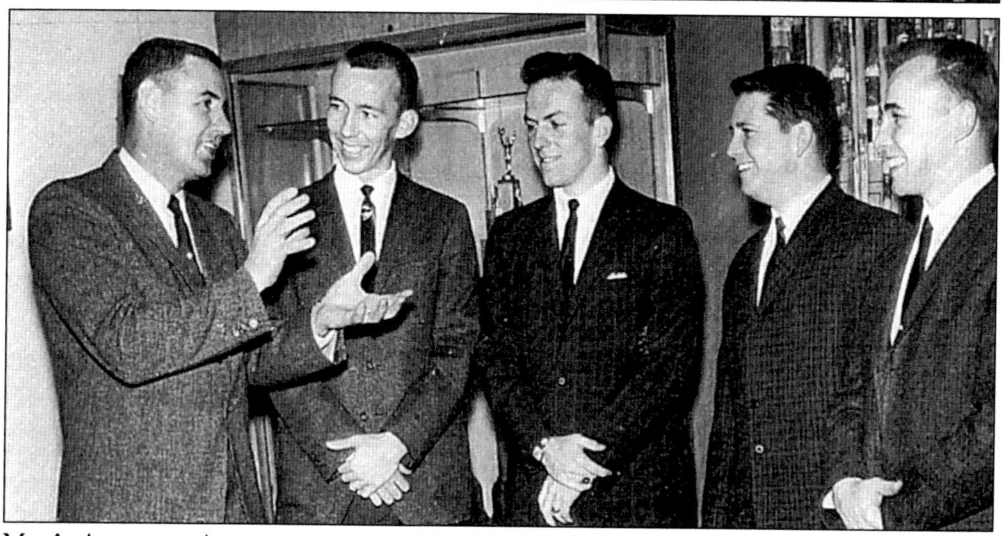

Men's Athletic Association, 1963. In 1957, the idea of a Men's Athletic Association was discussed by students who saw the need for such an organization. This idea became a reality in 1958 when a group of students organized and drew up a constitution. Athletics is accorded a very prominent place in the activity program of the college; thus, a broad intramural and intercollegiate program is carried on each year. The college strives to maintain a well-balanced program, designed to develop fair play and good sportsmanship; to create a sense of unity and loyalty among the students; and to establish friendly, competitive relations with other educational institutions. This organization is composed of male members of the student body who willingly donate their time and energy to help make our college an active one. In addition to the intramural program, this organization sponsors social activities such as the talent show, movies, and dances. The college is a member of the New England Teachers College Athletic Association. Seen, from left to right, are Coach John Foley (advisor), C. Chandler, P. Breckell, R. Barnaby, and P. Arold, later a PSC coach.

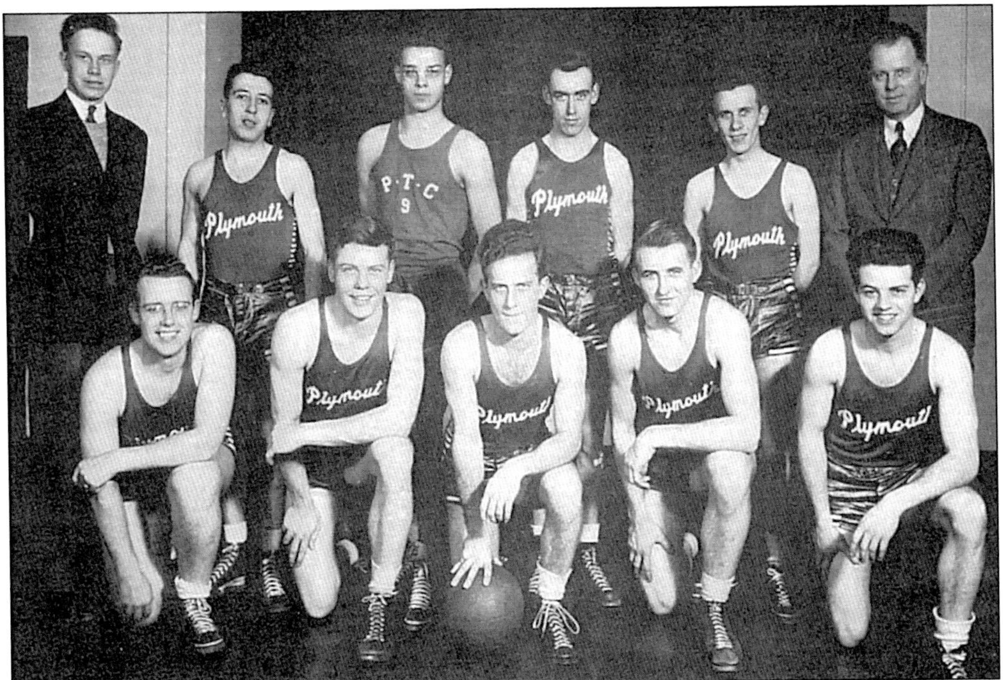

Boys' Basketball Team, 1942. Seen here, from right to left, are as follows: (front row) H. Annis, E. Conners, P. Tapply, B. Little, and W. Judkins; (back row) H. Vittum, P. Banios, A. Tufts, H. Evans, J. Zolner, and Mr. Stevenson. Henry Vittum returned to PSC as a professor of English.

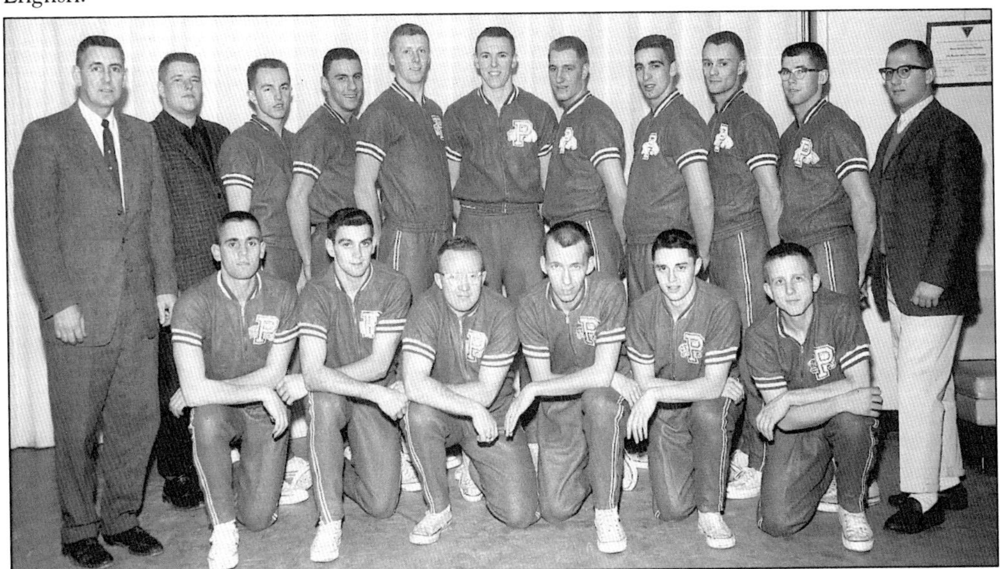

Boys "Plymouth Panthers" (or "The Foleymen") Basketball Team, 1962–63. In 1947, the college joined the New England Teachers College Athletic Association and soon earned an enviable record for its varsity teams. Seen here, from right to left, are as follows: (front row) Coach John Foley, D. Gilbert, G. Hunnington, P. Johnson, D. Chandler, and S. Lier; (back row) R. Hatch, D. Baker, K. Bernier, A. Blakely, S. Bamford, B. Coson, A. Nearey, J. Wescott, J. Connors, and B. Tkach.

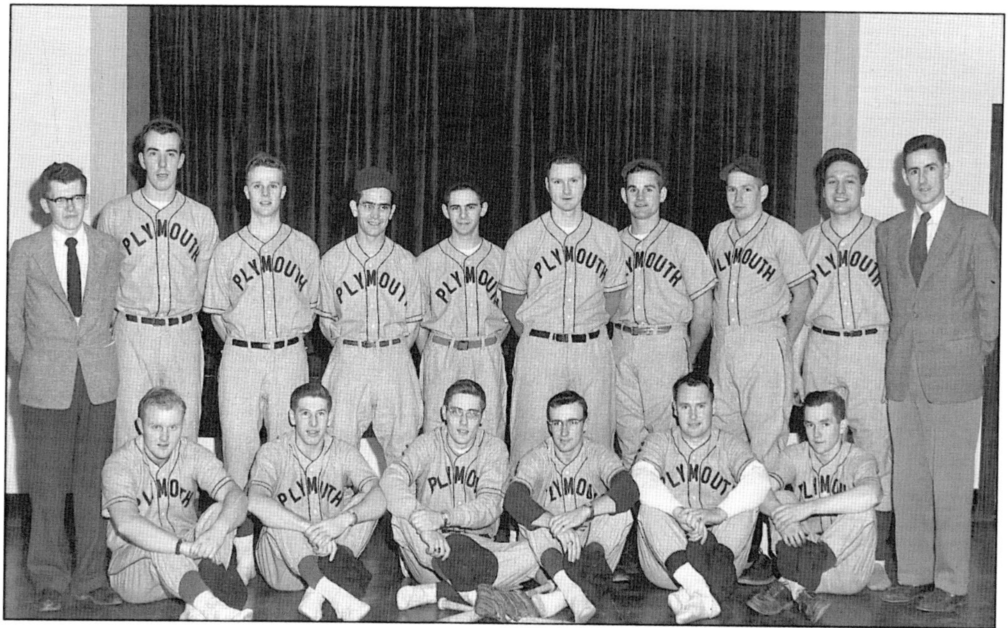

BASEBALL TEAM, 1953. In 1947, under the direction of John C. Foley, the department of education and the expansion of the men's varsity sports to include baseball brought new spirit and enthusiasm to the student activities. Seen here, from left to right, are as follows: (front row) E. Kenney, V. Bryant, W. Marston, E. Beals, R. Stickney, and D. Dole; (second row) R. Smith, D. Dearborn, W. Evans, R. Angers, F. Morin, J. Matthews, R. Parker, J. Callahan, and Mr. Foley (coach).

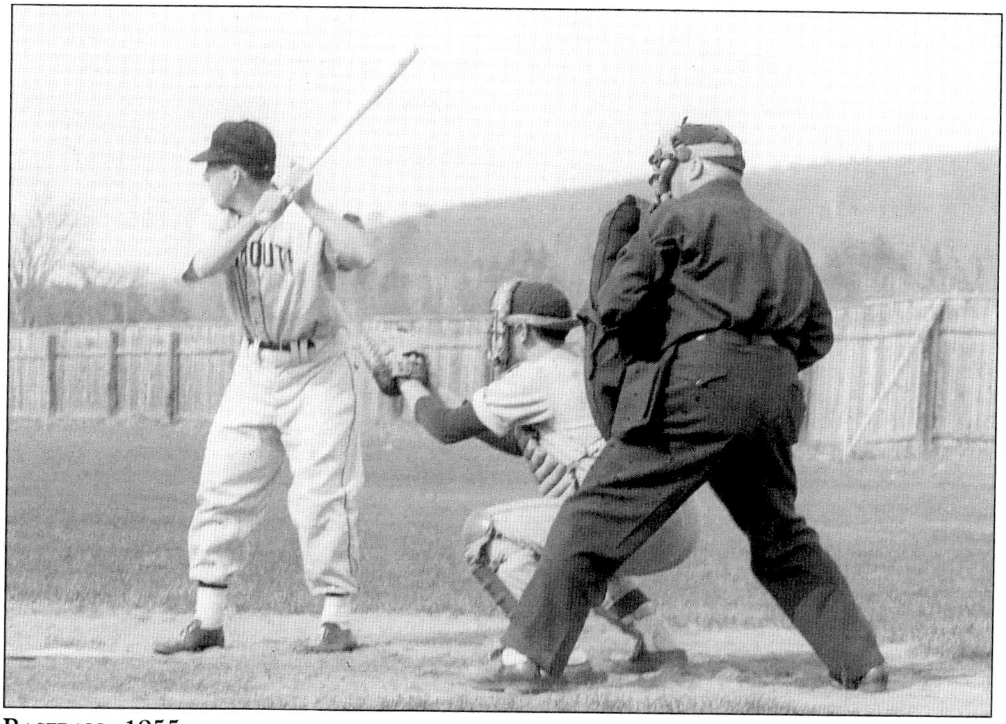

BASEBALL, 1955.

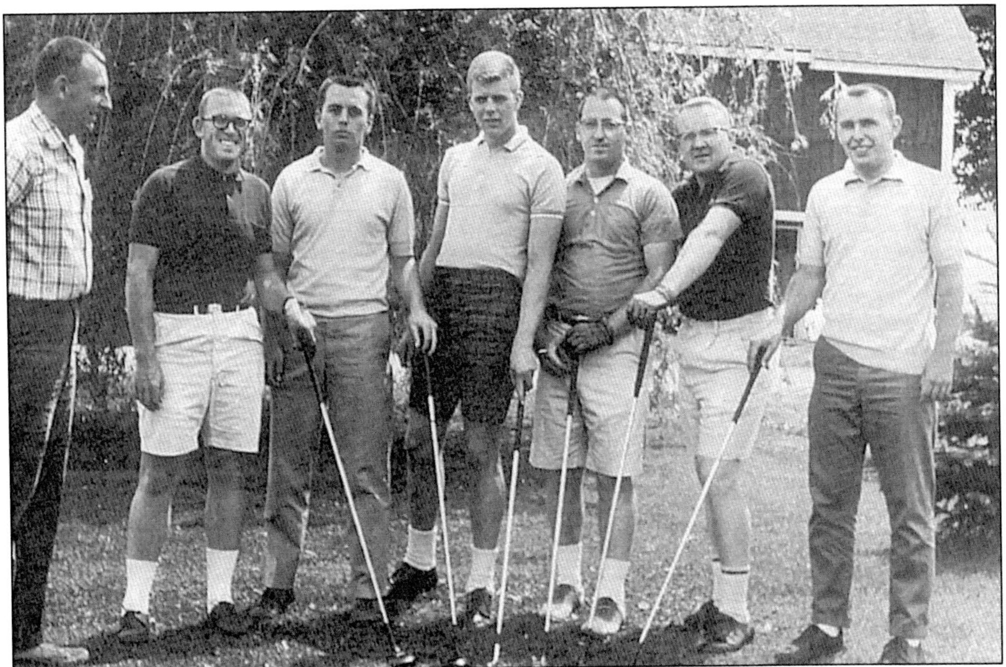

GOLF TEAM AT THE WAUKEWAN COUNTRY CLUB IN MEREDITH, 1963. Seen here, from left to right, are Dr. Frey (coach), D. Ross, W. Sidney, D. Ladieu, H. Noyes, P. Johnson, and E. Walker.

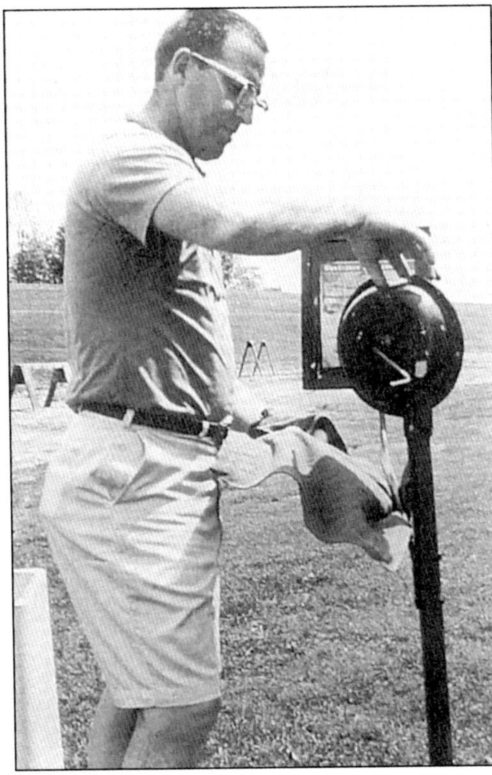

HOWARD NOYES. Noyes washes his golf ball in preparation for a match at Waukewan Country Club in Meredith, New Hampshire, 1963.

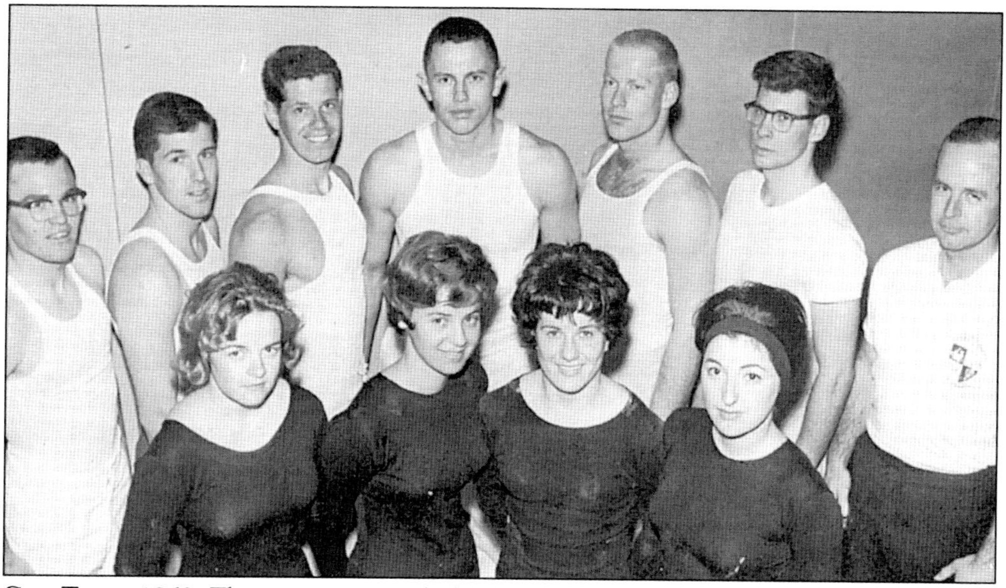

GYM TEAM, 1963. The team, composed of six men and four women, entered into competition with other schools for the first time in the history of PSC. The team worked toward excellence and precision through practice and exhibitions given for area audiences. Seen here, from left to right, are as follows: (front row) P. Dalton, A. Jones, J. Sinivori, and J. Barguin; (back row) B. Maguire, B. Wilson, J. Jablonski, M. Brown, D. Patnode, R. Butcher, and coach Charles Guemple.

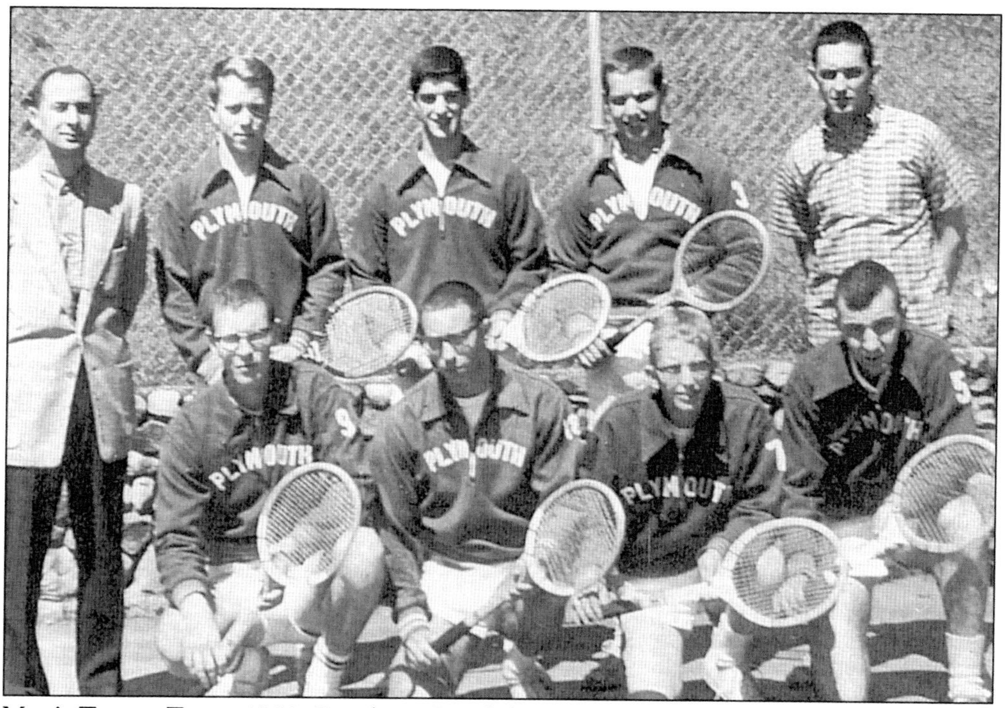

MEN'S TENNIS TEAM, 1963. Seen here, from left to right, are as follows: (front row) J. O'Wrill, D. Wzolek, R. Wilmont, and R. Shackett; (second row) Coach Goldman, R. Eames, B. Marshall, B. Damon, and manager J. Lavachia.

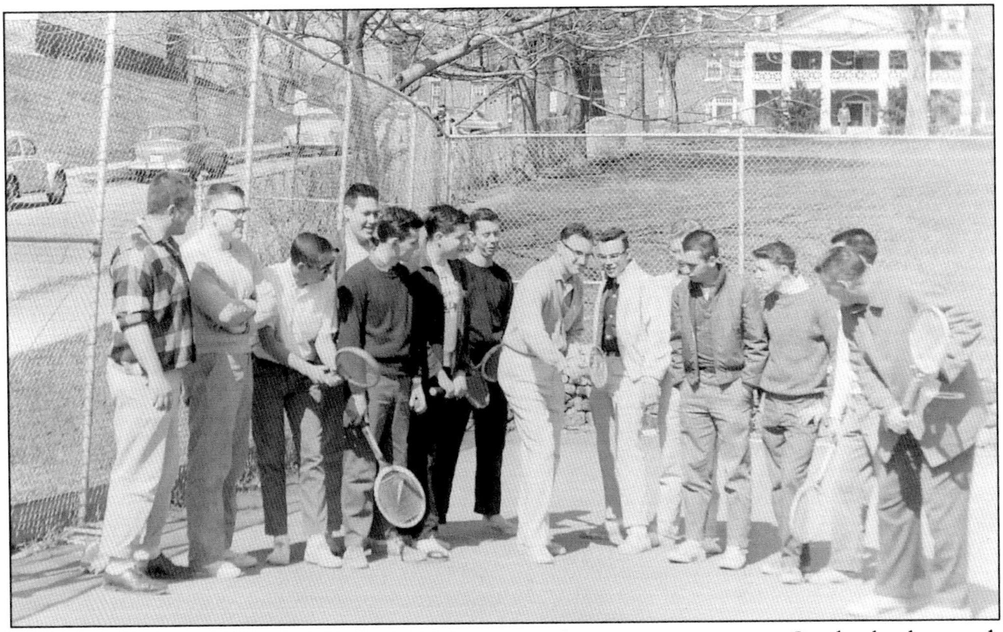

Men's Tennis Team, 1962. The team is getting last minute pointers. In the background, Mary Lyon Hall can be seen.

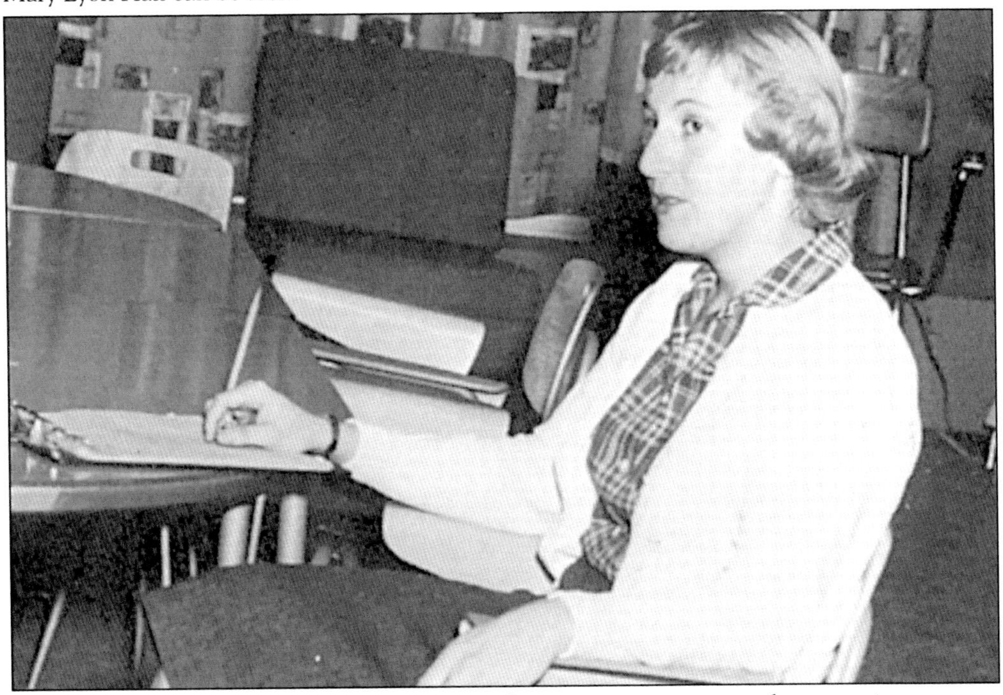

Women's Recreation Association, 1960. The association promotes the recreation program through Intramural sports, inter-class sports, varsity sports, co-recreational sports, sponsoring cheer leaders, encouraging tournaments in individual and dual sports, and sponsoring such activities as hiking, winter sports, sports days, and sports clinics. Ms. Priscilla Alden, the women's physical education director, was the advisor of the group; she worked closely with the advisors and members.

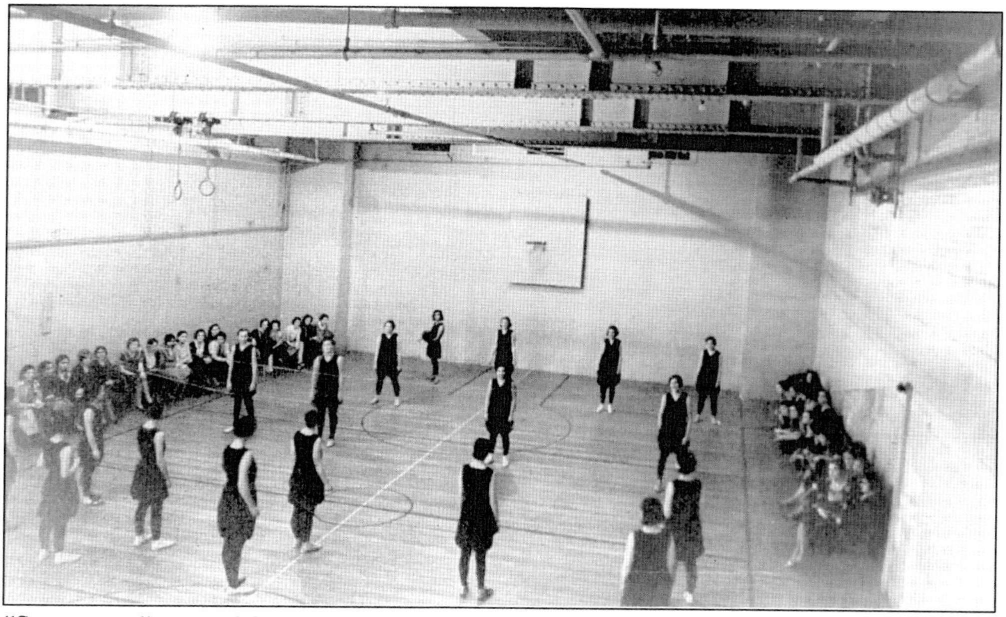

"SPEED BALL" IN THE MARY LYON GYMNASIUM, C. 1940S. Plymouth Teachers College women wear the despised gym suit and black cotton stockings for speed ball.

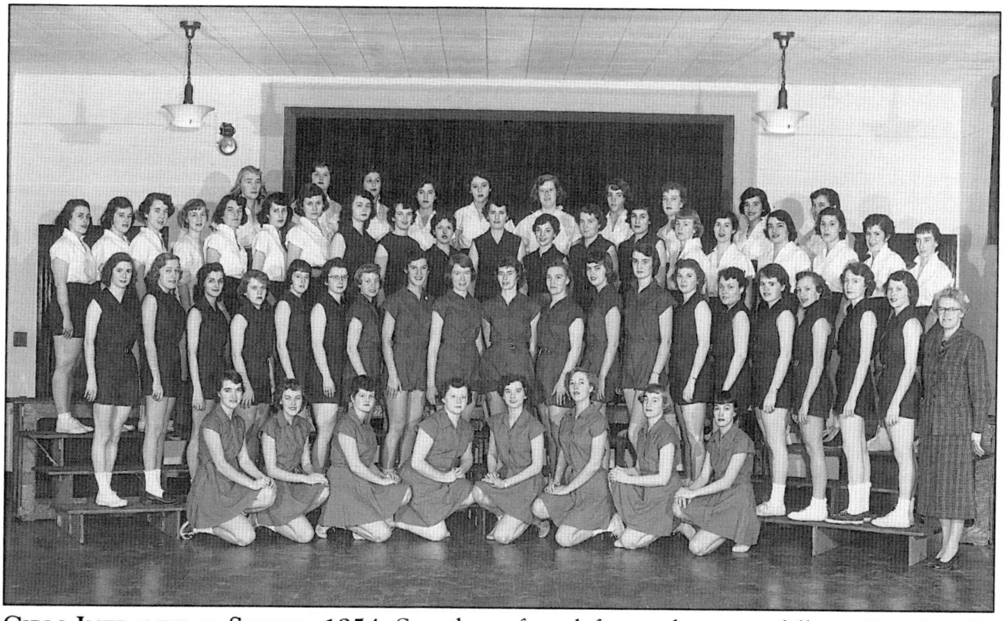

GIRLS INTRAMURAL SPORTS, 1954. Seen here, from left to right, are as follows: Kneeling: B. Callaghan, J. Stewart, C. Fowle, O. Blodgett, A. Bourey, J. Temperley, O. Chayer, and L. Little; (second row) E. Grant, M. Lewis, G. Cannistraro, R. Seaver, C. Shaw, H. Potter, E. Stewart, N. Bergeron, C. Crowley, E. Hayward, B. Ashley, M. Stratton, A. McAveeney, P. Elliott, A Welch, M. Stone, A. Binette, F. Martin, P. Jones, and Miss Alden (advisor); (third row) V. Souter, N. Ross, L. George, L. Avery, C. Clark, E. Clough, J. Fontaine, B. Vryant, E. Greenwood, J. Doyon, J. Harrison, N. Porretta, S. Dole, V. Samaha, P. Regan, M. Manary, E. DiBuono, S. Minichiello, S. Croteau, and L. Binette; (fourth row) P. Heath, E. Smith, B. Smith, D. Moffitt, N. Huggins, E. Brown, S. Thompson, C. Savage, D. Pitanis, and D. Wheatley.

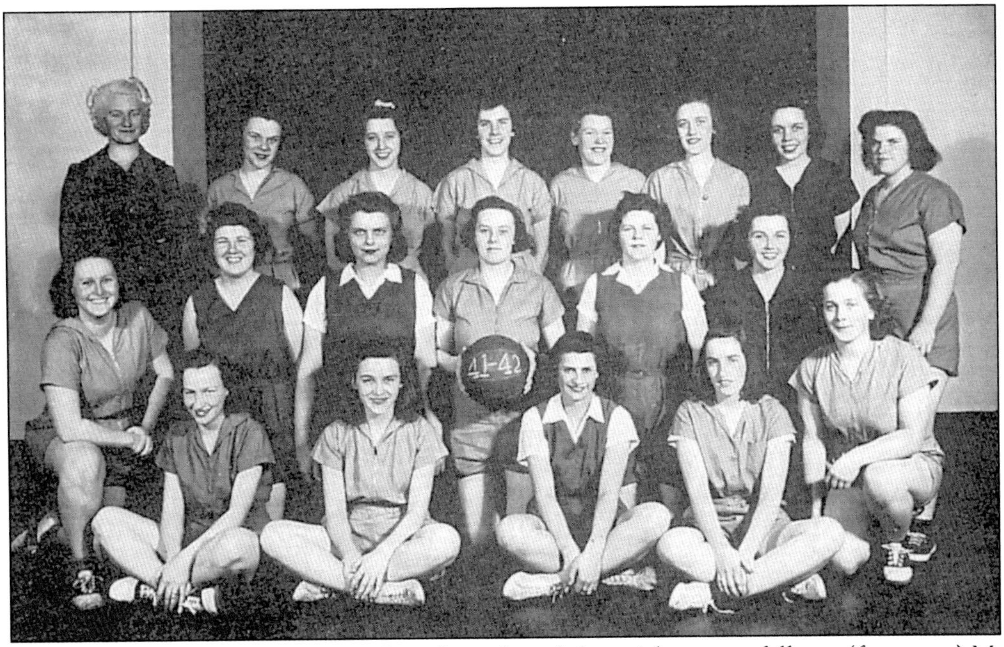

Girls' Basketball Team, 1942. Seen here, from left to right, are as follows: (front row) M. Powers, L. Nutting, R. Cannistraro, M. Durkee, and C. Mitton; (second row) K. Stulb, A. Huntress, R. Masavage, F. Weeks, M. Harrigan, and H. Brown; (third row) Coach Hodgdon, C. Crego, D. Jacques, B. Moffett, J. Nixon, F. Tarbell, L, Houle, and E. Johnson.

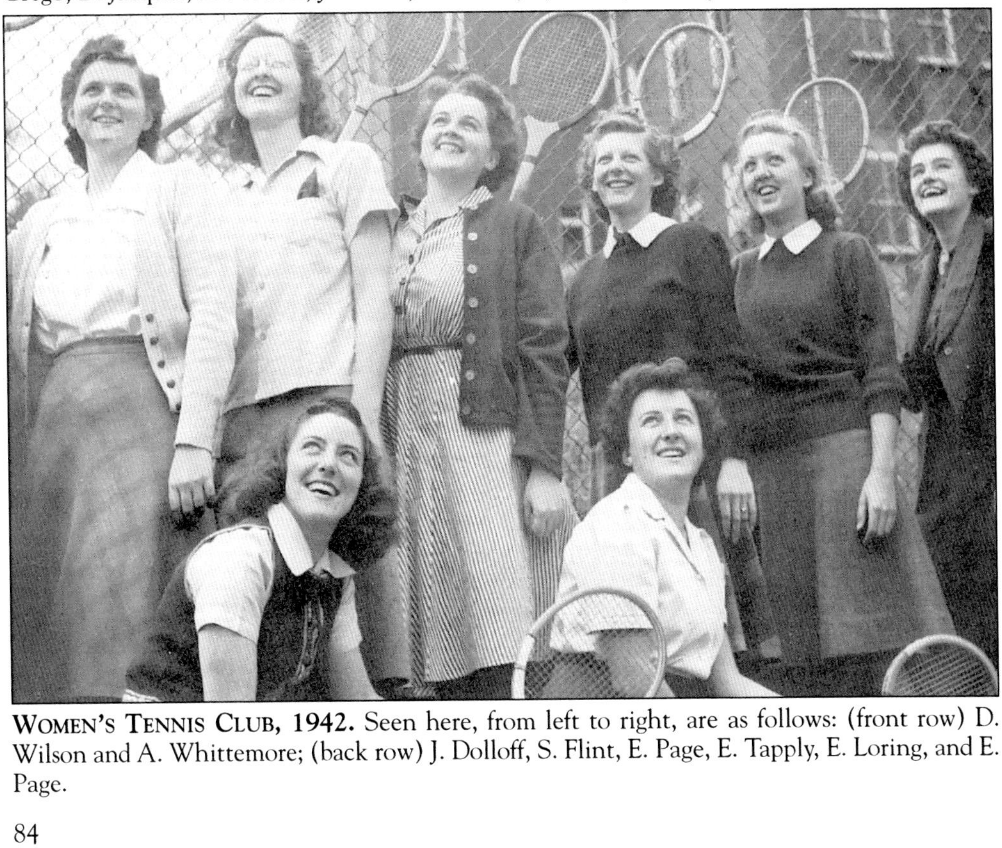

Women's Tennis Club, 1942. Seen here, from left to right, are as follows: (front row) D. Wilson and A. Whittemore; (back row) J. Dolloff, S. Flint, E. Page, E. Tapply, E. Loring, and E. Page.

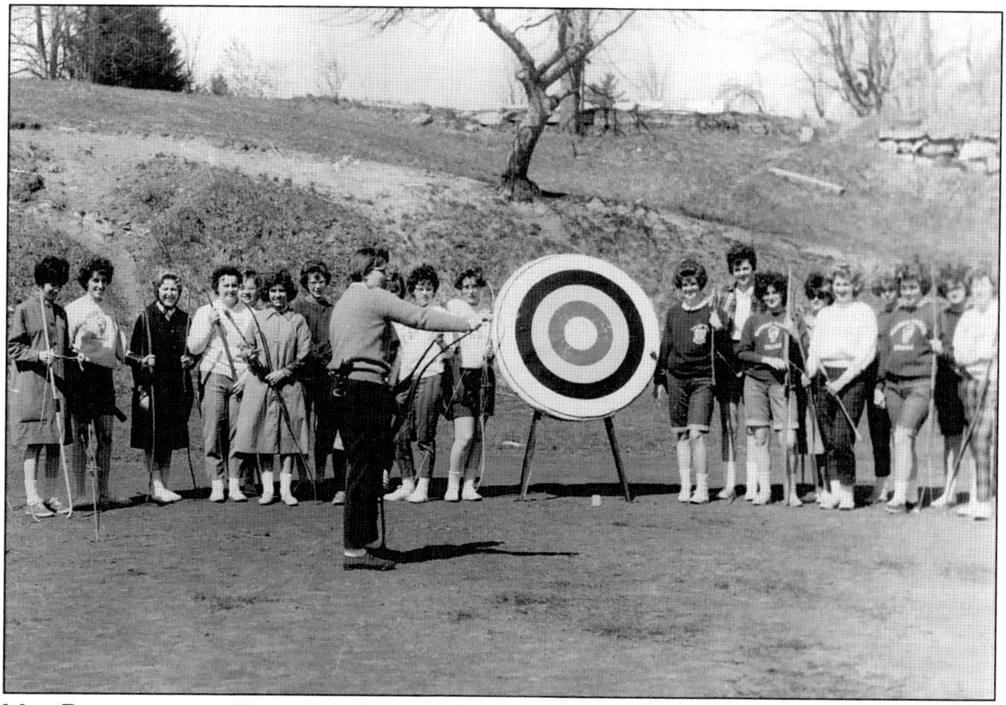

MISS PAUL AND THE "BOW AND ARROW CLUB," 1962.

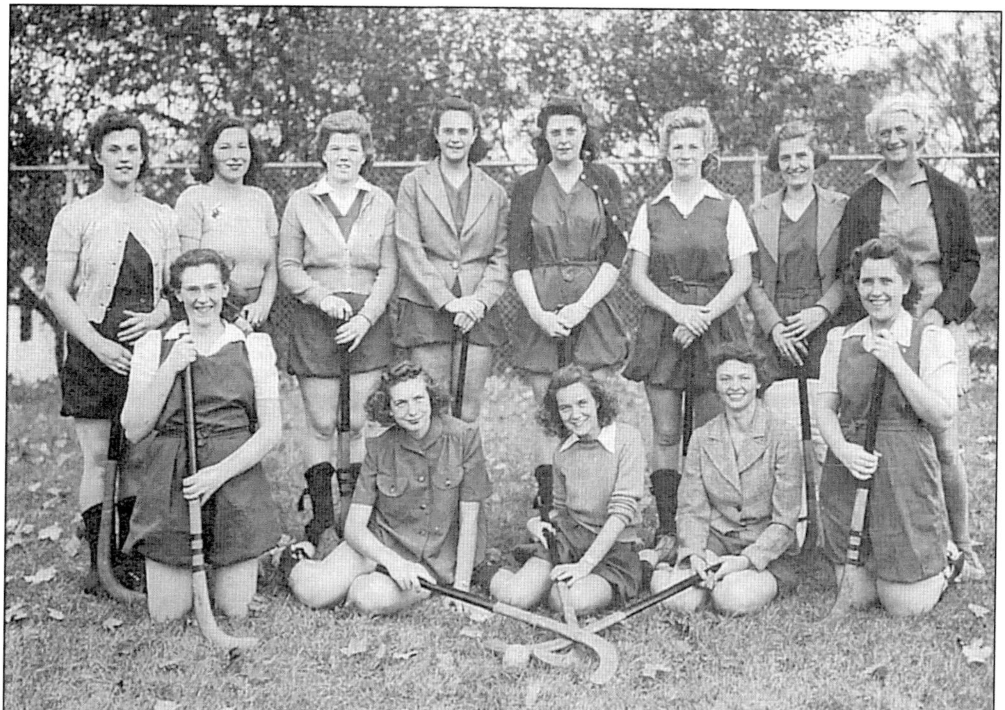

GIRLS' HOCKEY TEAM, 1942. Seen here, from left to right, are as follows: (front row) E. Nixon, E. Roy, J. Carr, F. Bachelder, and R. Dennis; (back row) M. Sawyer, J. Paulsen, P. Pushee, M. Brown, S. Huckins, P. Stickney, R. Wright, and Miss Hodgdon, coach.

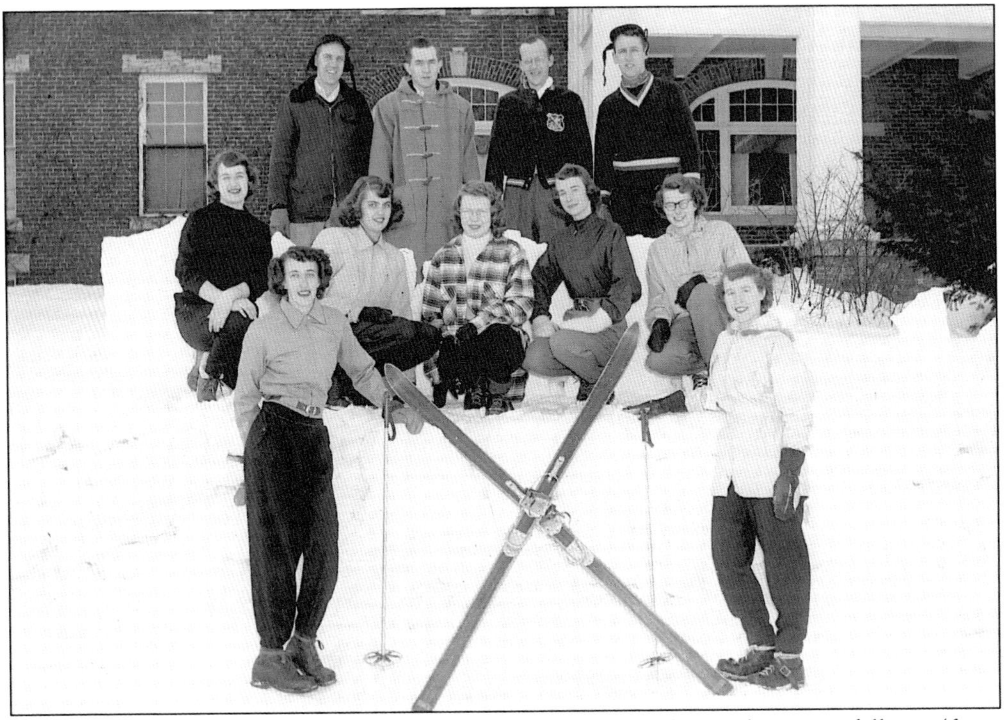

THE SKI TEAM, CONNING TOWER, 1952. Seen here, from left to right, are as follows: (front row) M. Bortree and M. Paris; (middle row) M. McKinney, M. Stratton, R. Bennett, K. Dow, and E. Hayward; (back row) H. Fay, D. Dole, R. Draper, and A. Rich.

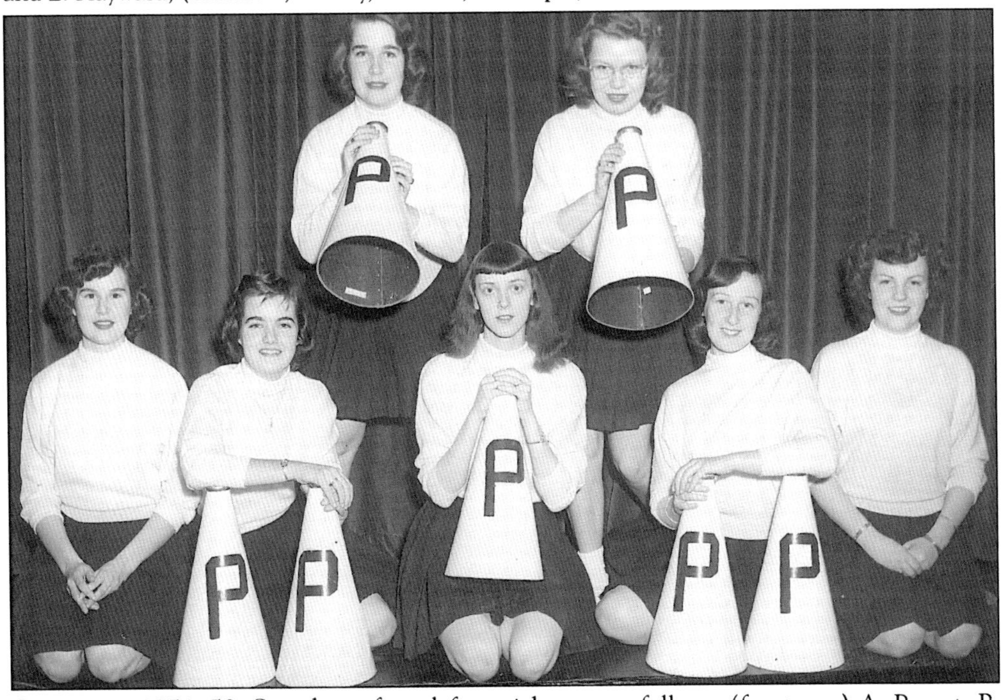

CHEERING, 1951–52. Seen here, from left to right, are as follows: (front row) A. Parent, B. Callaghan, H. Doyle (captain), P. Sinclair, and J. Homer; (back row) N. Heath and R. Bennett.

Three

Plymouth State College: 1963 to Present

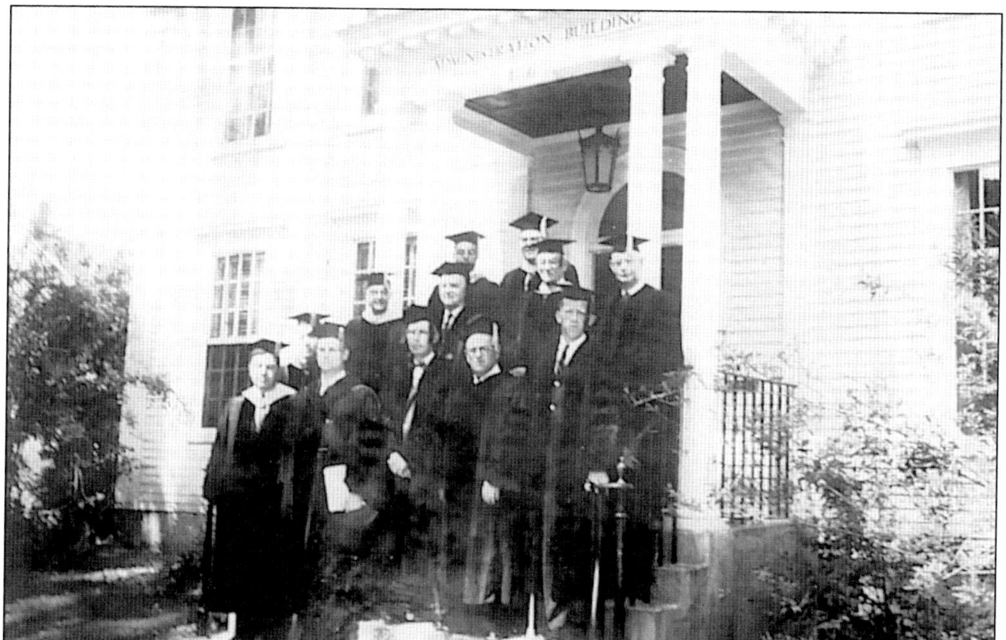

Faculty on the Steps of the Administration Building (Ellen Reed House). Dr. Hyde can be seen on far left.

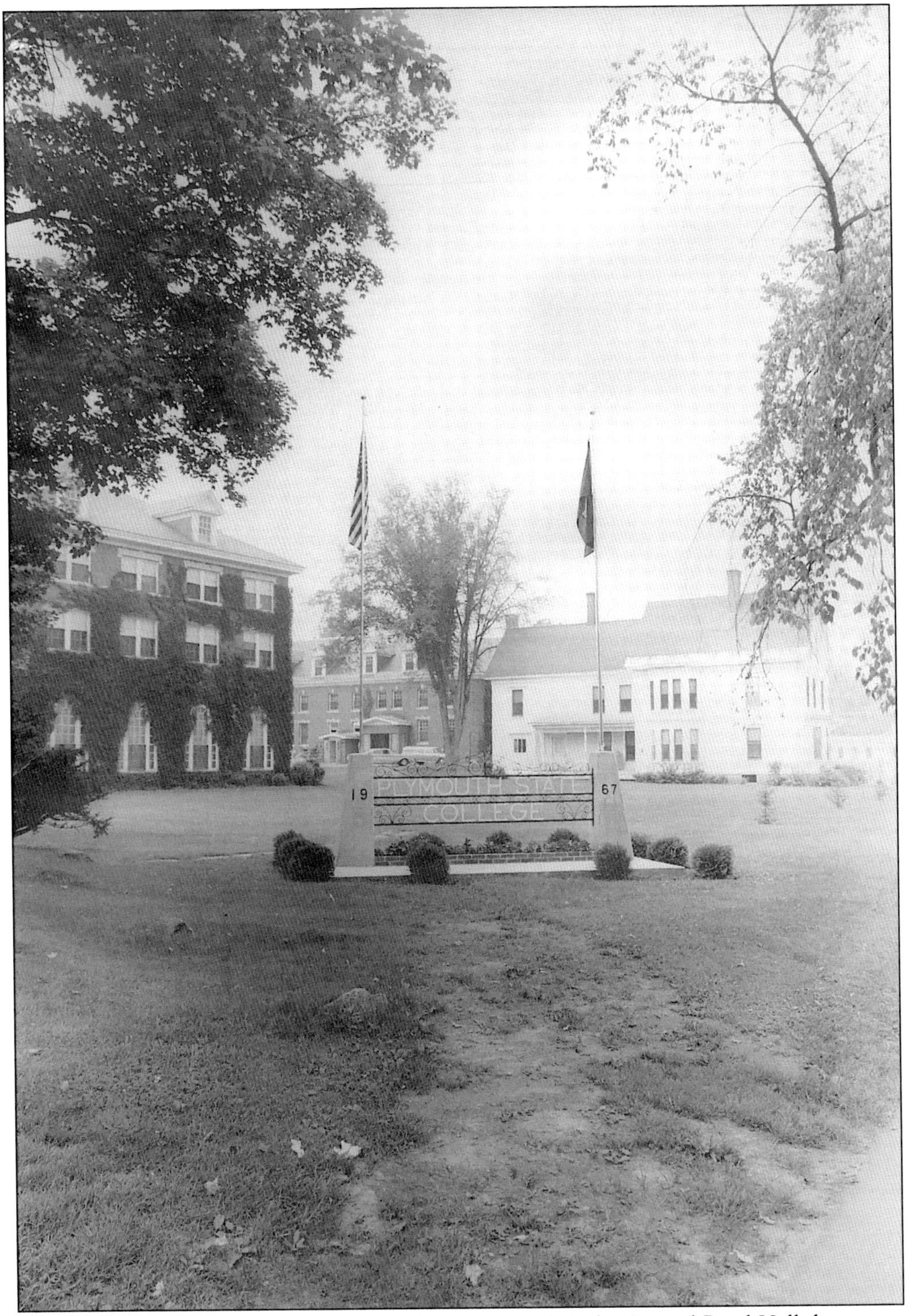

PLYMOUTH STATE COLLEGE CAMPUS, 1967. On the left is the Samuel Read Hall dormitory, Mary Lyon Hall in the center, and the old parsonage, later known as the Strafford Cottage dormitory, on the right.

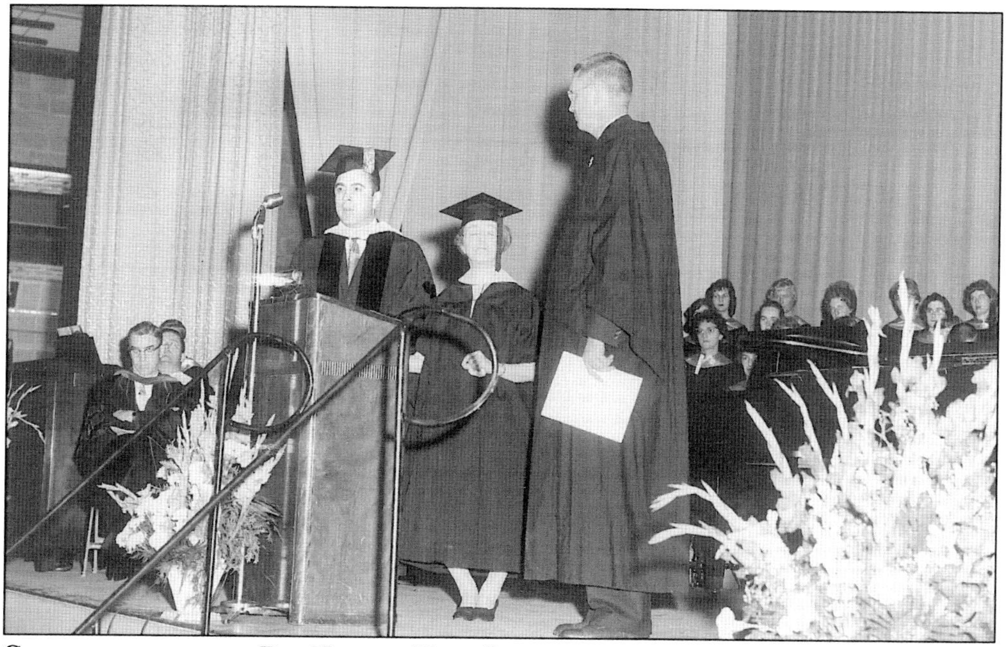

COMMENCEMENT WITH DR. HAROLD HYDE STANDING LEFT AT PODIUM. In 1963, the New Hampshire legislature changed the college into a multi-purpose institution, allowing it to award degrees in the liberal arts as well as business and secretarial science. Graduation honors have become an accepted part of Commencement in the various disciplinary fields for outstanding achievement, including *summa cum laude* graduates.

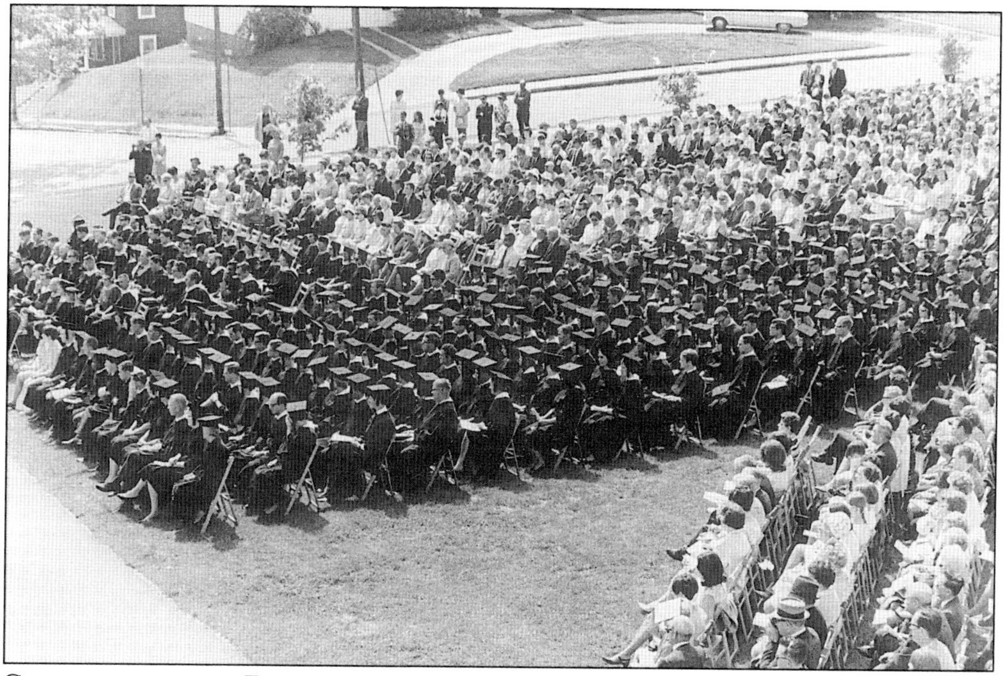

GRADUATION ON THE FRONT LAWN OF MARY LYON HALL, 1968. This was the first four-year class to receive degrees in the liberal arts major in English, music, history, as well as biological science, mathematics, and business administration and secretarial science.

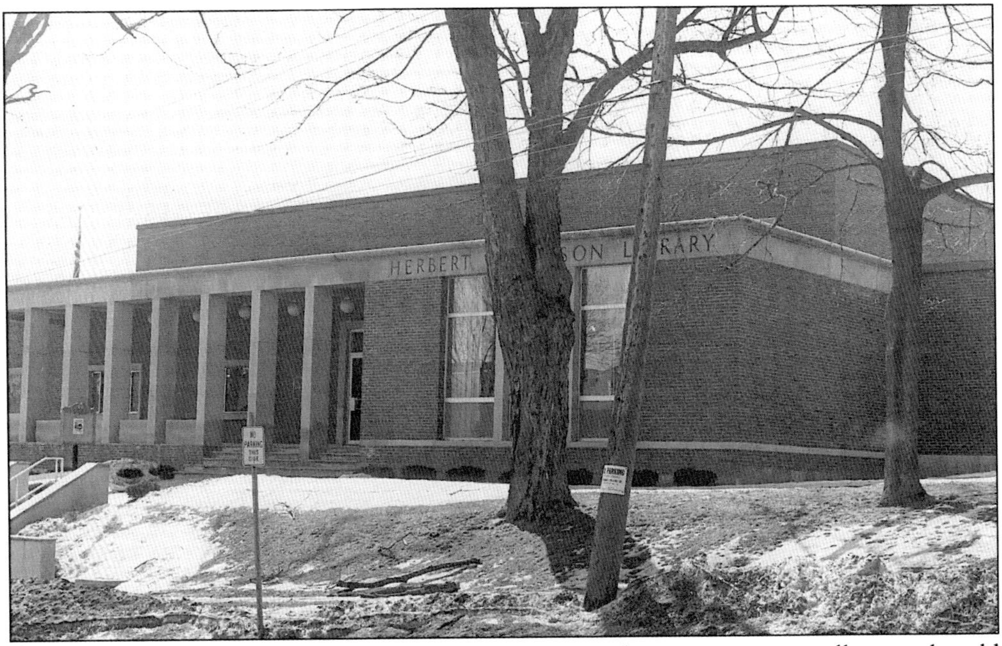

THE NEW HERBERT LAMSON LIBRARY, 1964. Due to the increase in enrollment, the old Lamson Library in Hall Dormitory rapidly became too small. Thus a new library that carried the same name was constructed across Highland Street and opened in 1964. This library witnessed a new addition in 1997, expanding it facilities to meet the growing need of the college.

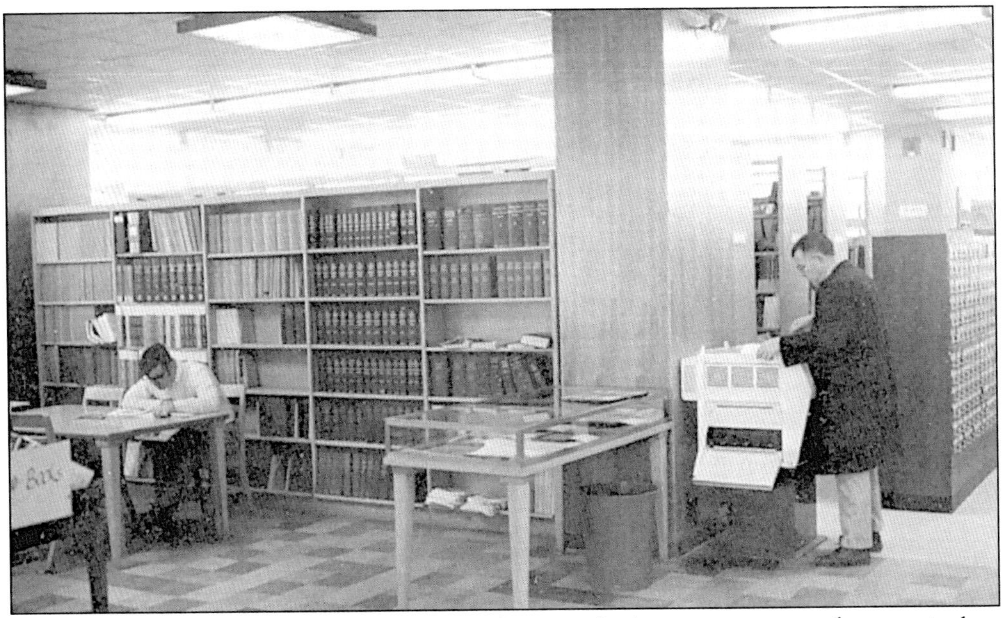

THE LAMSON LIBRARY (INTERIOR), 1968. This new facility contains a modern curriculum laboratory in addition to reading, study, seminar rooms, an audio-visual laboratory, and listening rooms. By 1968, it had already become too small to accommodate the many demands on its space. Thus, in 1969, the New Hampshire legislature authorized funds for expansion of the library.

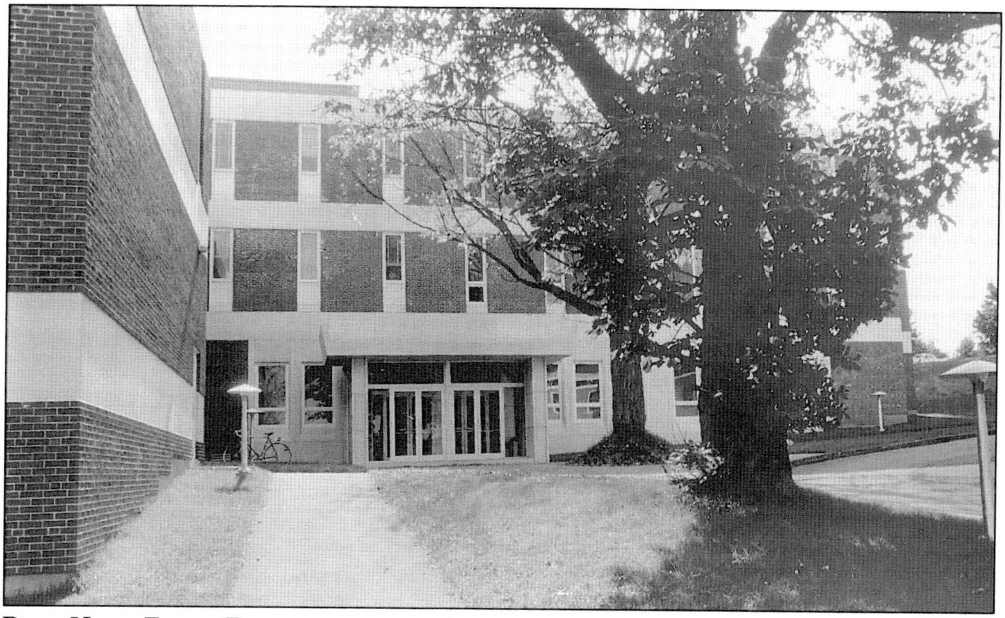

BOYD HALL, FRONT ENTRANCE, 1968. This facility houses both the Science Department and Foreign Languages. Boyd Hall, named for Robert L. Boyd, professor of science at the college for over 30 years, contains up-to-date science laboratories, a language laboratory, a greenhouse, and a planetarium.

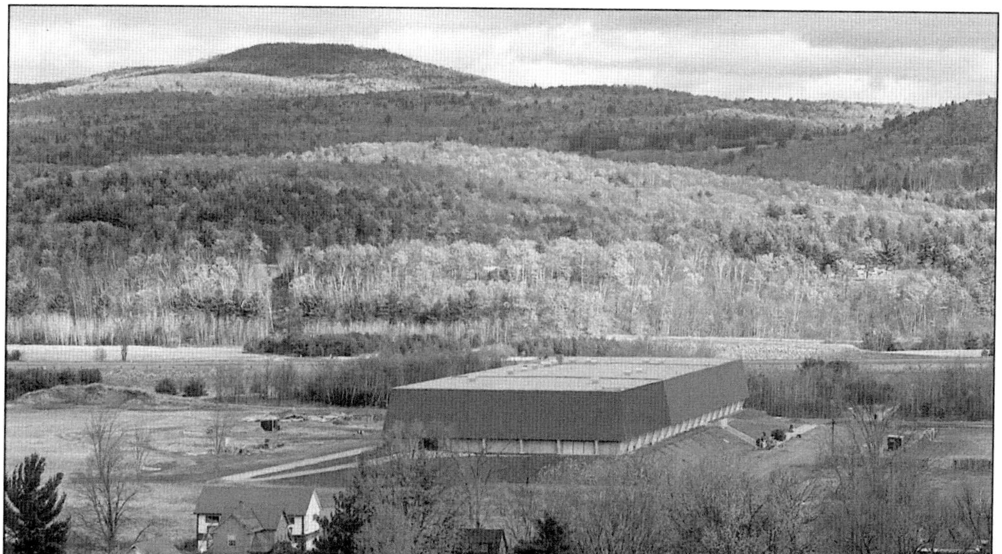

THE GYMNASIUM-FIELD HOUSE (FOLEY GYMNASIUM) WITH ROUTE I-93 DIRECTLY BEHIND, 1969. The new field house and gymnasium on the Holderness Road opened in the spring of 1969; in 1971, it was named the John C. Foley Field House for John C. Foley, chairman of the Athletic Department, coach, English professor, Dean of Instruction, and Dean of the College. The Field House contains an indoor track, gymnasium, swimming pool, and other facilities for the physical education program of the college. The field house has become the hub of activity at all hours of the day and night. More than 500 students and faculty participate in the program presented there.

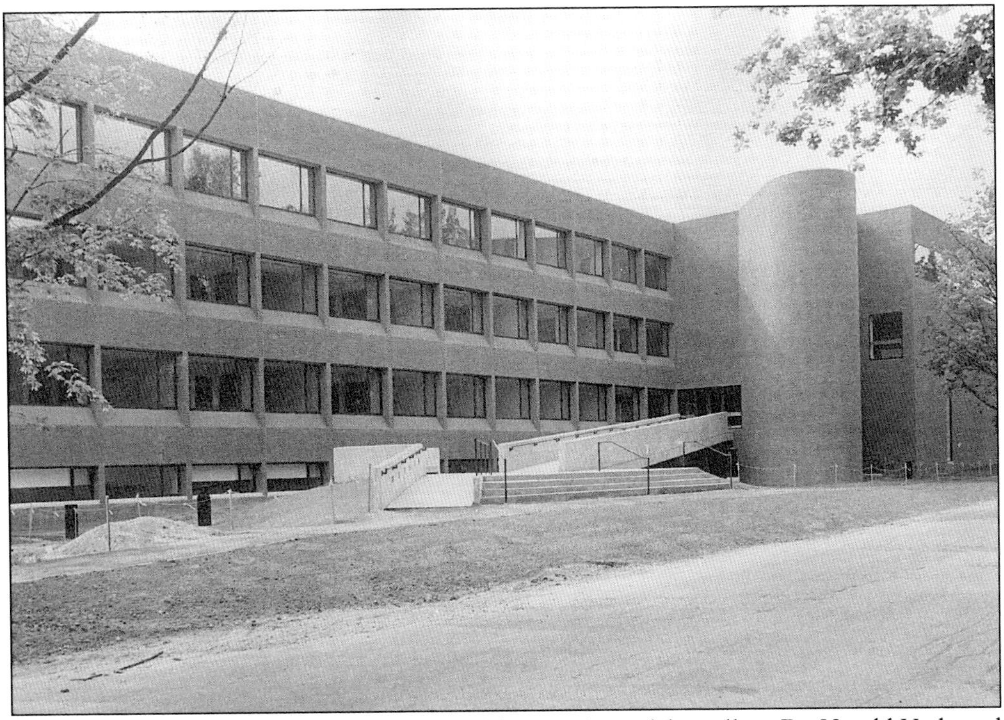

HYDE HALL, 1976. This building was named for president of the college Dr. Harold Hyde and for his "twenty years of total commitment." This building houses the following departments: Mathematics, Business, Psychology, Philosophy, and Foreign Languages.

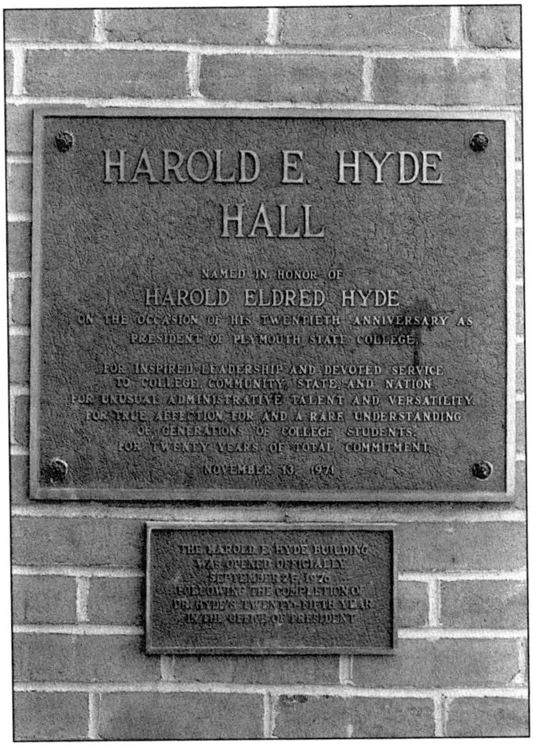

PLAQUE OF HYDE BUILDING, NOVEMBER 13, 1976. "In honor of Harold Eldred Hyde on the occasion of his twentieth anniversary as President of PSC. For inspired leadership and devoted service to college, community, state, and nation. For unusual administration talent and versatility. For true affection for a rare understanding of generations of college students. For twenty years of total commitment."

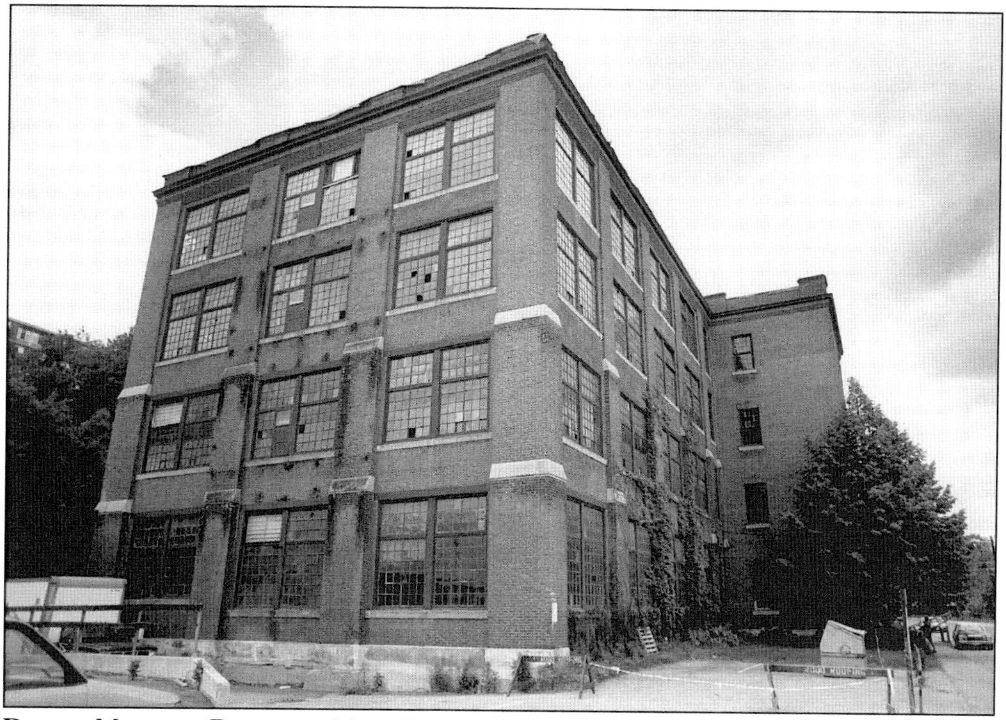

DRAPER MAYNARD BUILDING, MAIN STREET, PLYMOUTH, 1993. This four-story brick building was erected, c. 1912, and housed the Draper-Maynard Sporting Goods Company, which manufactured sporting items under the name of "*The Lucky Dog.*"

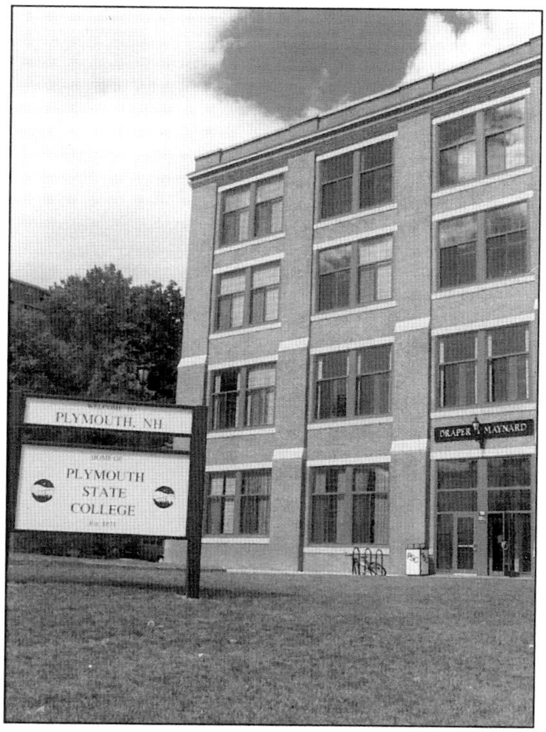

DRAPER MAYNARD BUILDING COMPLETELY CONVERTED, 1997. In this year, PSC moved the Art Department from Hyde Hall as well as the Health Department to this newly remodeled building.

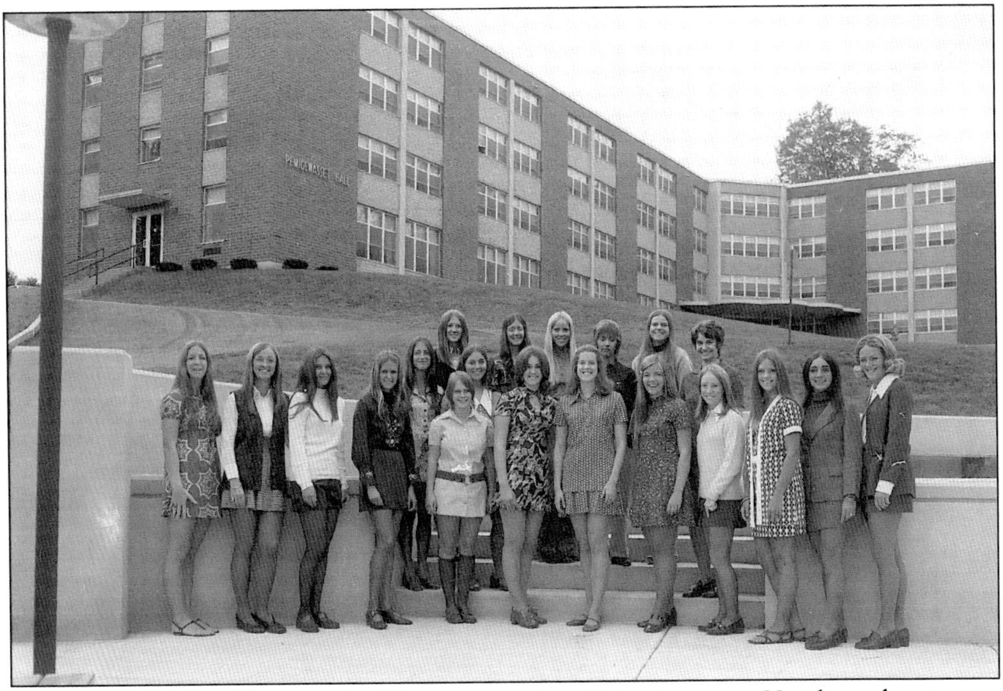

THE PEMIGEWASSET HALL, 1965. The property the old Pemigewasset Hotel stood on is now the site of a new dormitory for women, which was respectfully named the Pemigewasset Hall; this dormitory houses 225 students.

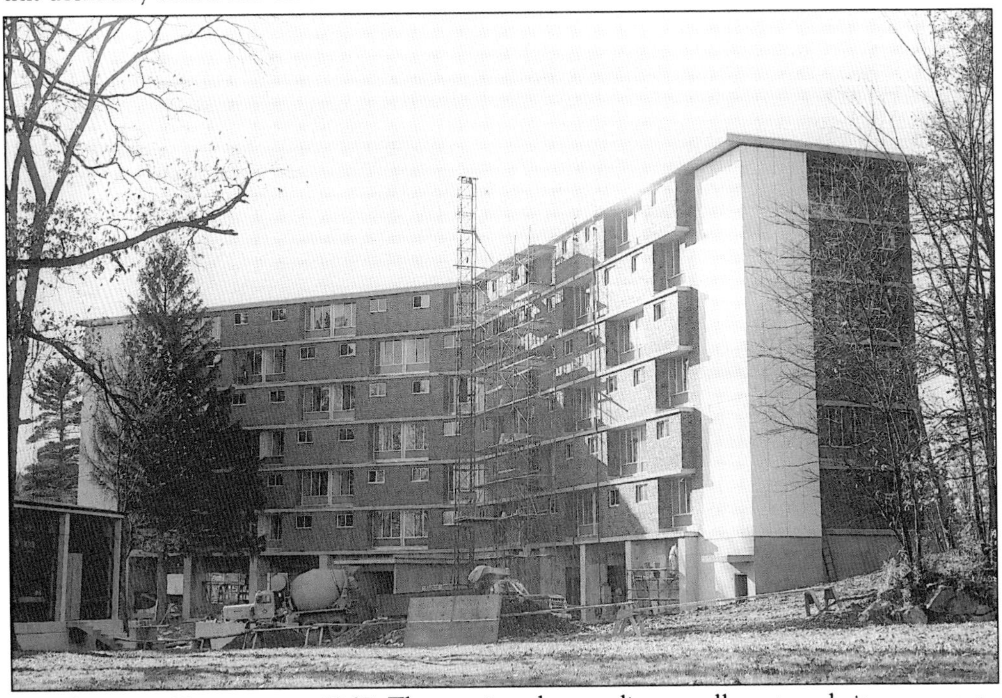

THE GRAFTON DORMITORY, 1967. The continued expanding enrollment made it necessary to build more dormitories. Pictured is the new Grafton Dormitory, named for Plymouth's county; it houses 200 students.

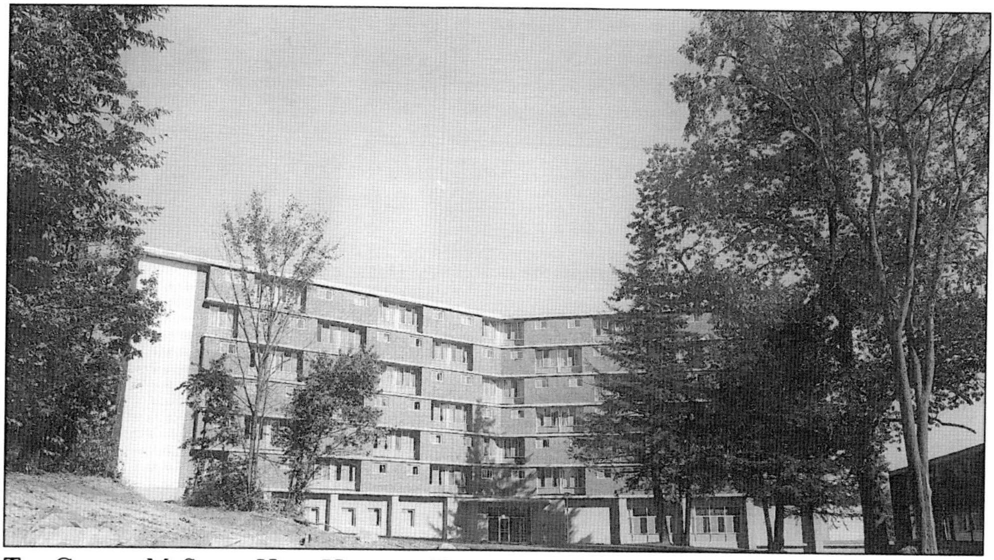

THE GENEVA M. SMITH HALL HIGHRISE DORMITORY, SPRING 1968. This hall was respectfully named for Geneva M. Smith, a longtime professor and chair of the Mathematics Department.

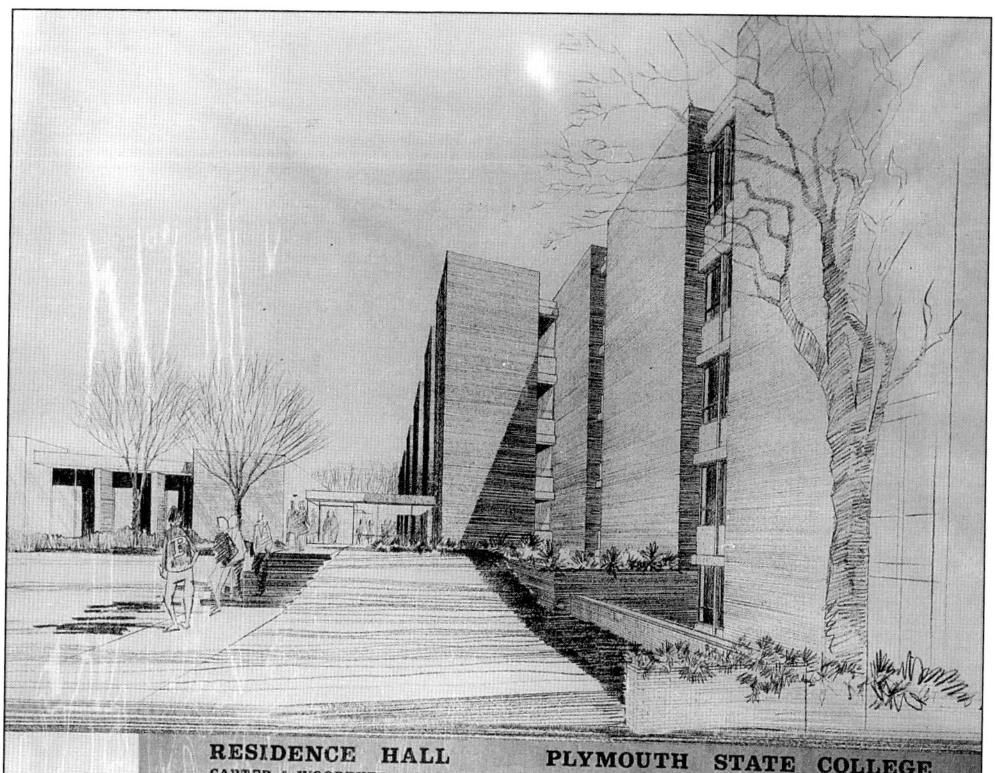

BELKNAP HALL, 1969. This dormitory was respectfully named for the neighboring county to the south.

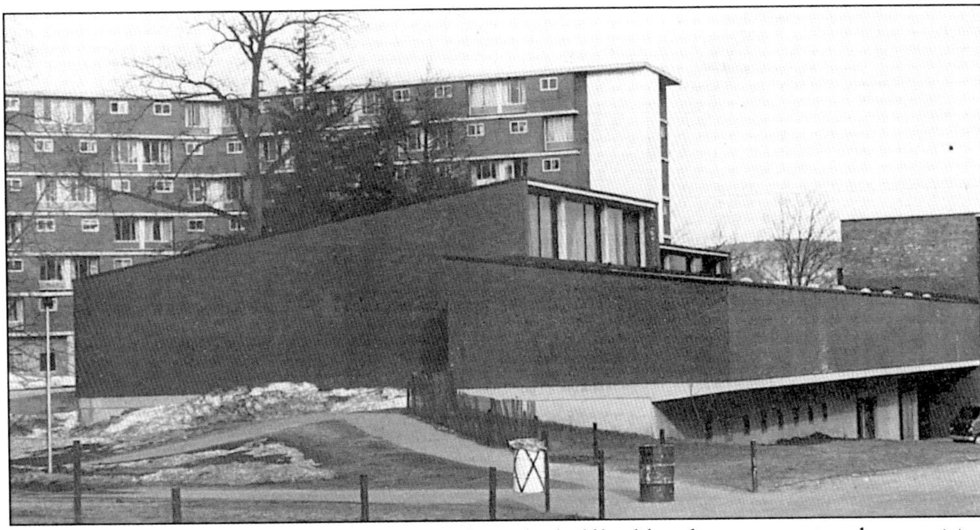

MT. PROSPECT DINING COMMONS, 1968. This split-half building has won national recognition for its architecture. It was built partly on land purchased by the Alumni and presented to the college. In the background is the Grafton dormitory for men. In 1981, a 2,600 square foot addition was created for more dining space.

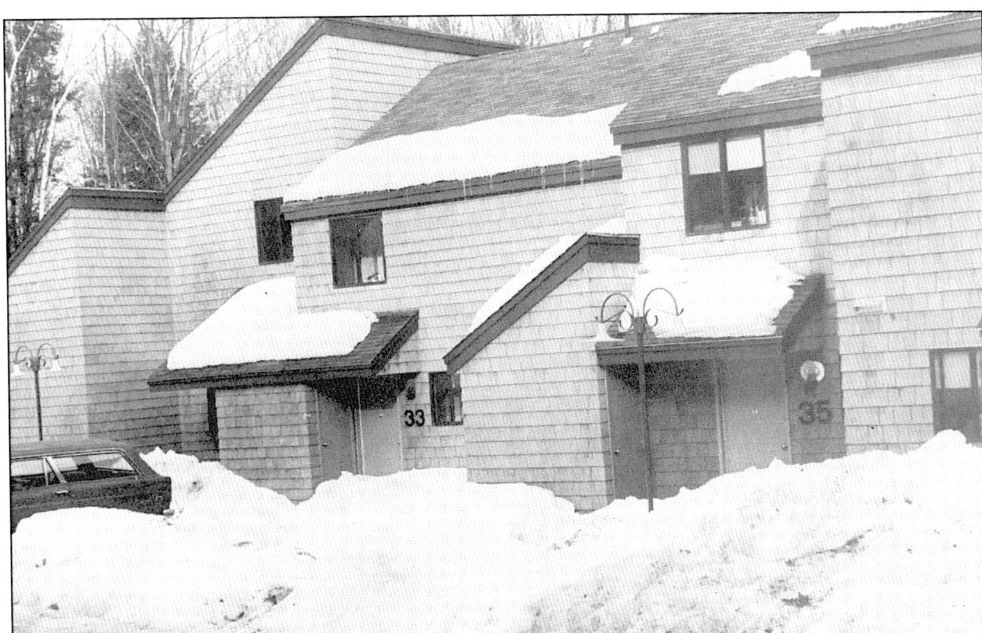

MARRIED STUDENT HOUSING, 1968. These living facilities, which are named for longtime physical education professor Beatrice Hodgdon and Dorothy B. O'Neill, professor and supervisor of student teachers in the laboratory school and professor of reading, opened in the fall of 1968. It is located on Merrill Street, on the northern edge of the campus.

FOOTBALL TEAM IN FULL ACTION. It was not until 1968 that the dream of football at PSC would become a reality, and then only to be an inter-squad sport. A club sport developed from a nucleus of 36 players coached by Paul Arold. Practices were held from 6:00 a.m. at D&M Park or behind the Field House at 4:00 p.m. on rough surface. Their uniforms were secondhand and their equipment purchased from other schools. Encouragement came from nearly every school in the state. The first game was on Homecoming Day in 1968 at D&M Park; it was an inter-squad game coached by Paul Arold and Don Drouin. That game was the only one played that year, but it was the beginning of a winning intercollegiate football team.

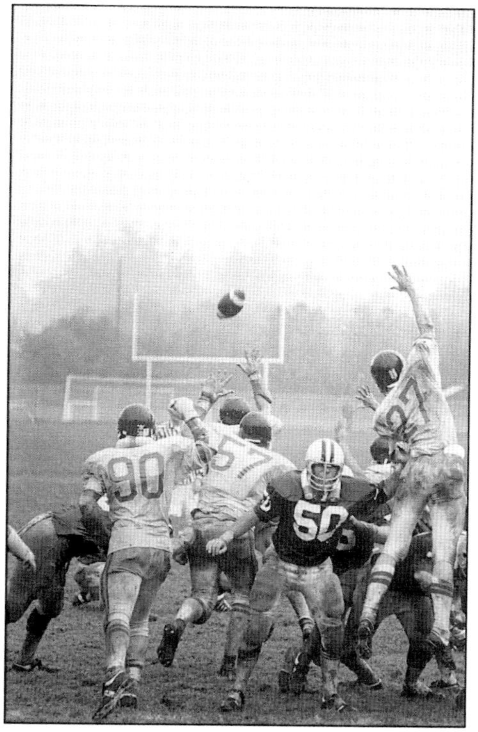

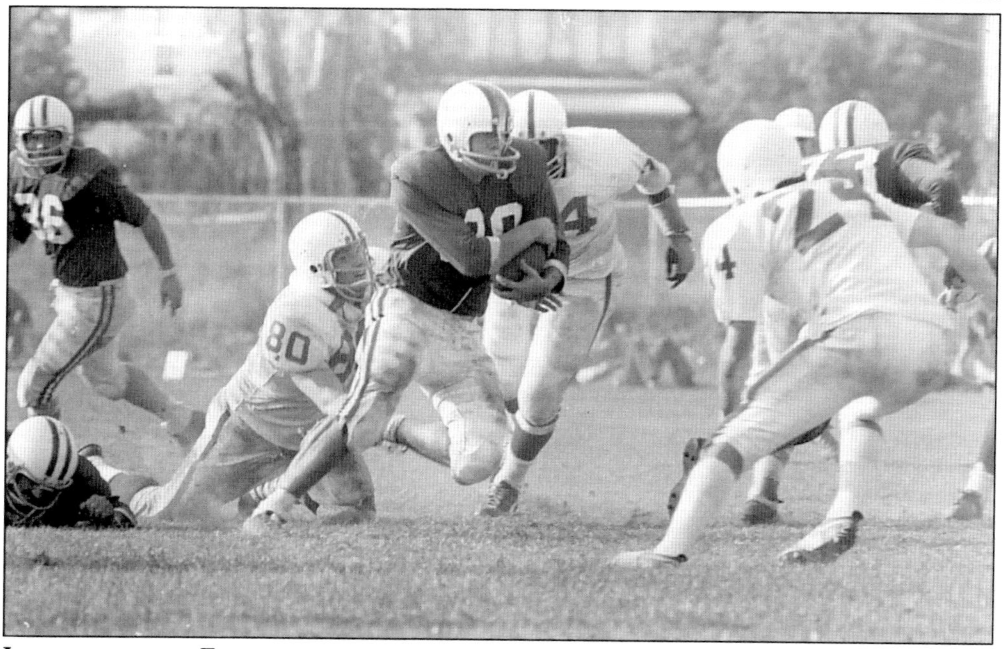

INTERCOLLEGIATE FOOTBALL AT PSC. Walter Murphy, a former Holy Cross gridster, prominent lawyer, and New Hampshire Superior Court Judge became head coach. His able assistants were Paul Arold and Charlie Currier. Homecoming Day in October marked the beginning of this official college team. For the first time, PSC had a full football schedule with Coach Walter Murphy. In 1984, the Panthers had the distinction of being the first Division III New England football team to ever be selected as one of the eight squads to play in the national playoffs.

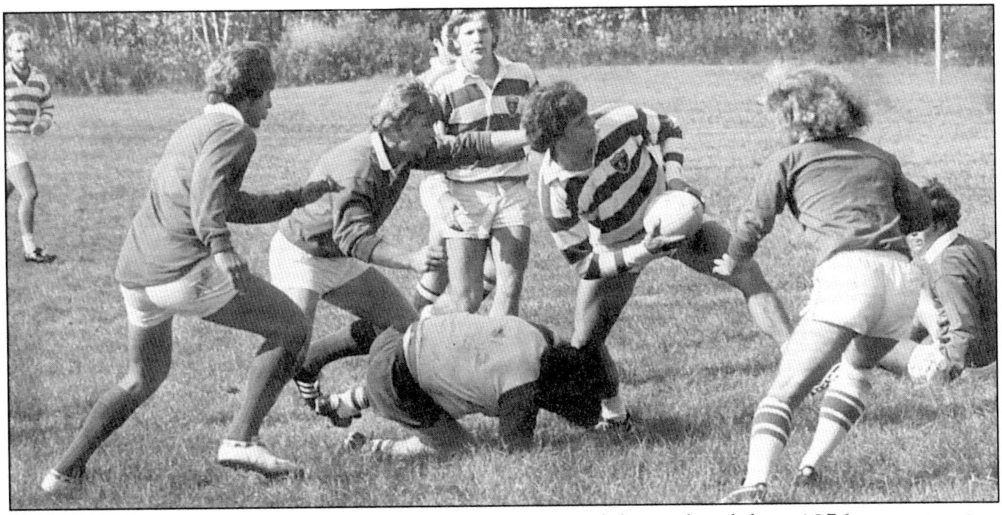

NORSEMEN RUGBY CLUB, 1979. Since the formation of the rugby club in 1976, participation and speculation of the game has increased greatly.

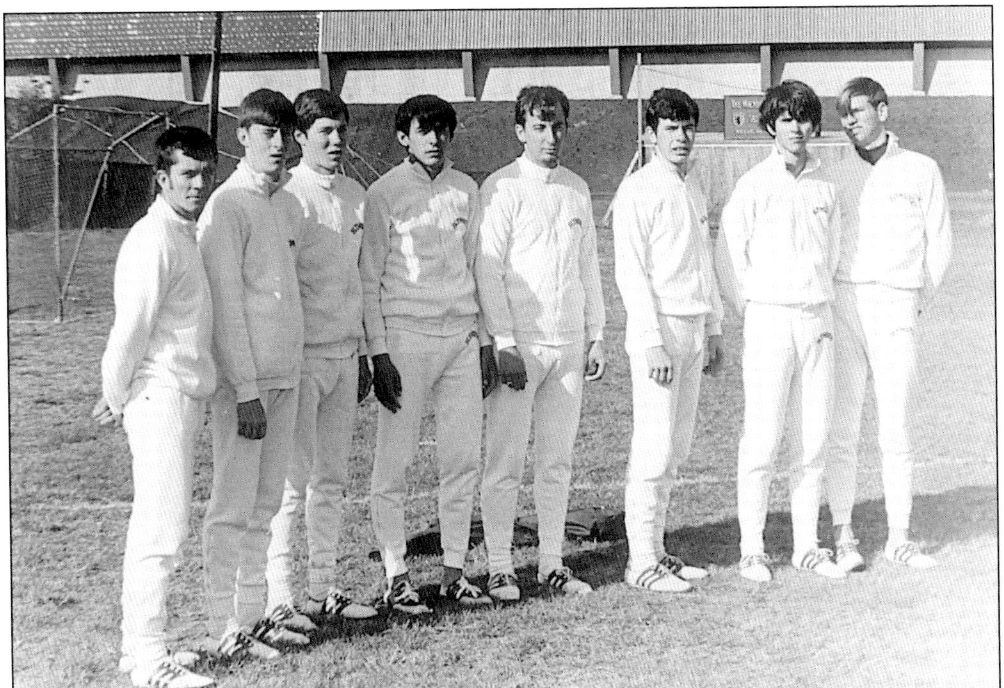

CROSS COUNTRY " HARTMAN'S HARRIERS," 1969. The team placed third in the annual New England State College Athletic Conference Championship held at Rhode Island College. Seen here, from left to right, are M. DeNies, D. Littlefield, B. Smith, A. Morin, J. Goulet, S. Heath, S. Eastman, and M. Donovan.

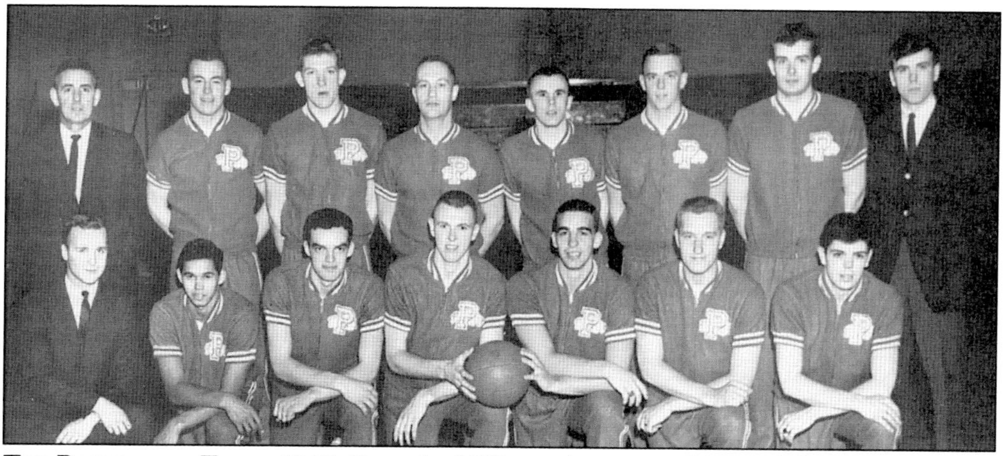

THE BASKETBALL TEAM, 1965. From the 1950s, to the present, Plymouth has produced some of the finest hoopsters, namely Steve Bamford '65 who was number one as Plymouth's best all-around basketball player. Seen here, from left to right, are as follows: (front row) manager K. Burrill, D. Araujo, C. McAllister, S. Bamford, A. Neri, R. Koson, and L. Childs; (back row) coach J. Foley, P. Sawtelle, E. Chevalier, J. Krug, K. Dunlap, R. Greenwood, J. Johnson, and manager R. Dumais. Steve Bamford returned to PSC as athletic director.

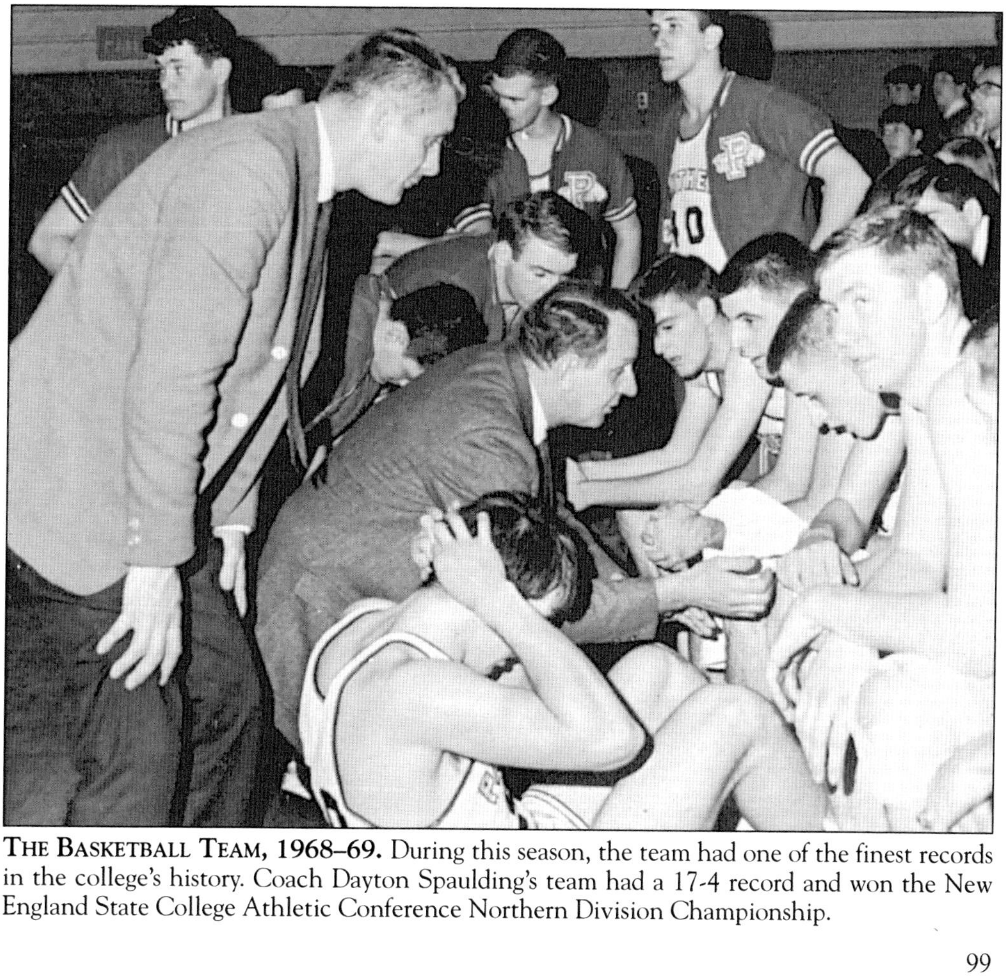

THE BASKETBALL TEAM, 1968–69. During this season, the team had one of the finest records in the college's history. Coach Dayton Spaulding's team had a 17-4 record and won the New England State College Athletic Conference Northern Division Championship.

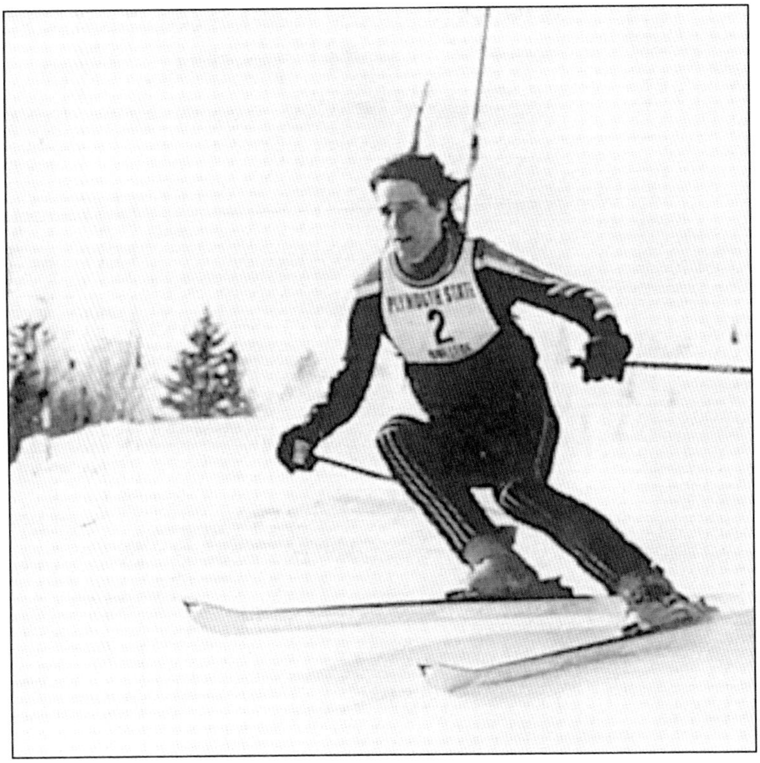

MENS' SKIING, 1981. This sport reached a high point in 1981 when PSC won the National Collegiate Ski Association Championship. This victory was the first time that PSC had ever won any national championship in any athletic endeavors. Coach Bob Sampson was heard to say, "We smoked the best competition in the country." This team was led by Doug Karwoski who was selected as an All-American.

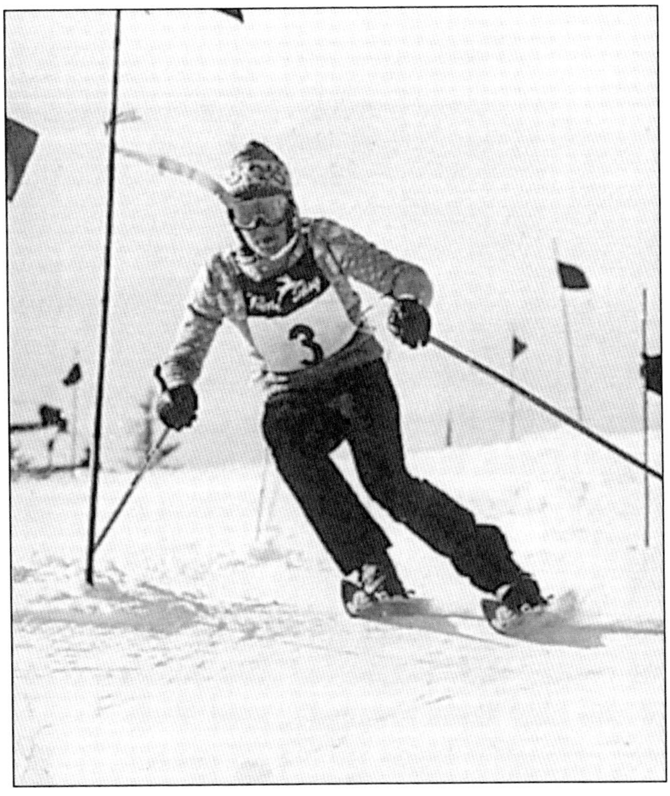

WOMEN'S SKIING, 1981. Under coach Bob Sampson and assistant Nancy Guilfoy, the 1980–81 PSC women's ski team completed the most successful season in the team's history, finishing second in the Osbourne Division of the Women's Intercollegiate Ski Conference (WISC).

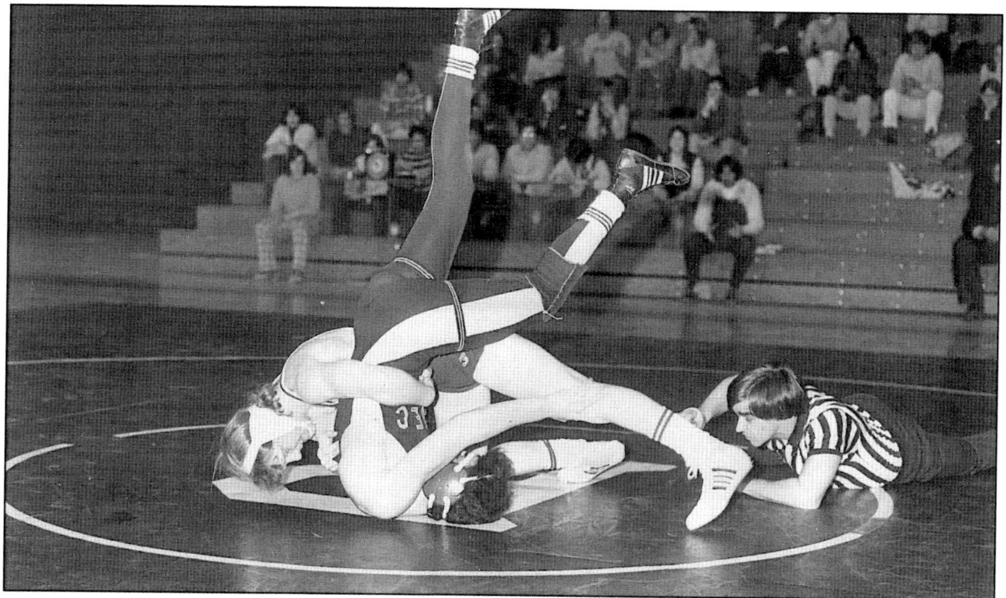

Wrestling Match. This sport began during the 1966–67 season under Doug Wiseman; it was later continued under Paul Arold, Jim Beals, and later by Jim Aguiar in 1974. Under Coach Jim Aguiar, PSC won the Northern New England Championship and the NAIA District V Championship in 1975. Coach Aguiar was selected the Coach of the Year for NAIA District V. In November 1976, Alan Potter of Keene stacked his opponent for a pin in the Western New England College at Springfield, Massachusetts.

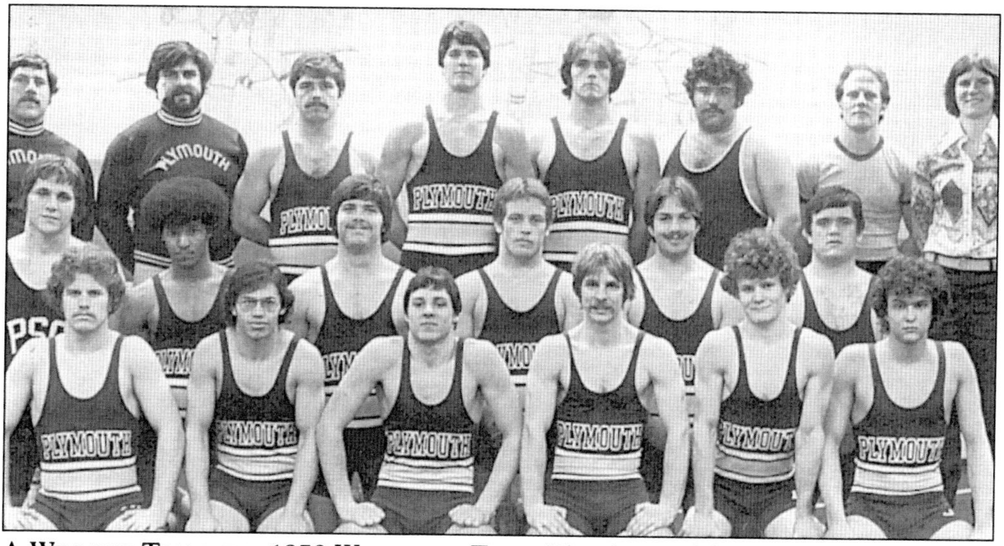

A Winning Team: the 1979 Wrestling Team. The climax of the season came at the New England Intercollegiate Championships. The team had five wrestlers named to the All-New England Team and had their best finish ever; Matt Staples and Bruce Gabriel qualified for the NCAA III National Championships by placing first and second in New England. Seen here, from left to right, are as follows: (front row) B. Gabriel, A. Madera, J. Giarrusso, B. Vermouth, H. Phelps, and M. Hudson; (middle row) F. Matyiko, K. Rowlette, B. Partridge, B. Ford, D. Smith, and B. Mitchell; (back row) assistant coach L. Didenzo, coach James Aguiar, C. Baker, M. Staples, M. Smith, V. Ferretti, A. Potter, and K. Zemaitis.

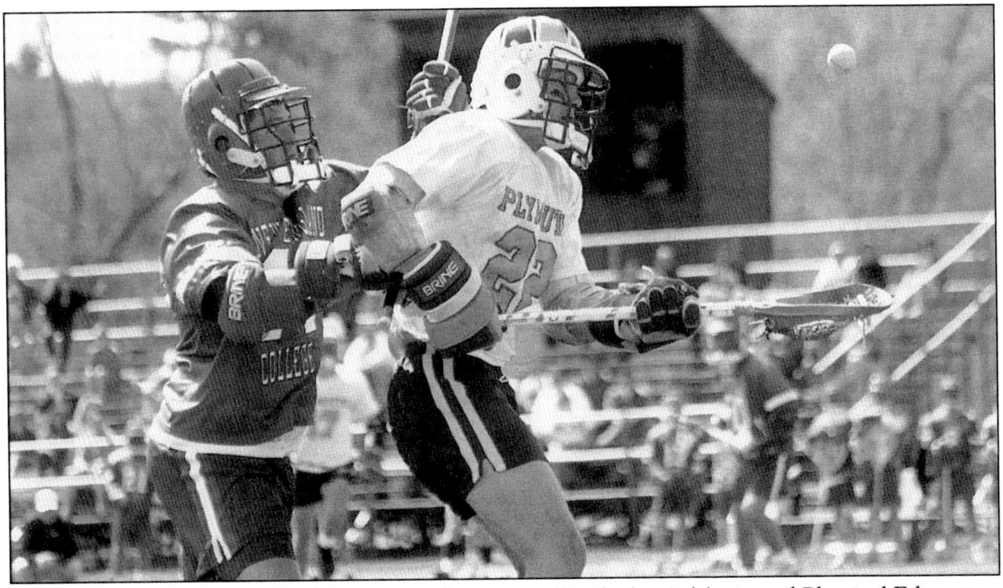

MENS' LACROSSE, 1967. Paul Hartman, chairman of both the Athletic and Physical Education Departments, is considered the father of lacrosse here at PSC. Men's Lacrosse competed annually during the early- and mid-70s for the Colonial Division Championship under the direction of Coach Ted Kolva.

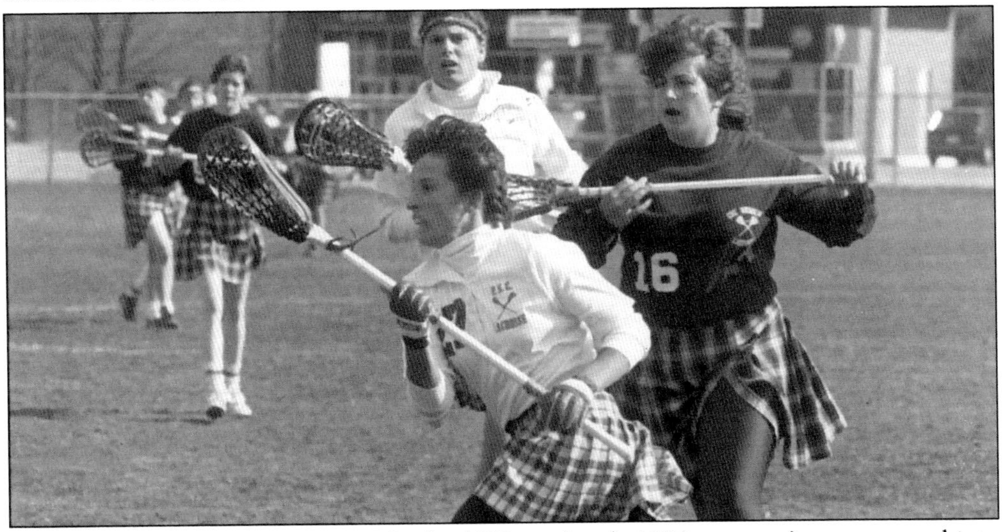

WOMEN'S LACROSSE TEAM, 1979. In the 1970s and early 1980s, women's sports moved into high gear. The dean of the women's coaching staff, Janet Nell, played an important role in its progress. She coached five different sports: field hockey, soccer, lacrosse, basketball, and tennis. Under her tutelage, the women's lacrosse team had undefeated seasons in 1972, 1976, and 1979. This team made history twice during the season. Led by senior tri-captains Leslie Freeman, Patty Morgan, and Laurie Williams, the Panthers won their first division II tournament in the New England tournament that May. They and their opponents in the finals, Springfield College, became the first women's teams to ever play in the Yale Bowl in New Haven. Coach Nell said, "I compliment the players for an outstanding season... it's one of the best Lacrosse teams I've ever coached...the players deserve all the praise, they worked hard, put it together, and accomplished the winning record that they did."

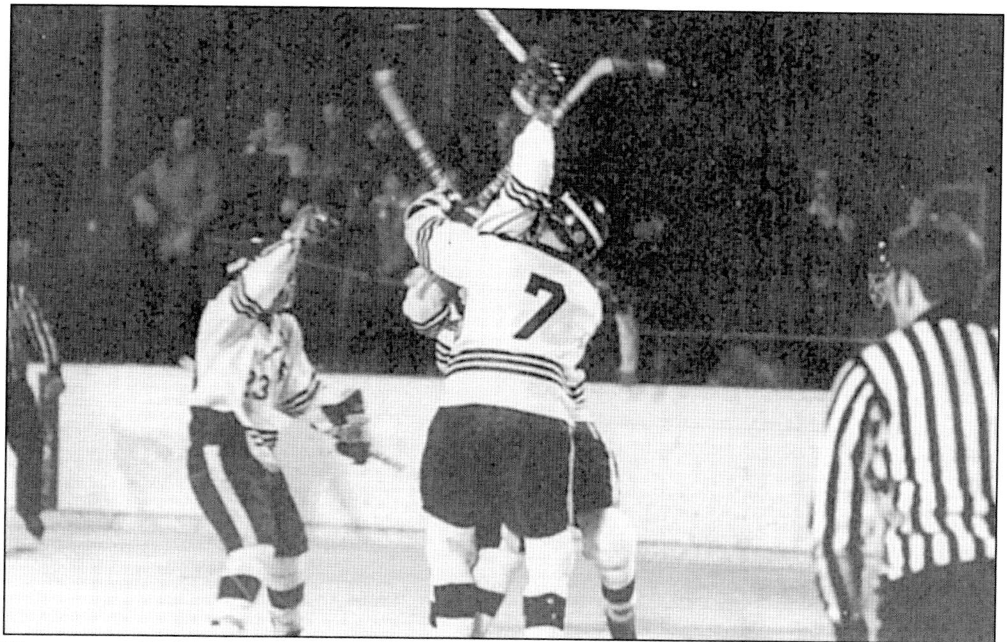

HOCKEY AT PSC, 1970. Hal King, then Principal of Holderness Central School, became its first hockey coach. Under him and, later, Rick Hutchins, the team players were enthusiastic and displayed their talents to local hockey fans at their home games at the Holderness School rink. Since 1977, it has gained an outstanding record that included being one of the top ECAC Division III teams in 1981.

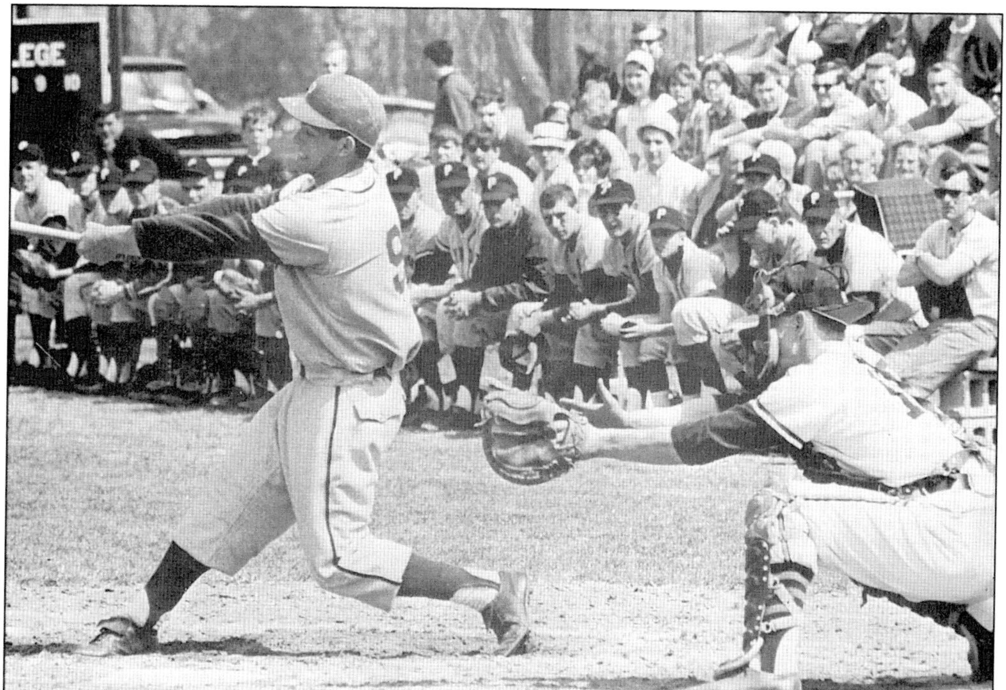

THE BASEBALL TEAM WITH DICK KENT AT BAT, 1966. From 1963 to 1972, this team sported a winning percentage of 75%. They were New England Baseball Conference champs in 1966.

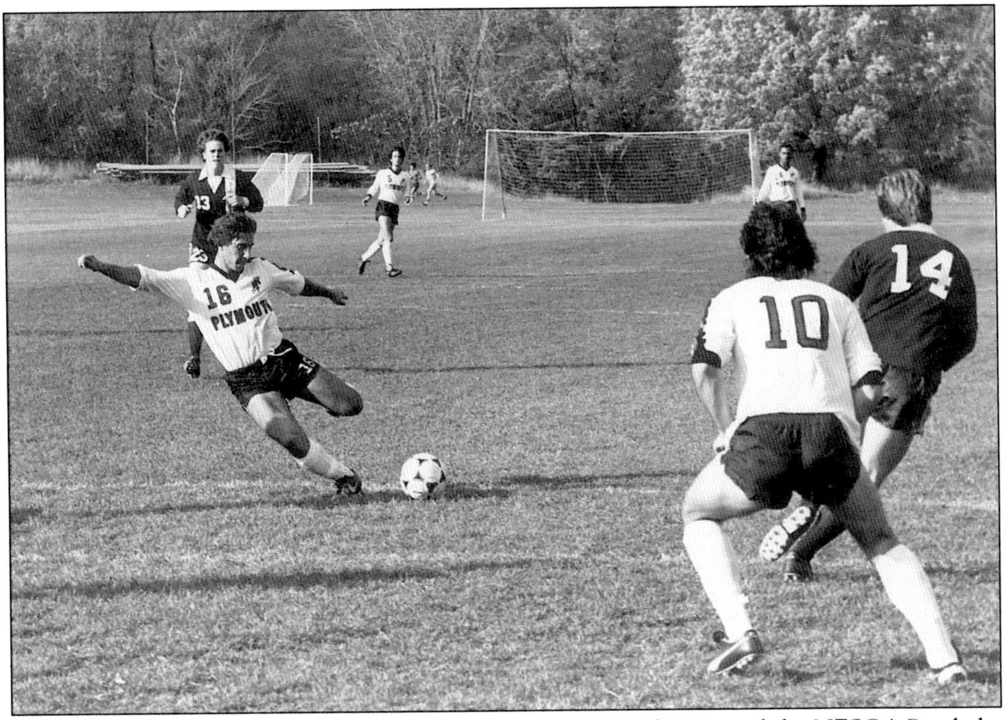

MEN'S SOCCER TEAM, 1978. For the first time ever, Plymouth captured the NESCAC title by defeating arch-rival Keene State College. As a result the Panthers were chosen for the NCAA Division III playoffs for the third time in four years.

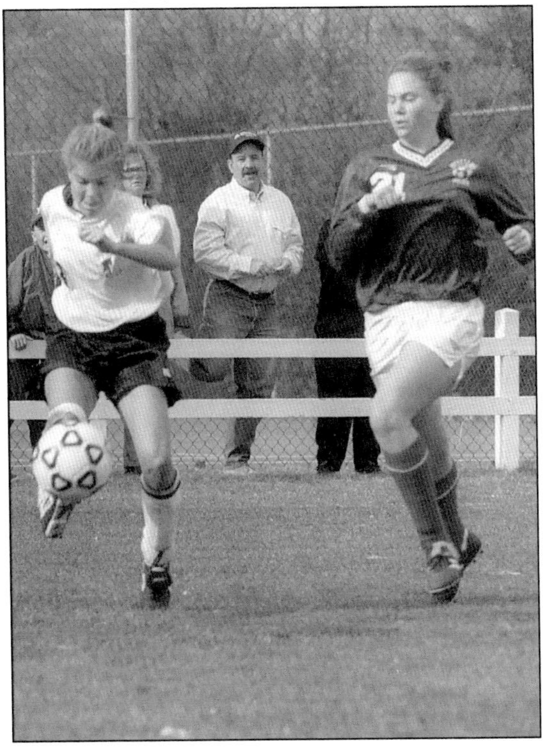

WOMEN'S SOCCER TEAM, 1978. Women played in Division II ranks until 1983. During that time, Plymouth was a member of the AIAW (Association of Intercollegiate Athletics for Women). This organization has since become defunct. Since 1983, the women's teams have become members of Division III.

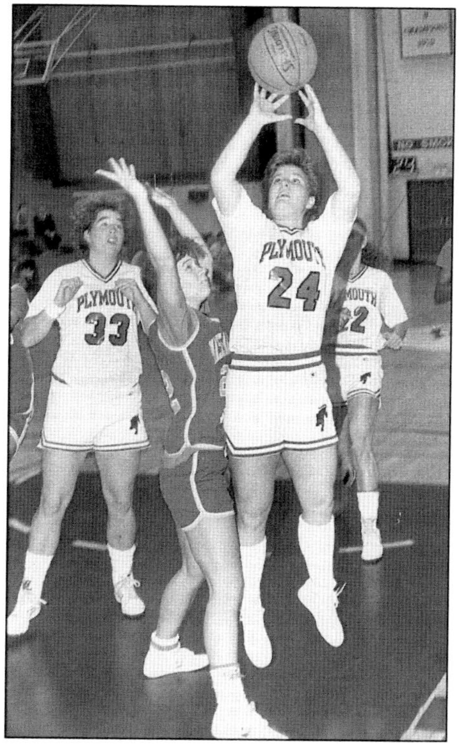

WOMEN'S BASKETBALL, PSC VERSUS UMASS AT BOSTON, 1986–87. Ellen Griffin is No. 33; Heather Boyce is No. 24.

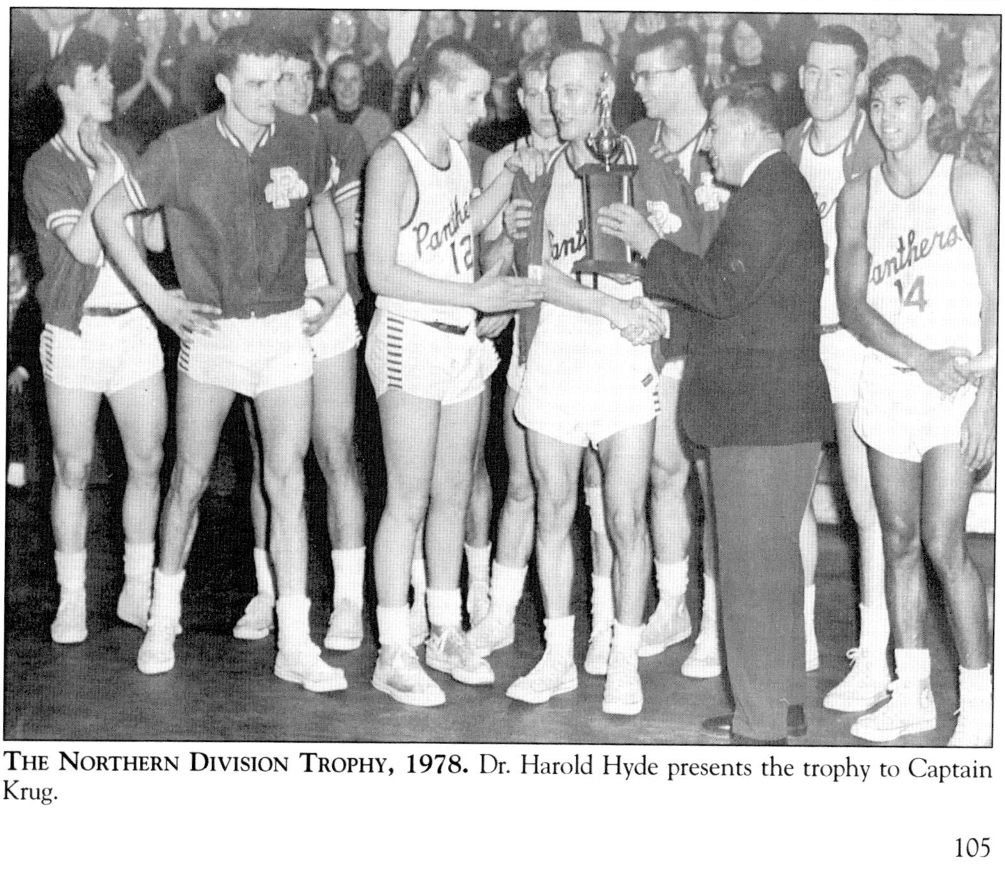

THE NORTHERN DIVISION TROPHY, 1978. Dr. Harold Hyde presents the trophy to Captain Krug.

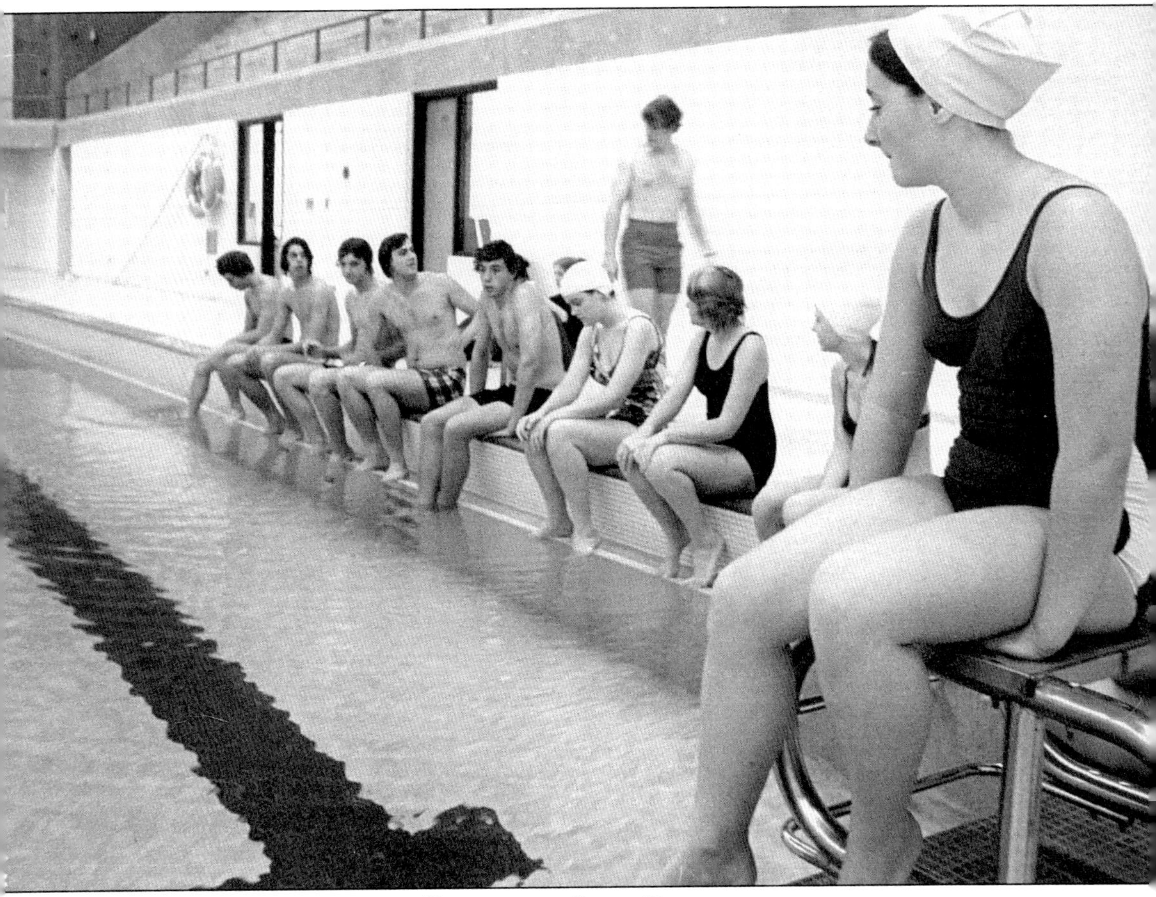

A MOMENT TO RELAX IN THE POOL IN THE FOLEY FIELDHOUSE.

Four

Moments of Reflection

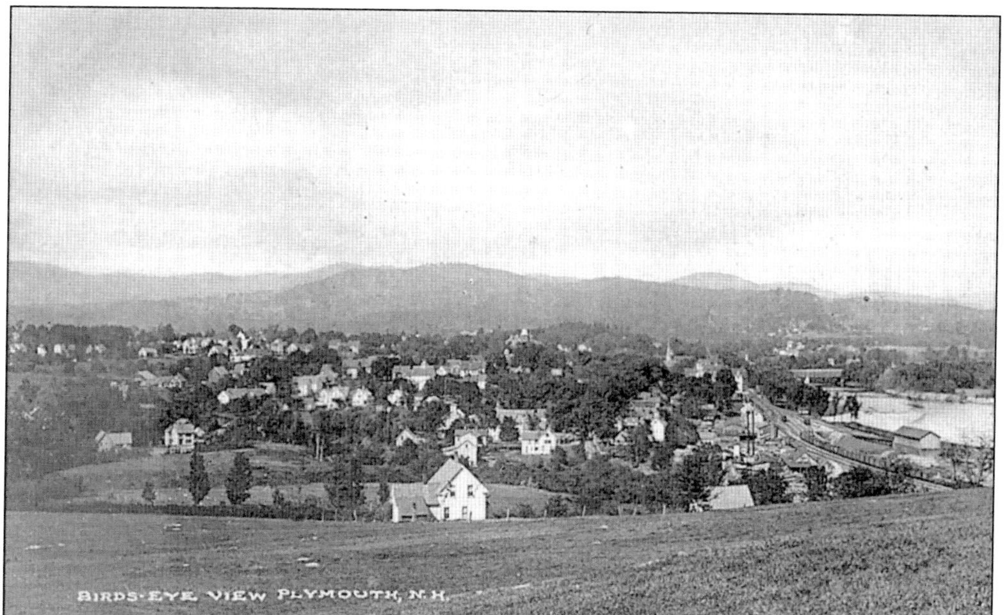

Bird's Eye View of Plymouth, c. 1900s. On the brow of the hill, in the far center, the Conning Tower on Rounds Hall can be seen.

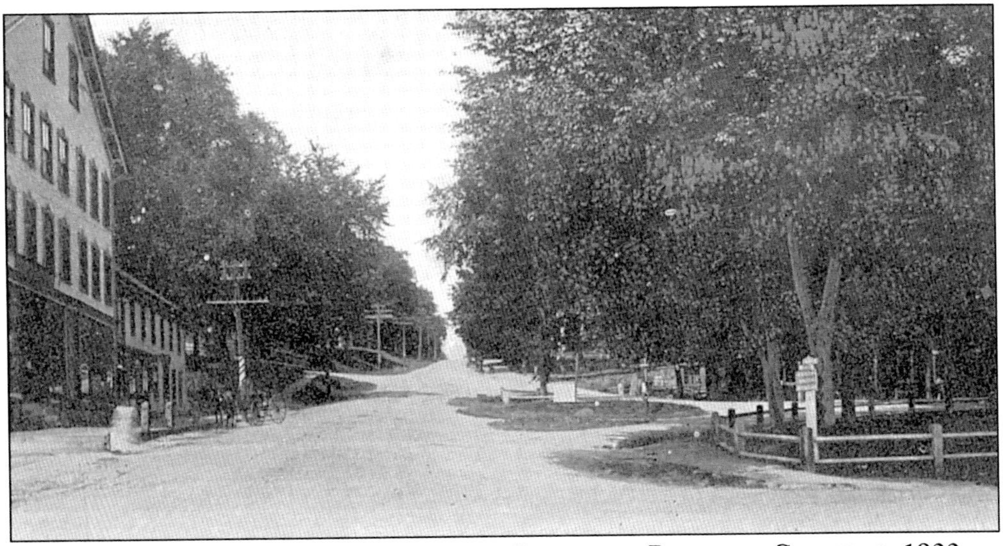

HIGHLAND STREET LOOKING WEST FROM THE COMMON IN PLYMOUTH CENTER, C. 1900.

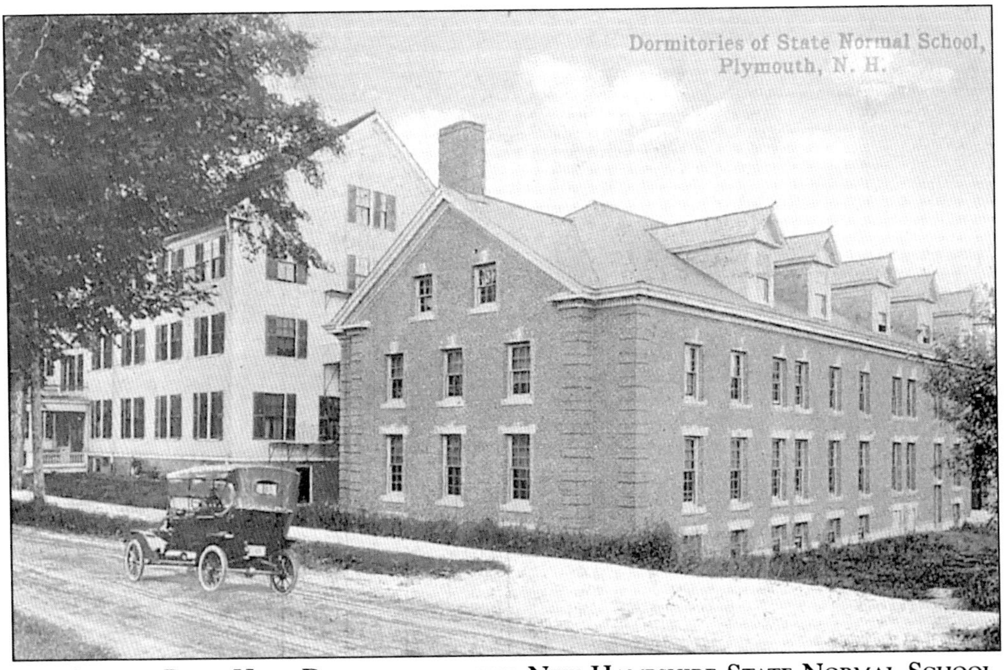

THE SAMUEL READ HALL DORMITORY OF THE NEW HAMPSHIRE STATE NORMAL SCHOOL, HIGHLAND STREET, 1915.

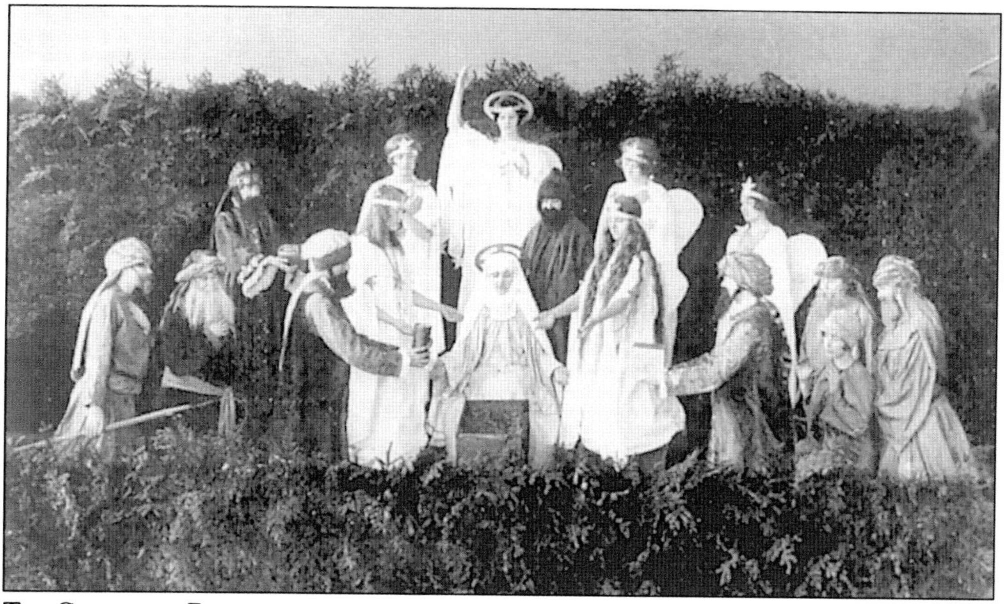

THE CHRISTMAS PAGEANT, 1928.

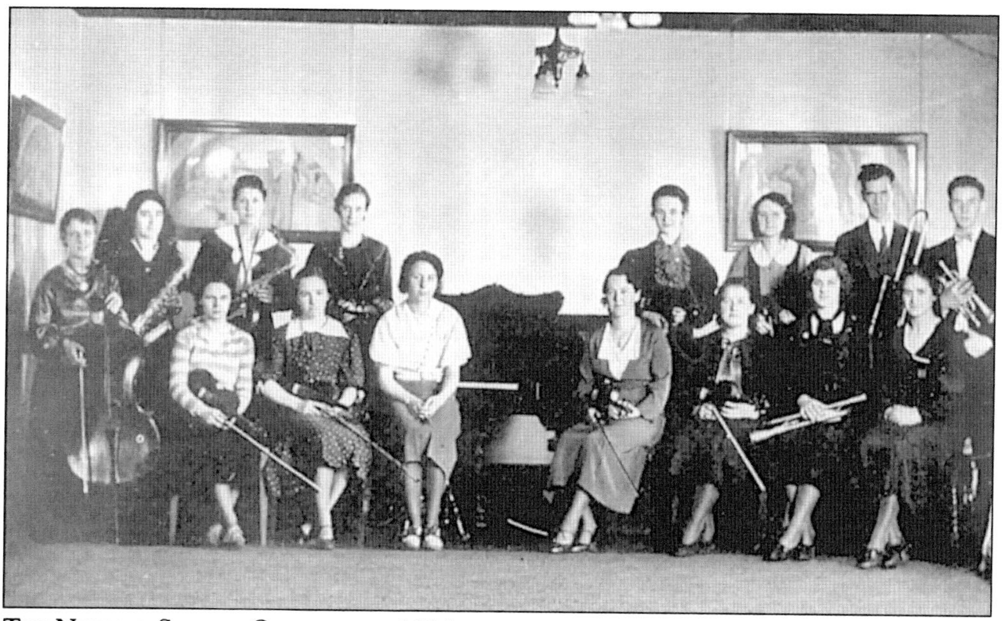

THE NORMAL SCHOOL ORCHESTRA, 1934.

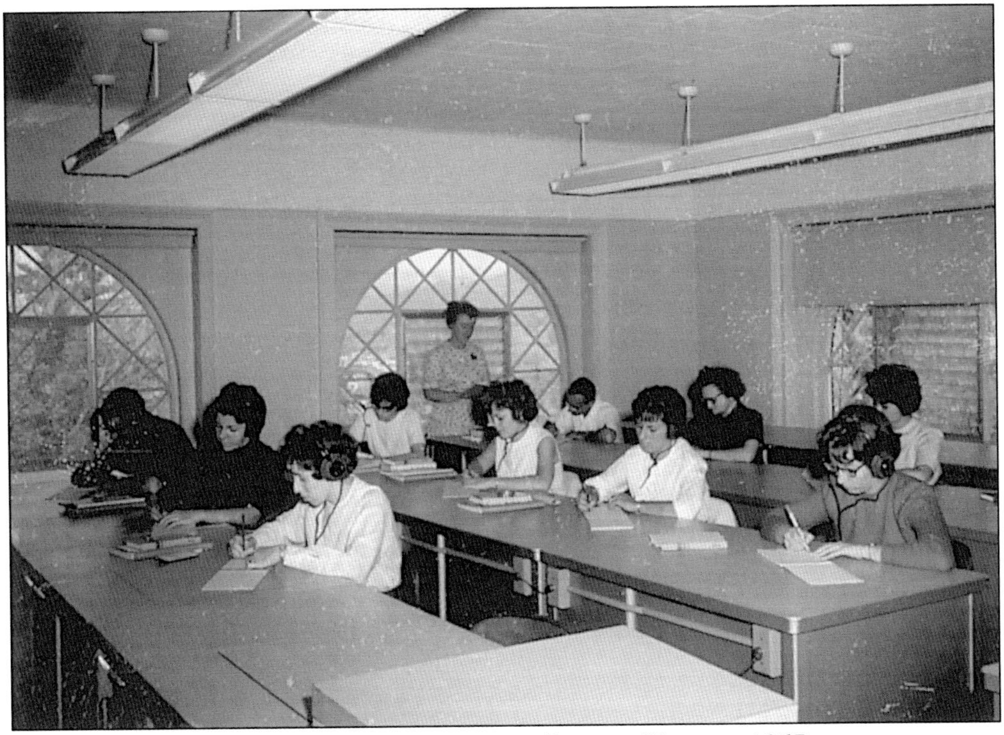

BUSINESS DEPARTMENT ON THE THIRD FLOOR OF ROUNDS HALL, c. 1967.

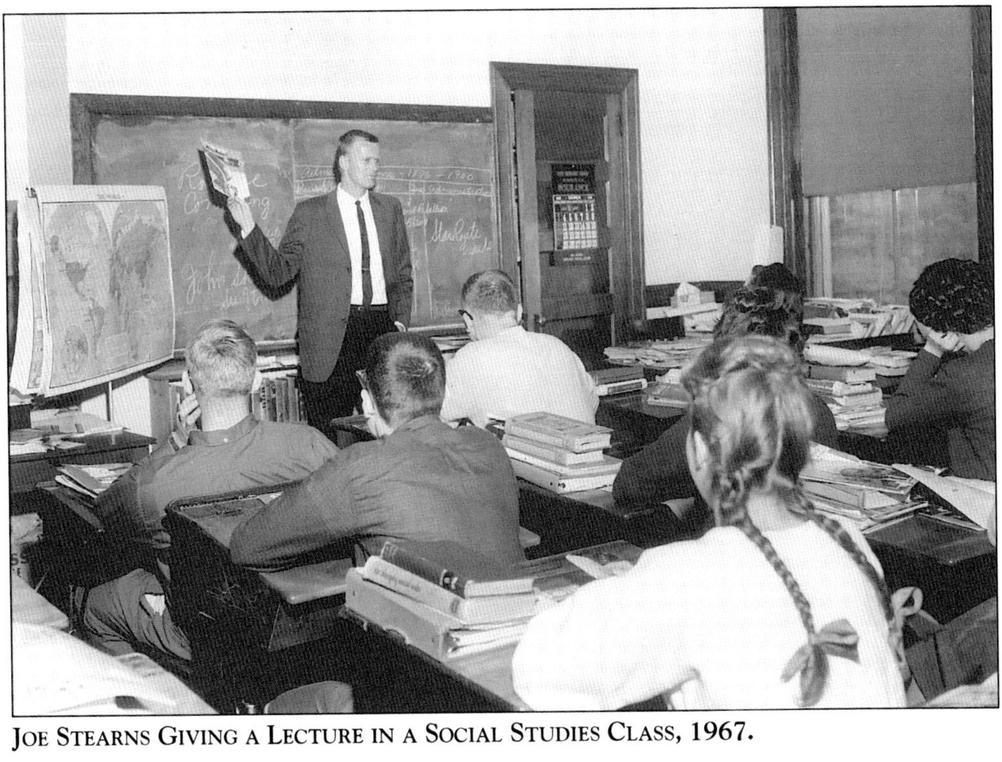

JOE STEARNS GIVING A LECTURE IN A SOCIAL STUDIES CLASS, 1967.

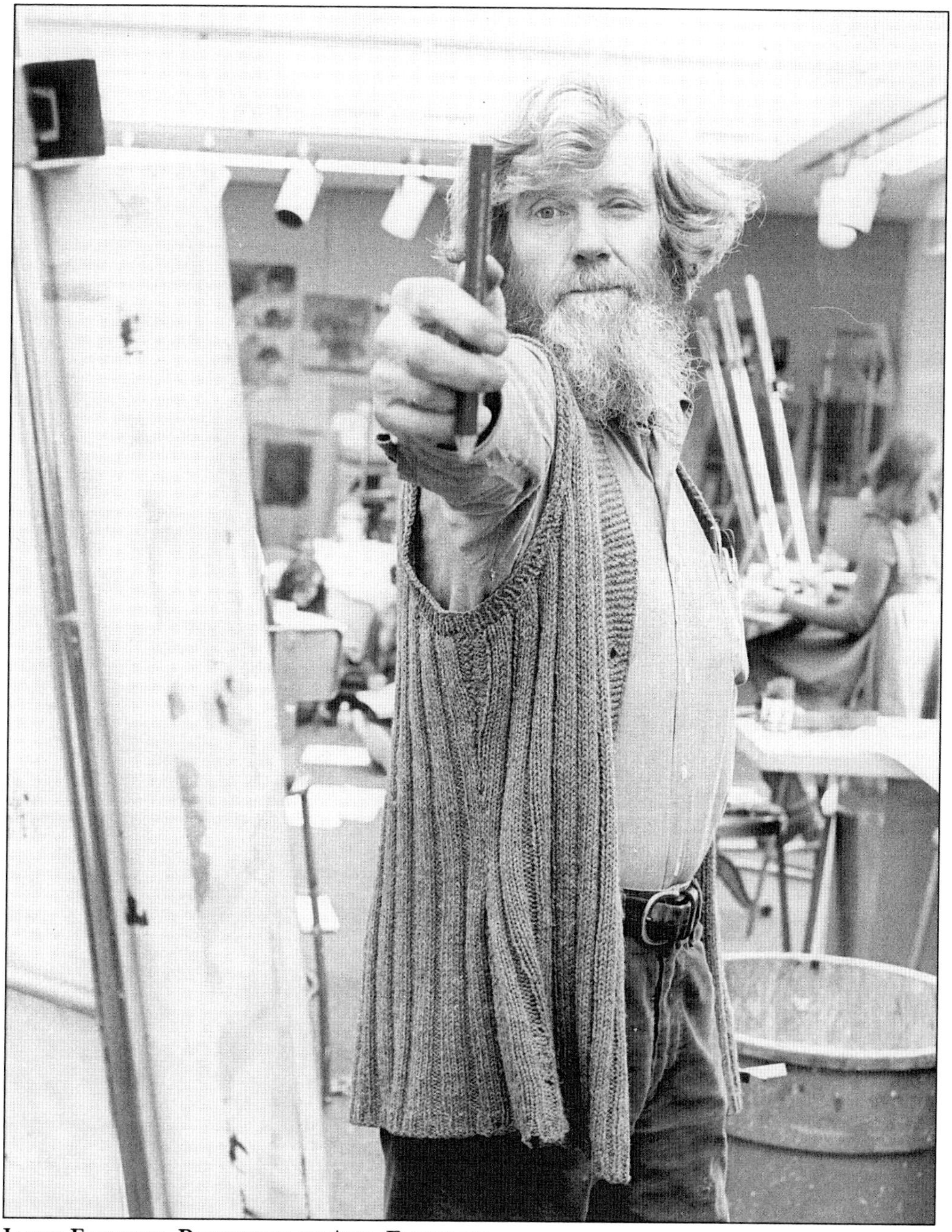

JAMES FORTUNE, PROFESSOR OF ART, EMERITUS.

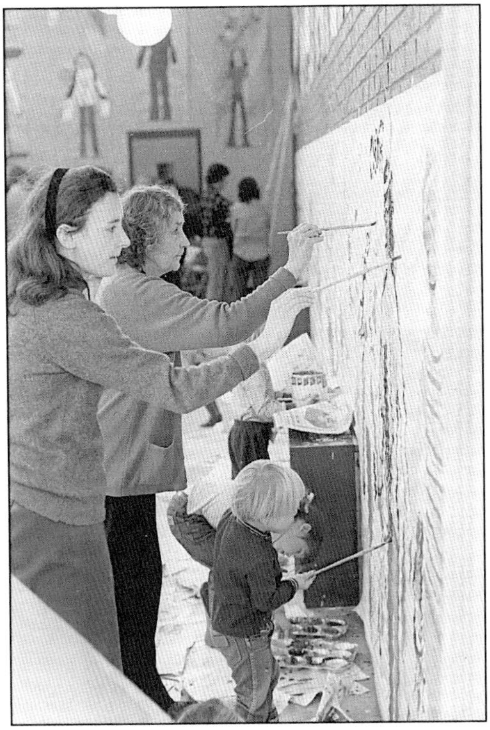

ART EQUALITY. Art is for everyone and at Plymouth, this is no exception.

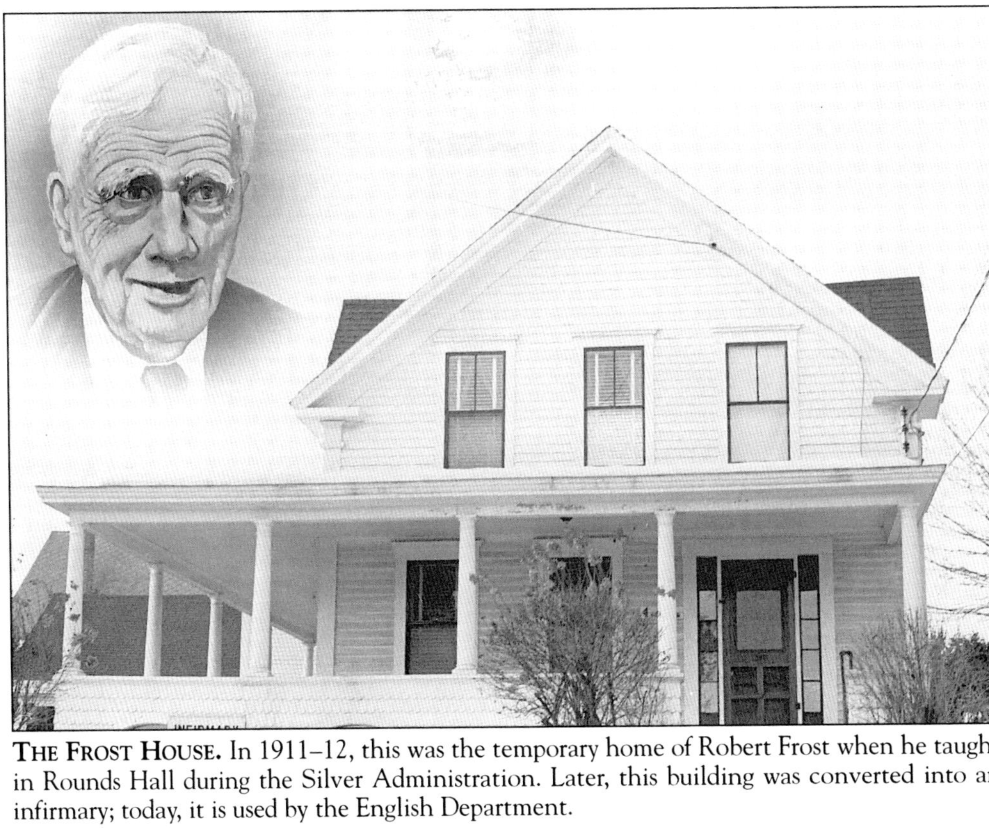

THE FROST HOUSE. In 1911–12, this was the temporary home of Robert Frost when he taught in Rounds Hall during the Silver Administration. Later, this building was converted into an infirmary; today, it is used by the English Department.

LOUIS ARMSTRONG, 1968. He performed in Silver Hall to a record crowd; a moment to be cherished.

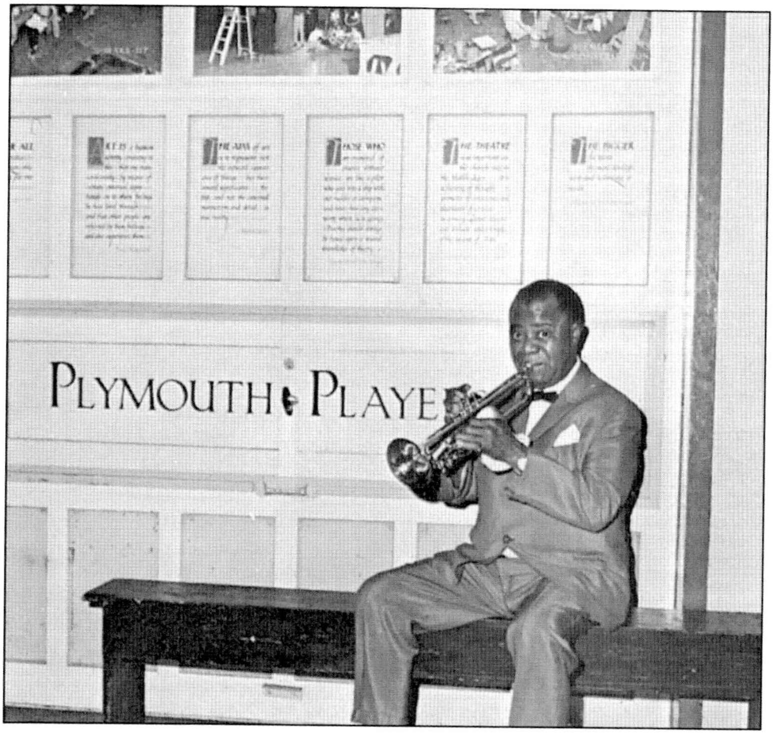

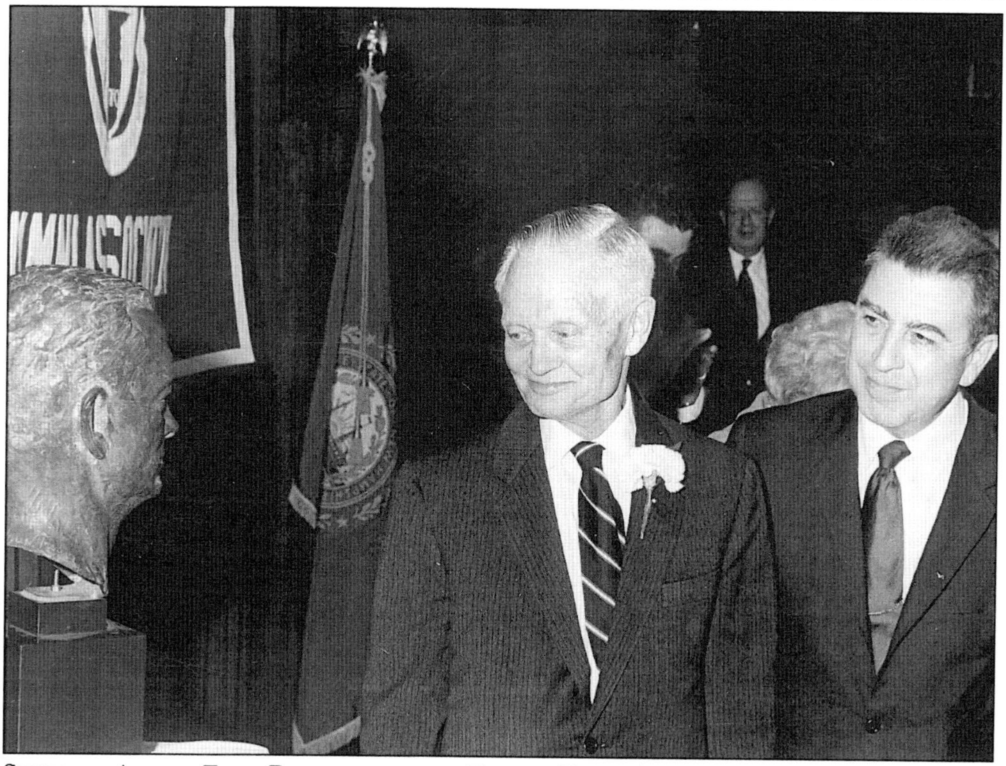

SHERMAN ADAMS, FIRST RECIPIENT OF THE ROBERT FROST AWARD, AND PRESIDENT HAROLD HYDE. These distinguished men look at the *Bust of Adams* exhibited at the college.

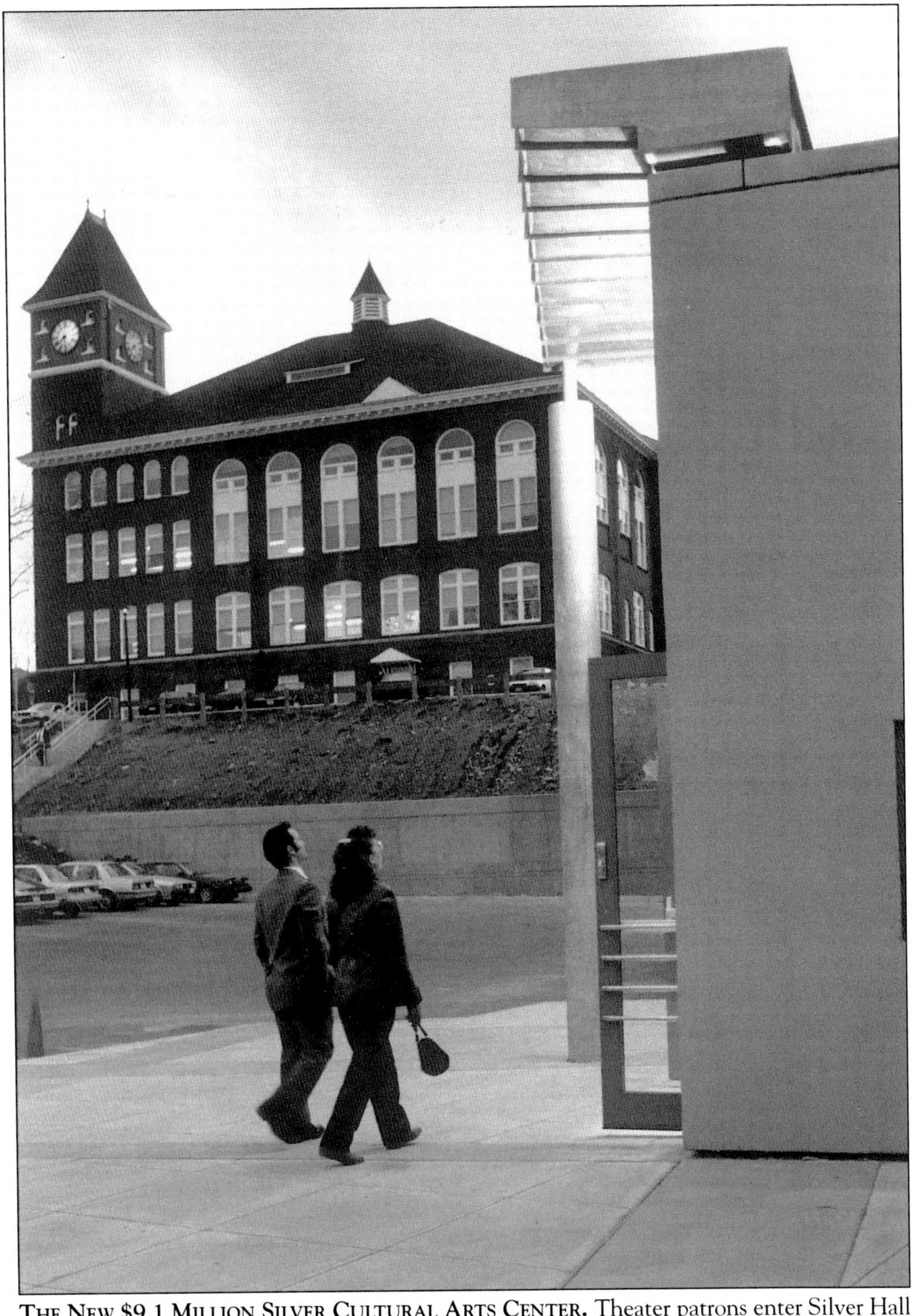

The New $9.1 Million Silver Cultural Arts Center. Theater patrons enter Silver Hall for the opening night performance of the musical "Working," the theater's first public performance. In the background is Rounds Hall, the college landmark, with its clock tower illuminated, April 9, 1992.

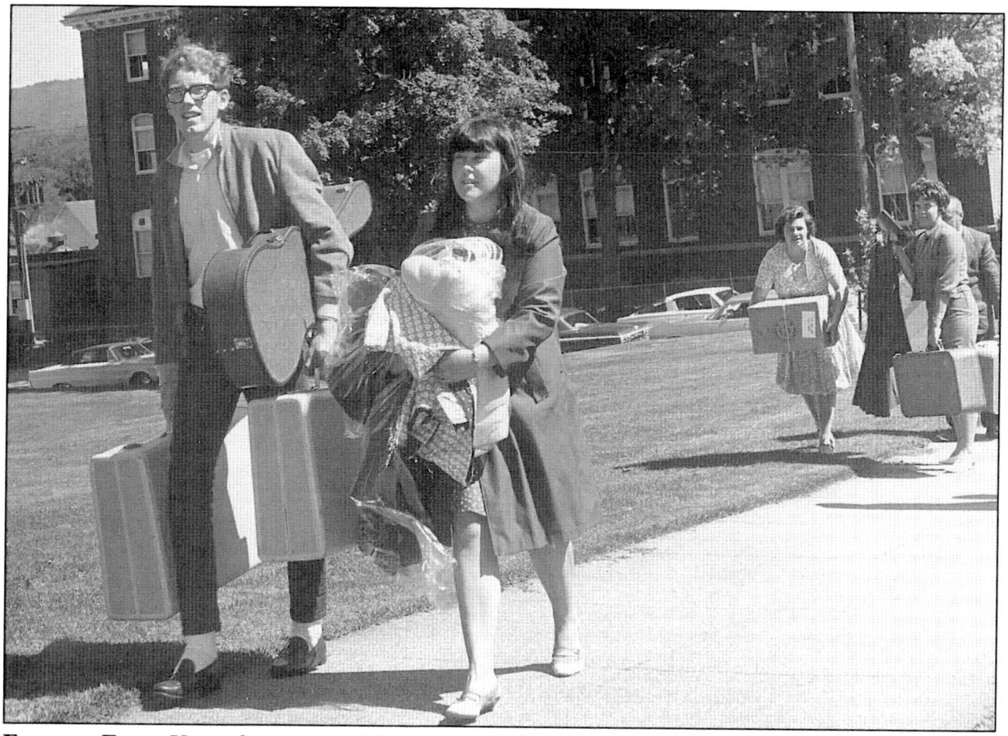

Excited First Year Students. These new students move with parents into Mary Lyon Hall, 1968.

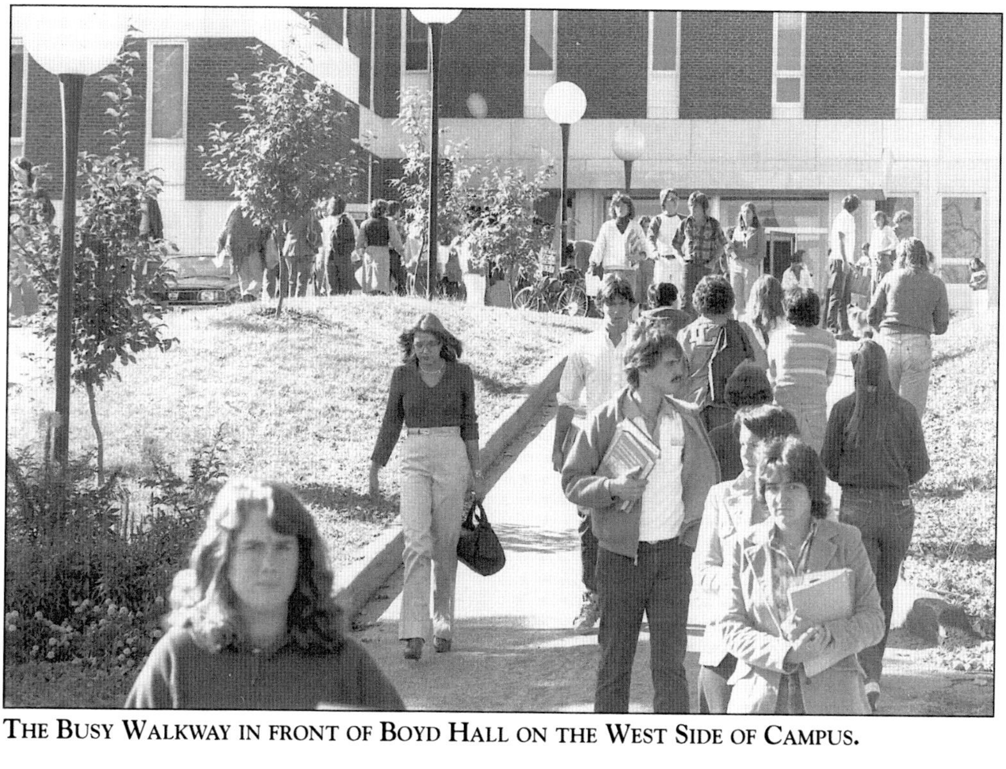

The Busy Walkway in front of Boyd Hall on the West Side of Campus.

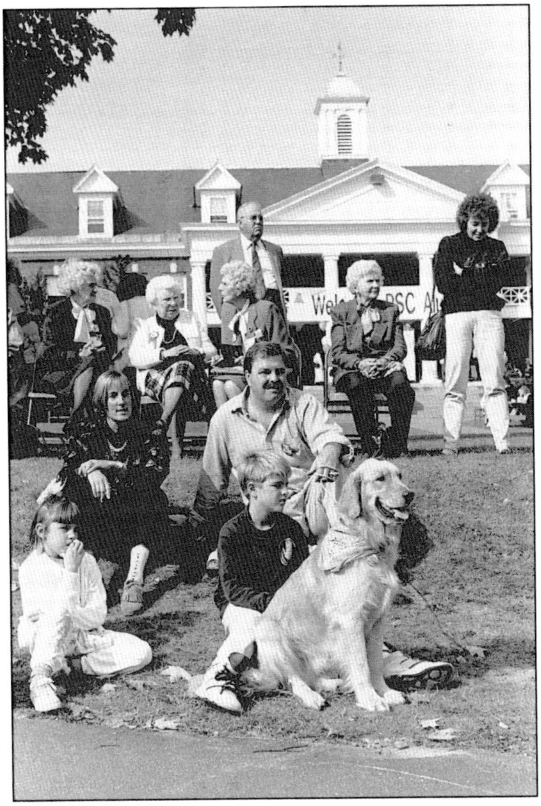

Alumni, Parents, and Friends Patiently Waiting for the Homecoming Parade to Pass in front of them at the Mary Lyon Hall.

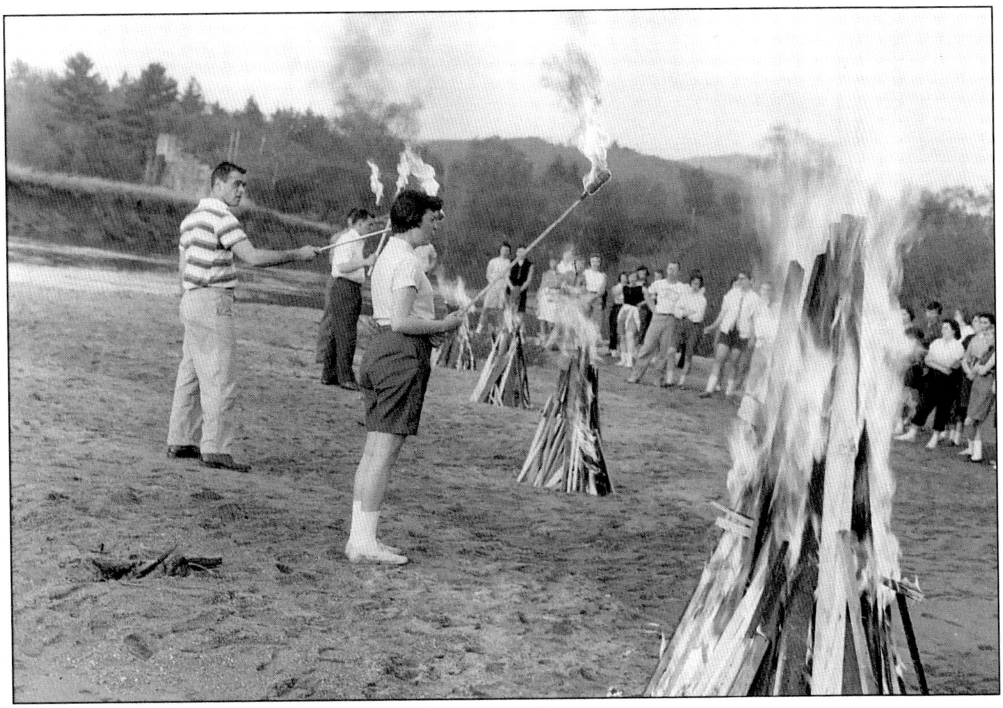

Symbolic Passing of the Torch at Langdon Park.

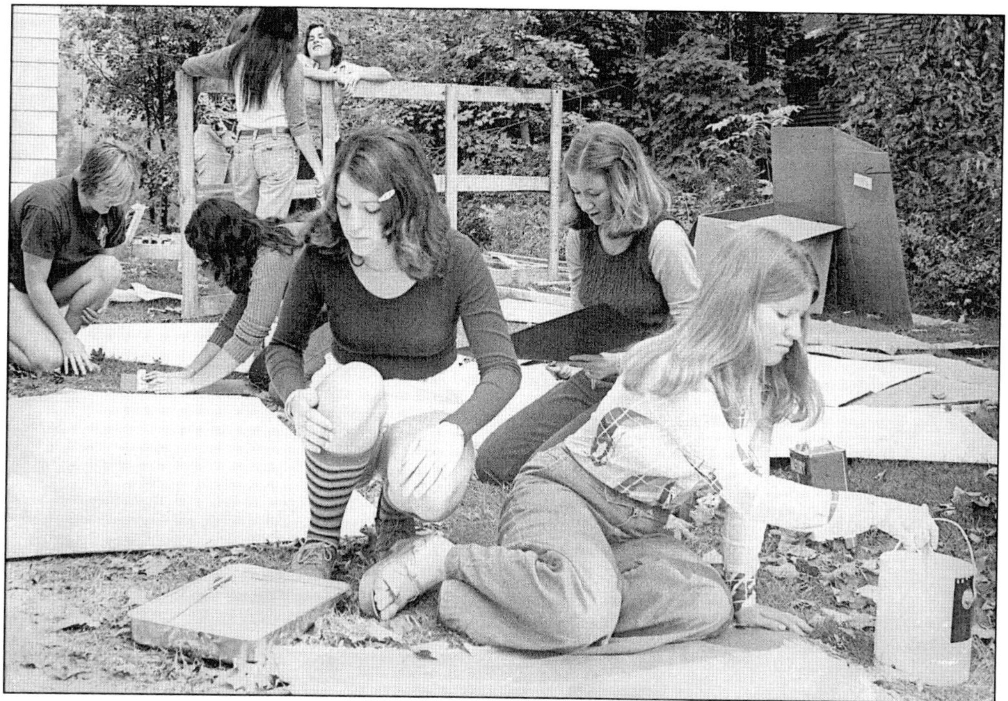

CHI ALPHA ZETA SORORITY, 1975. With cardboard, paint, and glue, the sisters are building one of the 20 floats that will wend their way through the Plymouth State College campus as part of the ninth annual Homecoming. Getting started are, from left to right, Sue Fuller, Colleen O'Leary, and MaryJane Young.

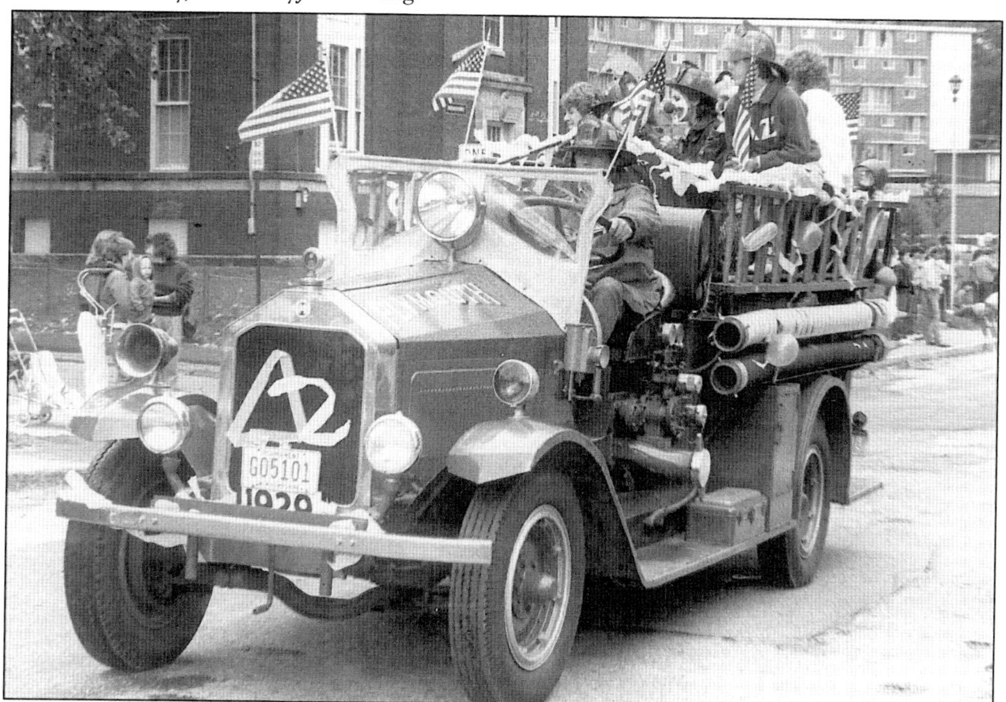

A 1929 PLYMOUTH FIRE TRUCK IN THE HOMECOMING PARADE.

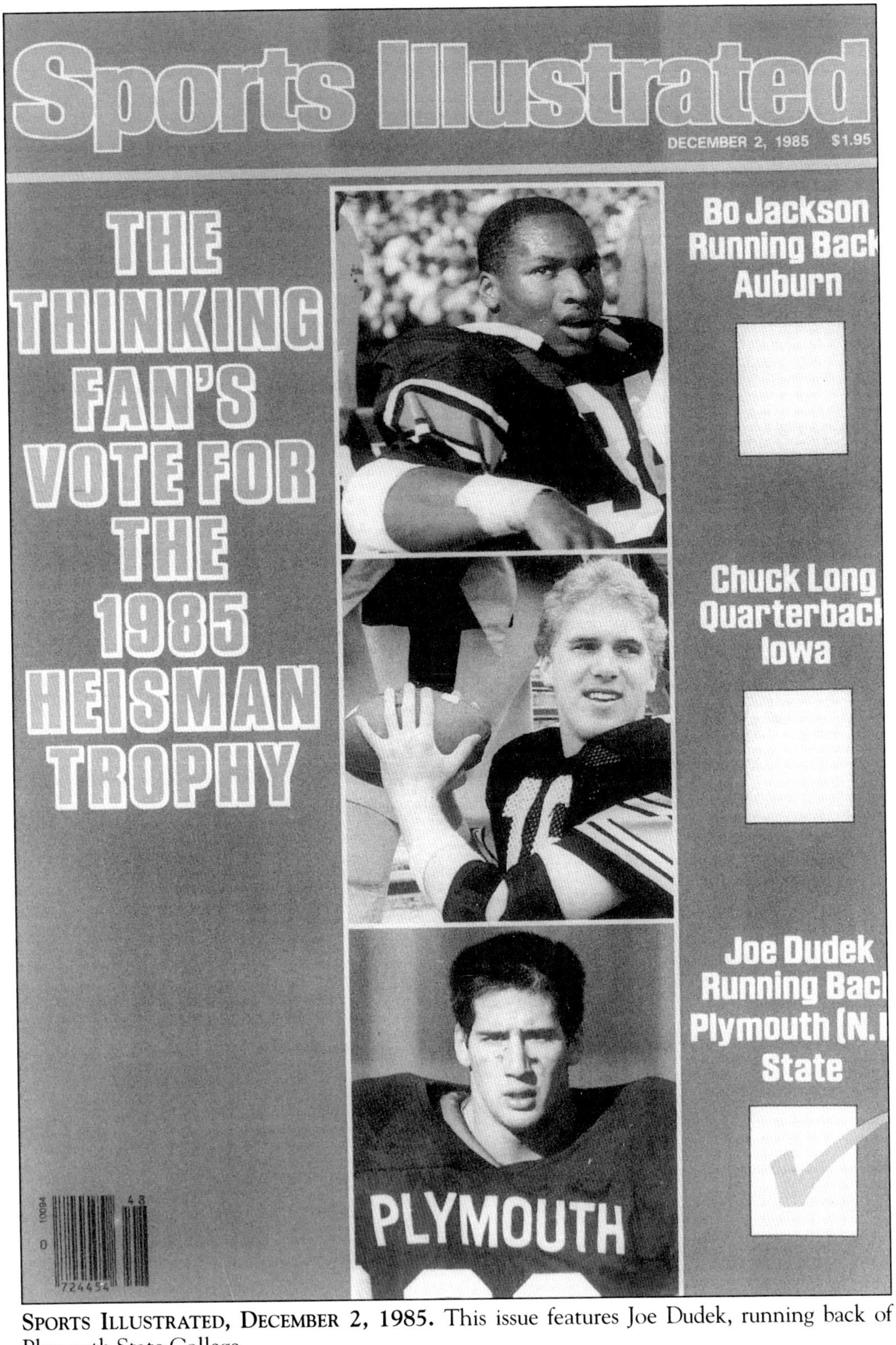

SPORTS ILLUSTRATED, DECEMBER 2, 1985. This issue features Joe Dudek, running back of Plymouth State College.

SWIM MEET, 1976. Steve "Harpo" Hadley is set for the dive in this photograph.

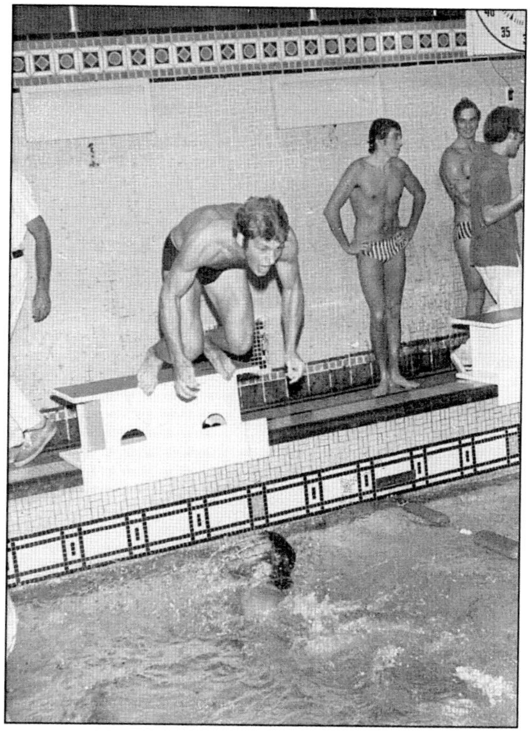

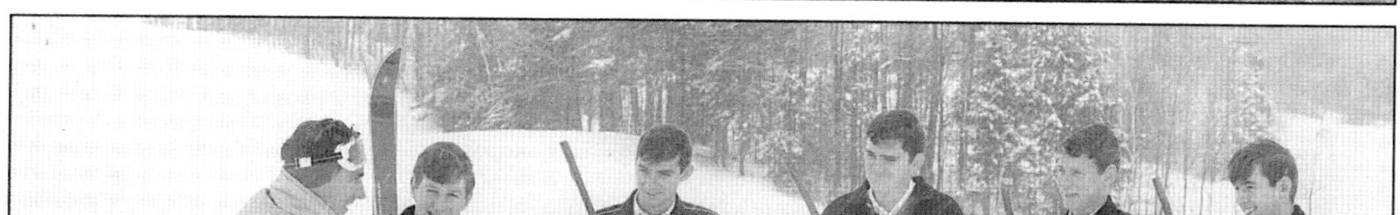

KAPPA DELTA PHI FRATERNITY RUNNING THE TORCH, SATURDAY, FEB. 10, 1968. Members needed to run a torch from the top of Gunstock Mountain to downtown Laconia to open the gala Kawartha Cup International Snowmobile Championship parade. Seen here, from left to right, are former Austrian Olympic skiing champion Egon Zimmerman, Robert "Skip" Whitmore, George Provost, Daniel Andrews, Richard Woodward, and Dale Woodward.

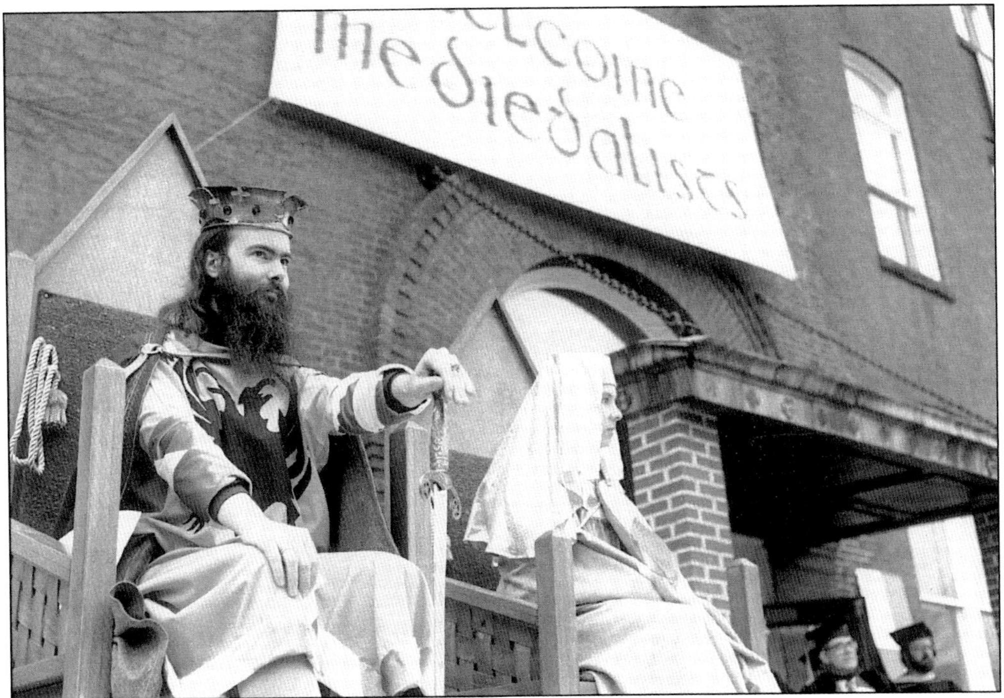

MEDIEVAL FORUM AT PSC APRIL 14-15, 1988, IN FRONT OF ROUNDS HALL. Shown here, from left to right, are Angus MacDonald and April O'Keefe. Next to April is Dr. Manuel Marquez-Sterling, one of the organizers of the Medieval Forum.

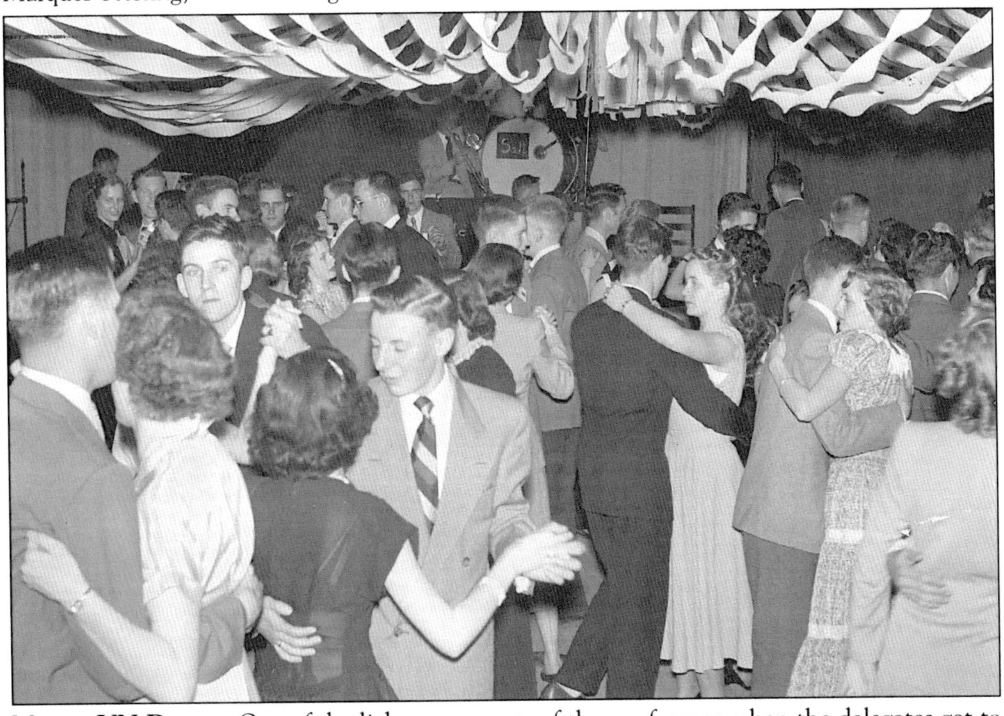

MODEL UN DANCE. One of the lighter moments of the conference when the delegates get to know each other at the "Cafe Internationale," the dance is generally held on the first night.

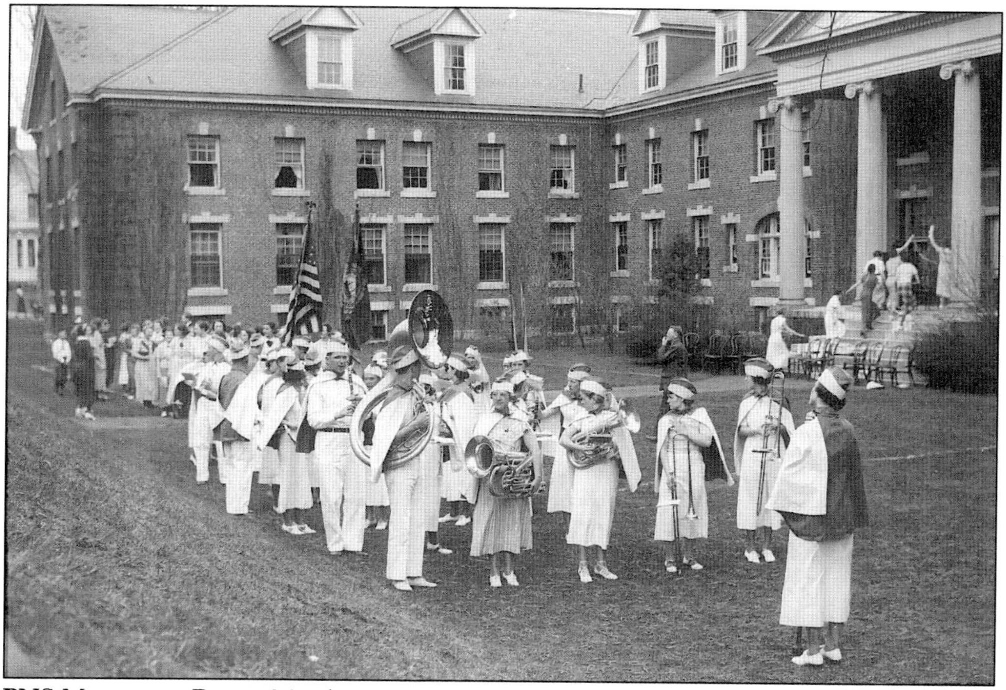

PNS MARCHING BAND. Members practice for graduation on the west lawn of the Mary Lyon Hall, *c.* 1930s.

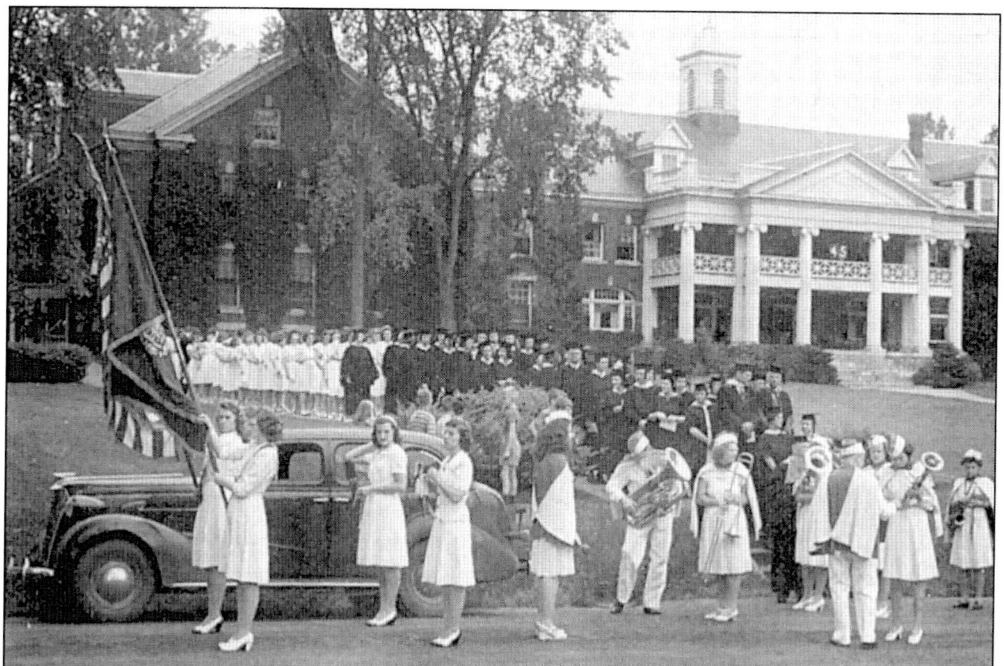

FORMING THE PROCESSION OF THE GRADUATING CLASS C. 1930S. The procession moves from the Mary Lyon Hall to the theater.

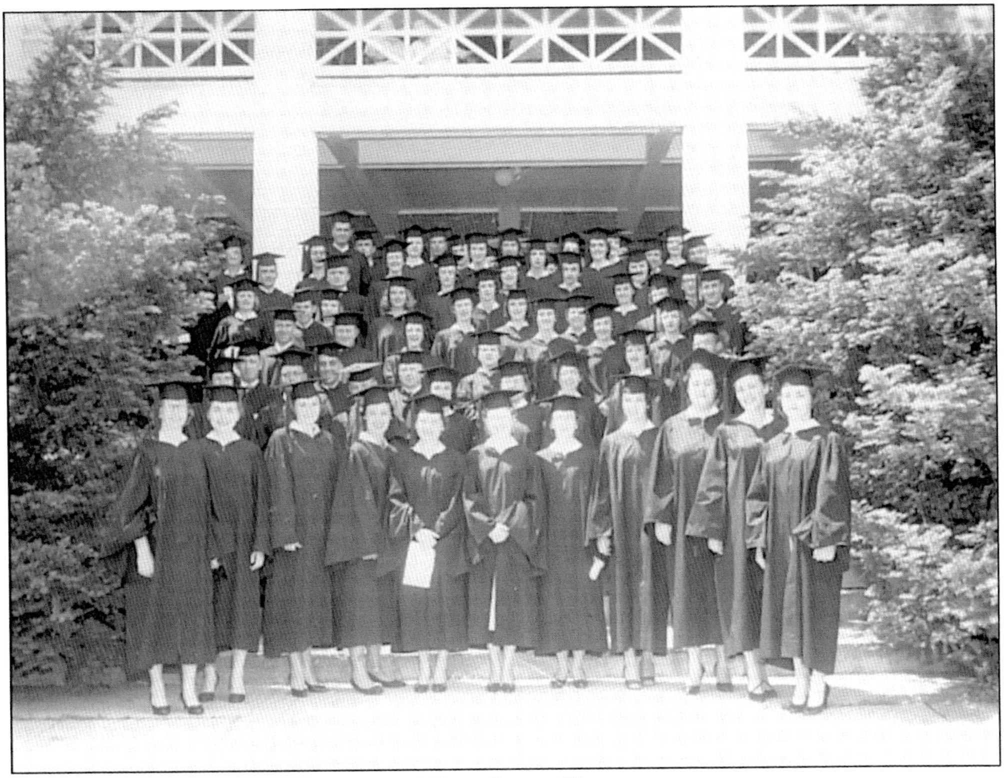

CLASS OF 1959 ON THE STEPS OF THE MARY LYON HALL.

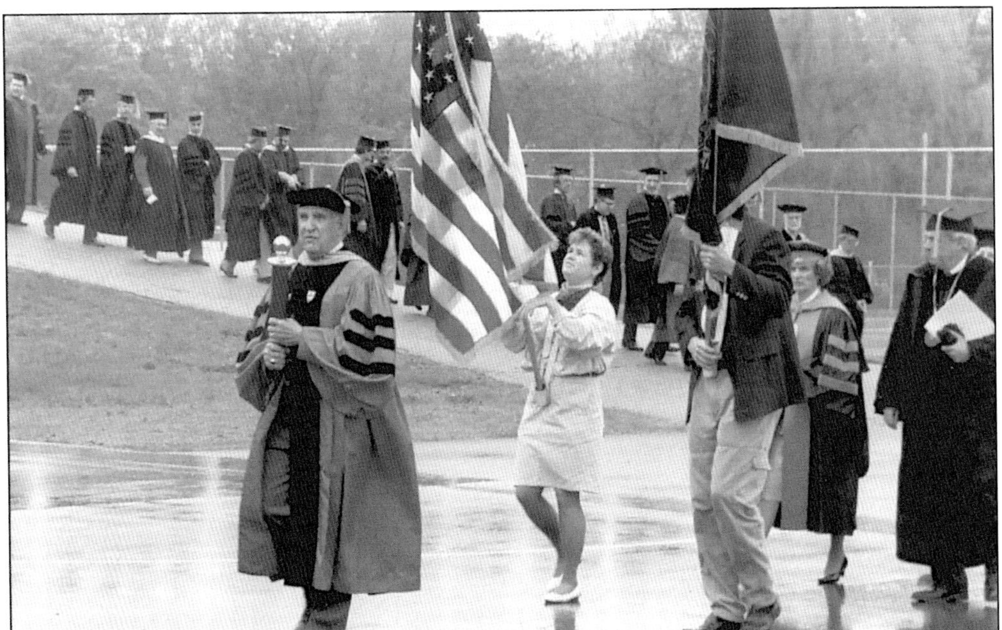

ACADEMIC PROCESSION. This procession was led by the distinguished teacher of the year, Professor Emeritus Mark Sylvestre, PSC, May 21, 1988. William J. Farrell, 13th president, is at the far right.

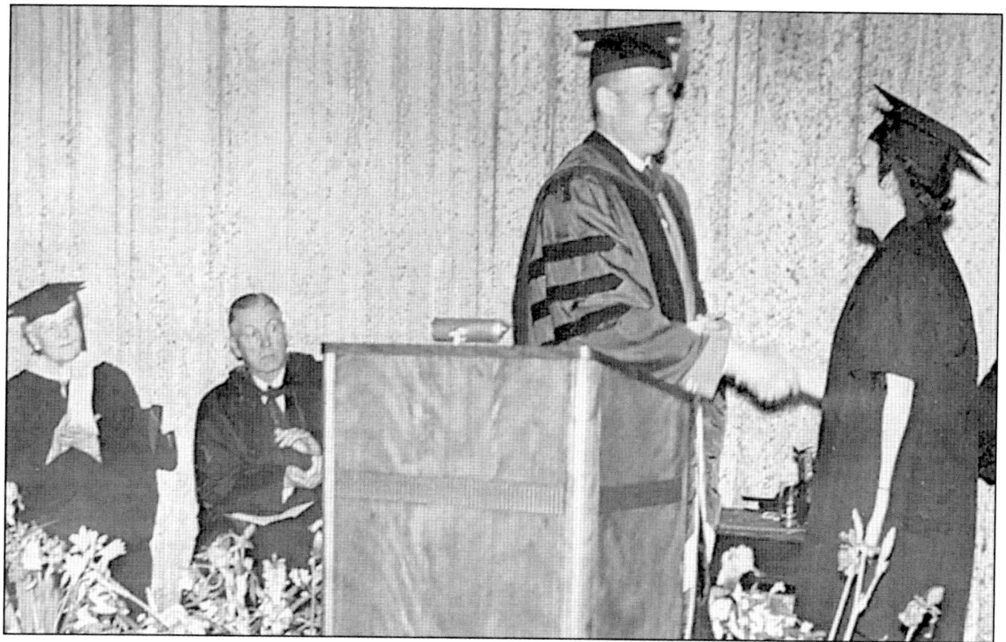

The First Master's Degree. Dr. Jones awards the first master's degree at PSC.

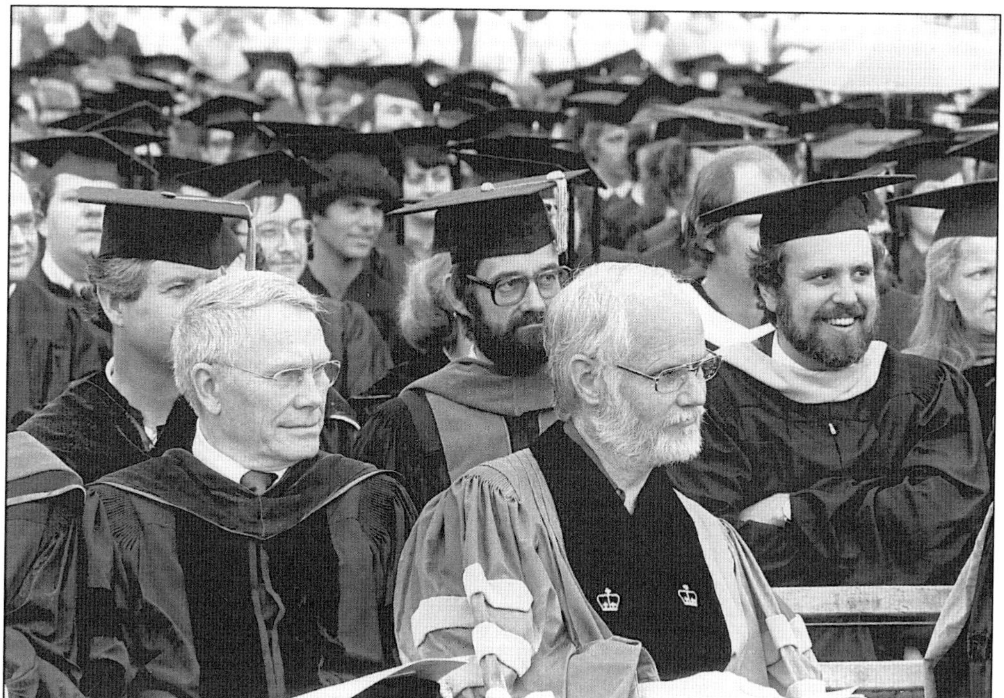

Henry Vittum and Richard M. Chisholm. (These veteran faculty members intently watch the proceedings at graduation.)

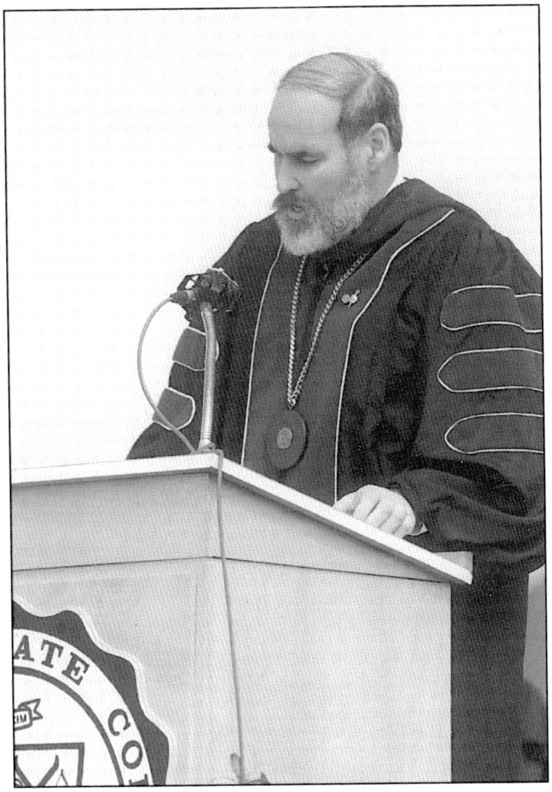

PRESIDENT DONALD P. WHARTON, PH.D. Wharton addresses the graduates, their families, and friends.

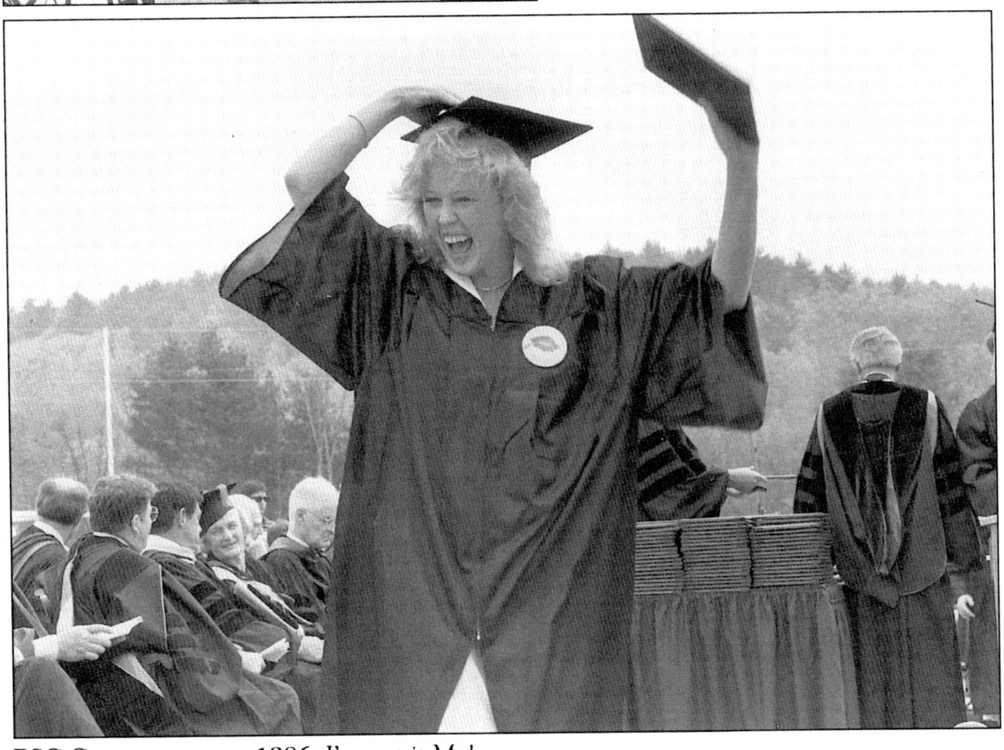

PSC COMMENCEMENT 1986. I've got it Ma!

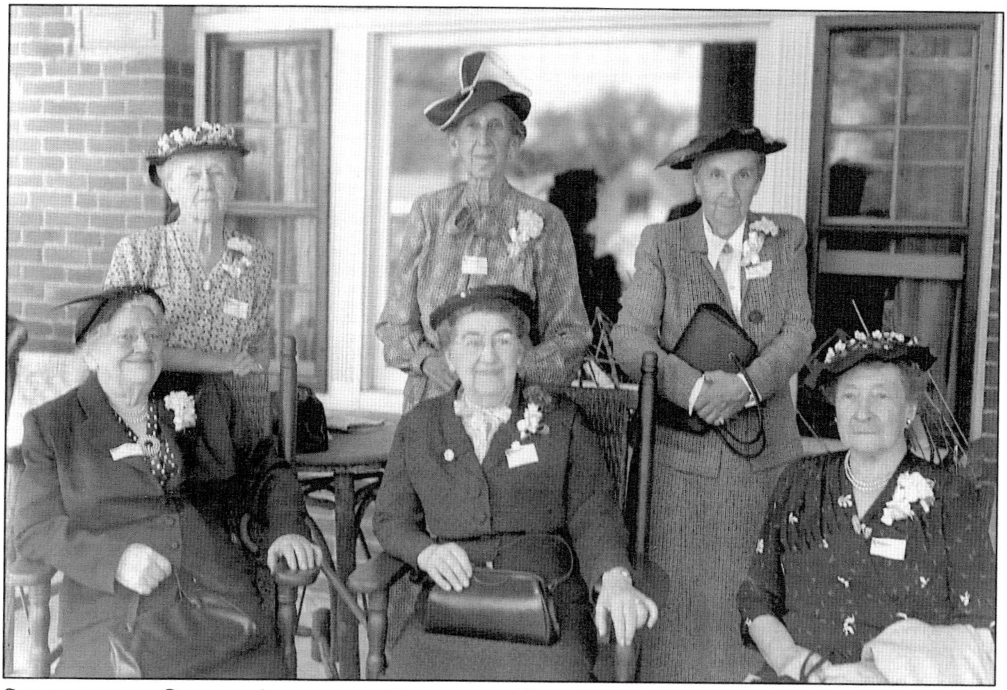

Some of the Oldest Alumni of Plymouth Teachers College. Seen here, from left to right, are as follows: (standing) Florence Johnson Houston of Bath, 1901; Mabel Gardner of Bradford, 1900; and Carolyn Stevens of Salmon Falls, 1904; (sitting) Christabel Allen Foster of Plymouth, 1902; Maud Smart Prince of Lancaster, 1898; and Carolyn Blount Bowles of Plymouth, 1891.

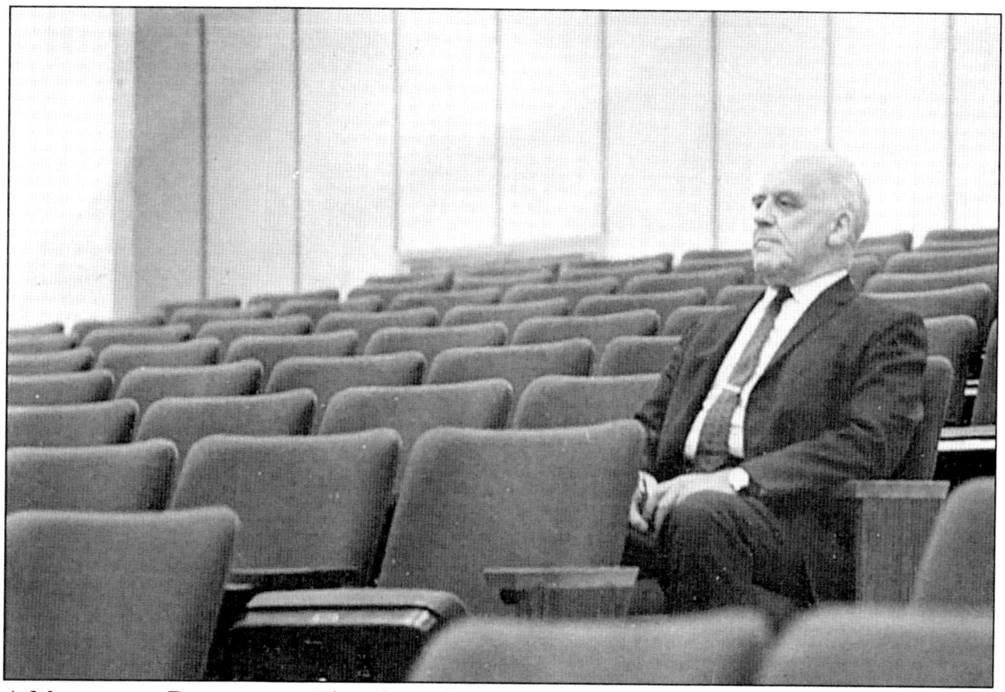

A Moment of Reflection. This photo shows Mr. Robert L. Boyd in Boyd Hall Auditorium.

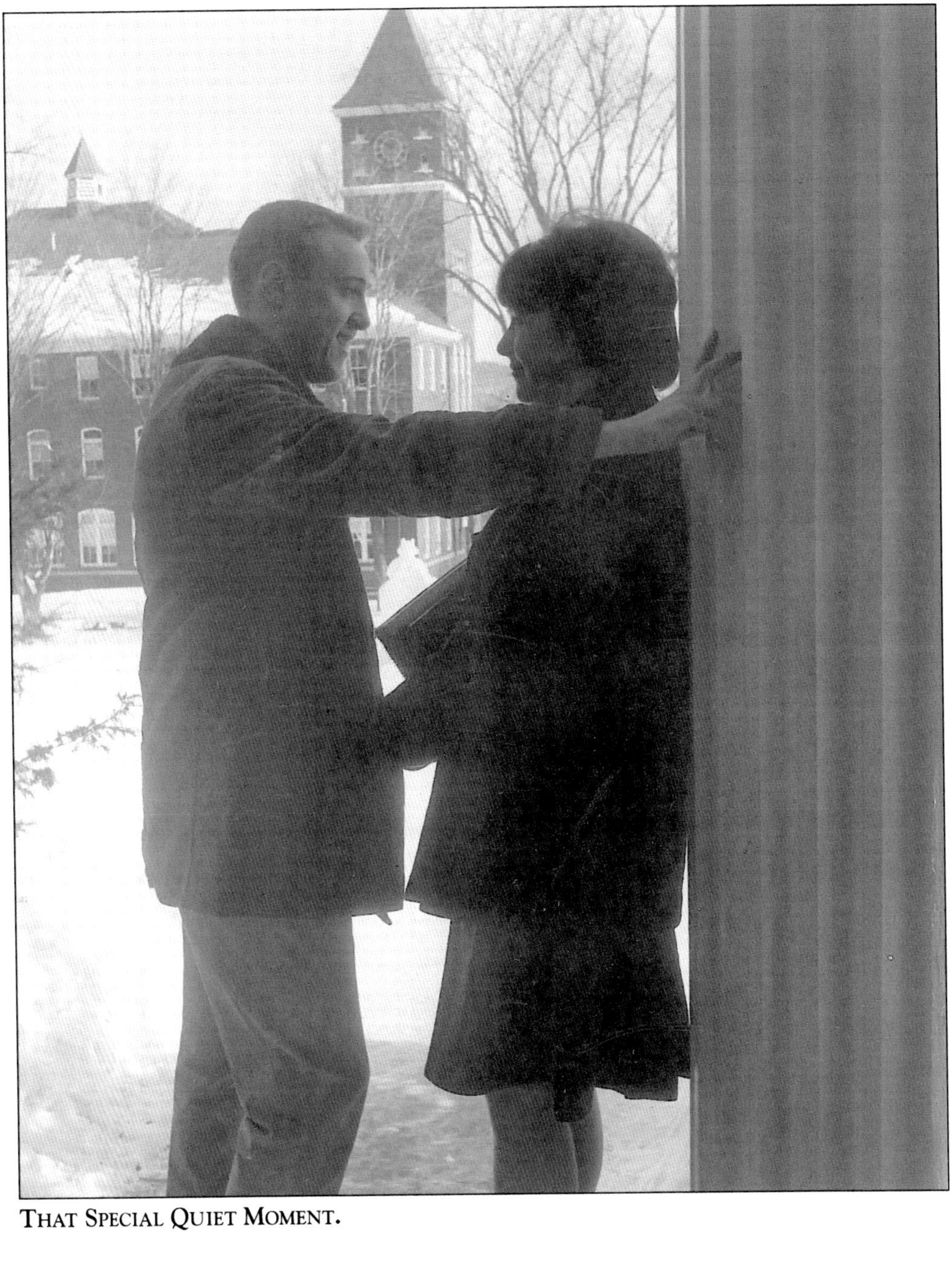

THAT SPECIAL QUIET MOMENT.

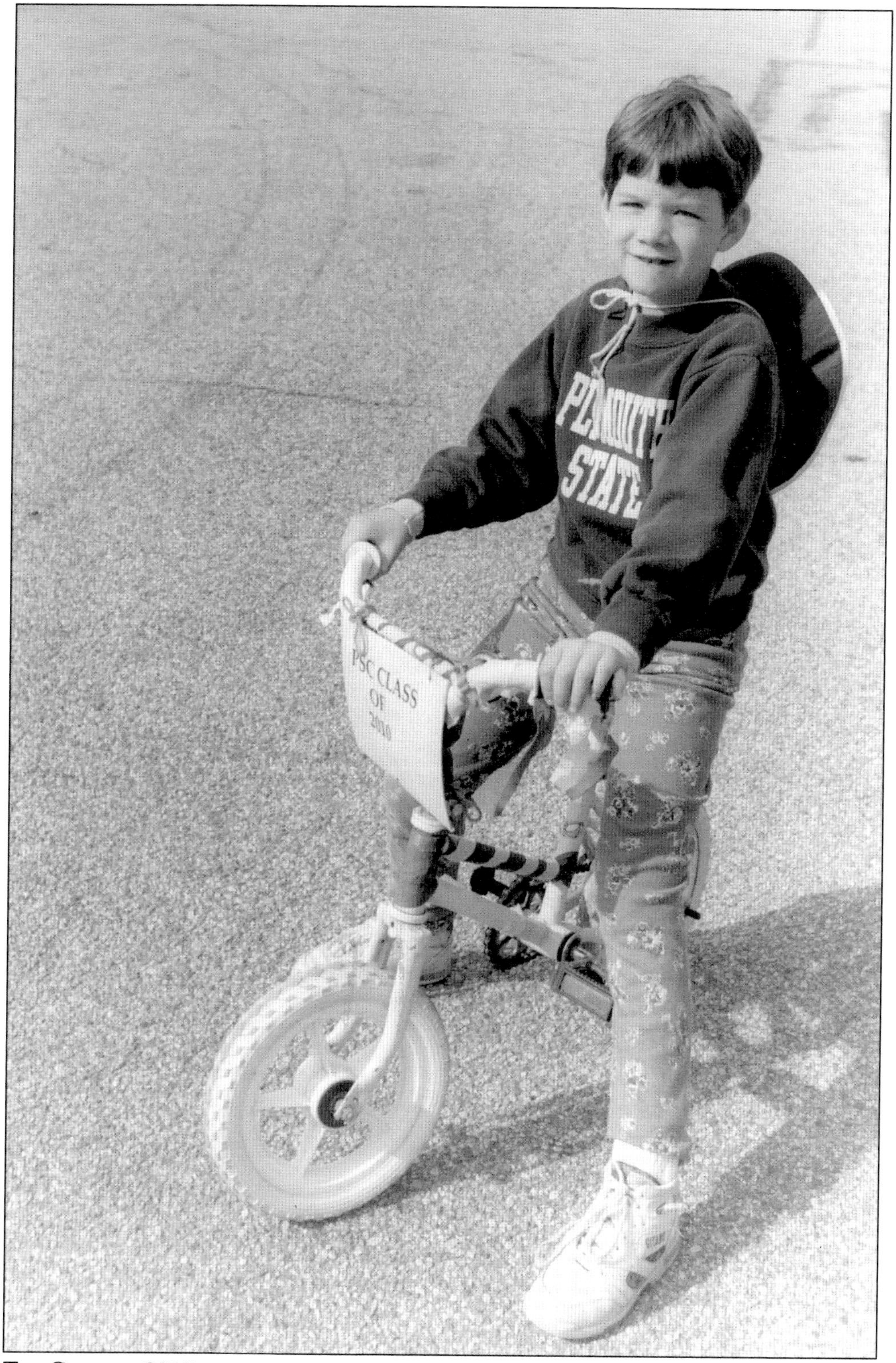

THE CLASS OF 2010.

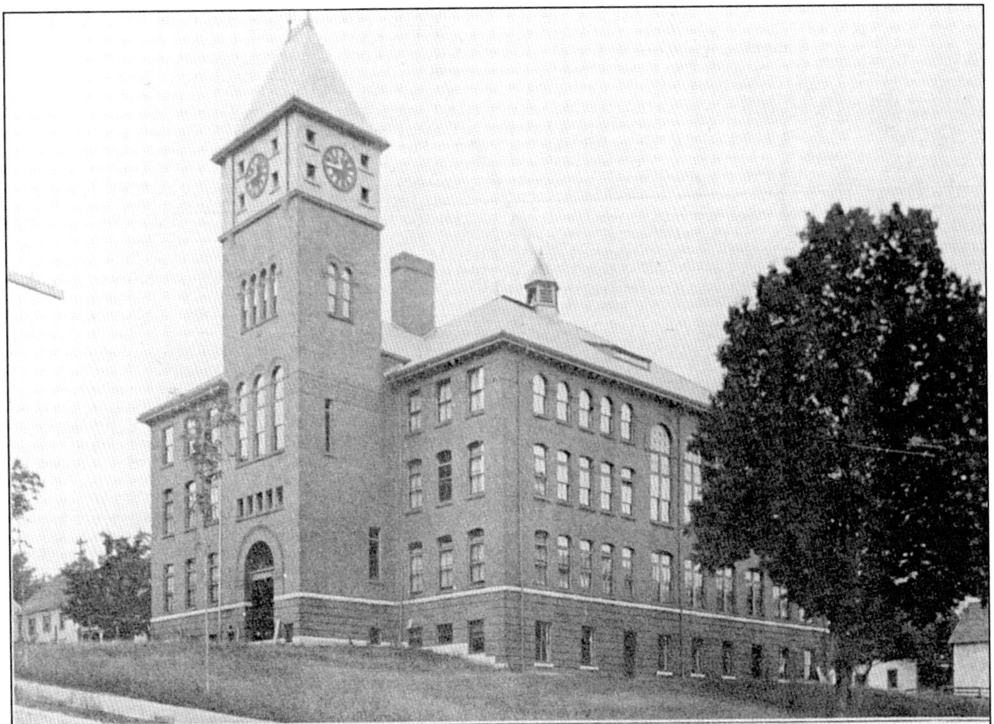

State Normal School.

1908 April 1908

SUN.	MON.	TUES.	WED.	THU.	FRI.	SAT.
			1	2	3	4
5	6	7	8	9	10	11
12	13	14	15	16	17	18
19	20	21	22	23	24	25
26	27	28	29	30		

STATE NORMAL SCHOOL, C. APRIL 1908.